What Algorithms Want

What Algorithms Want

Imagination in the Age of Computing

Ed Finn

The MIT Press
Cambridge, Massachusetts
London, England

This book was set in Stone Sans and Stone Serif by Toppan Best-set Premedia Limited. Printed and bound in the United States of America.

Library of Congress Cataloging-in-Publication Data

Names: Finn, Ed.
Title: What algorithms want : imagination in the age of computing / Ed Finn.
Description: Cambridge, MA : MIT Press, [2017] | Includes bibliographical references and index.
Identifiers: LCCN 2016030924 | ISBN 9780262035927 (hardcover : alk. paper)
Subjects: LCSH: Information technology--Social aspects. | Computers--Social aspects. | Algorithms--Social aspects.
Classification: LCC HM851 .F5565 2017 | DDC 303.48/34--dc23 LC record available at https://lccn.loc.gov/2016030924

10 9 8 7 6 5 4 3 2 1

Contents

Acknowledgments

This book owes its existence to the generosity and support of many people and institutions. I count myself very lucky to have the support of my academic home, Arizona State University, in a tremendous range of large and small ways. Thanks go to President Michael Crow, for hiring me and making my unique position possible, and to the many university leaders who continue to support our strange experiment in imagination. I am especially thankful to the School of Arts, Media & Engineering, Director Sha Xin Wei, and Deans Steven Tepper and George Justice, for granting a vital research leave during the early composition phase of the book.

I am deeply grateful to my colleagues at the Center for Science and the Imagination who have supported my long and solitary sojourn as I carved out time to work on this book among many other pressing projects. Thanks to Ruth Wylie for taking on a huge burden of leadership during this period, and to Joey Eschrich, Michael Bennett, Brian David Johnson, Nina Miller, Bob Beard, Cody Staats, and Chelsea Courtney for making CSI such an exciting and rewarding place to work. A special thank you to Joey for heroic editorial efforts as I revised the manuscript, and to Joseph Bianchi for assisting me with image permissions.

A number of people gave me vital feedback on the work as it emerged: Lee Konstantinou, Corey Pressman, Jacqueline Wernimont, Sam Arbesman, G. Pascal Zachary, and George Justice. Nathaniel Greene and Connor Syrewicz were invaluable as research assistants for the project. I'm also grateful to the students of my Arts, Media & Engineering graduate seminar, Reading the Algorithm, for helping me clarify a number of ideas relating to the book. Perhaps the single greatest day for feedback came from a tremendous event titled "The Tyranny of Algorithms," organized by my wonderful colleagues at Future Tense, a partnership of ASU, New America, and *Slate* magazine. Thanks to Torie Bosch and Will Oremus at Slate and Richard Gallant at CNN for feedback, conversation, and the chance to publish some of my thoughts along the way. And finally, I am very grateful to my collaborators at MIT Press: my editor, Doug Sery, for believing in this book; Michael Sims for his dedicated copyediting; and director Amy Brand for her support and enthusiasm of our multiple editorial projects.

All of these interventions, redirections, shows of support, and good advice vastly improved the book and I could not have finished it without them. All remaining imperfections are entirely my own.

Finally, I thank the Finns of Phoenix, my own intrepid band of adventurers, dancers, ad-hoc parade leaders, and dessert aficionados. Anna, Nora, Declan: I love you more than numbers can count or words can say.

Introduction

"Remember the first time you learned binary code?"
"Sure."
"You were forming pathways in your brain. Deep structures. Your nerves grow new connections as you use them—the axons split and push their way between the dividing glial cells—your bioware self-modifies—the software becomes part of the hardware. So now you're vulnerable—all hackers are vulnerable—to a *nam-shub*. We have to look out for one another."
Neal Stephenson, *Snow Crash*, p. 126

Codes and Magic

The myth is probably as old as language itself. There are spells in the world: incantations that can transform reality through the power of procedural utterances. The marriage vow, the courtroom sentence, the shaman's curse: these words are codes that change reality. It is an old and attractive idea.[1] From the *logos* of Genesis to the many religious traditions identifying the "true names" of God, humanity has persistently believed that certain invocations do not merely describe the world but make it. And why not? Language has always operated at the troubled boundary between reality and the description of reality. The more structured, abstract, and esoteric an idea, the less likely we are to divine its substance without first gleaning a name to call it by.

Today our languages sprawl across many registers: procedural computer languages, critical languages of film and new media, creoles, fictional languages, newspeak, emoji. In our perception, each of those registers ascribes certain magical powers to symbols and meaning; each of them generates cultural power based on the inherent tension between reality and representation. The link between spoken language and abstract symbolic systems, particularly mathematics, has created new avenues for mystical connections between numbers, universal truths, and the fundamental structure of reality. Jewish kabbalah, Isaac Newton's fascination with alchemy, and biological examples of mathematical figures like the Golden Ratio all reinforce a particular metaphysical notion that some logical order, some grammar and symbolic vocabulary, underlies the universe.

In debating these questions, philosophers and mathematicians developed increasingly sophisticated understandings of symbolic languages, laying the groundwork for the contemporary era of computation. From its bones in set theory and symbolic logic to the latest articulations of data-driven machine learning, computation casts a cultural shadow that is informed by this long tradition of magical thinking. As computation transforms almost every aspect of cultural life, the stories we tell about it, the balance of myth and reason, will play a major role in determining what we can know and think. Language has power in the world, and may in some sense define the world. When enacted, symbolic logic can effect procedural alterations to reality.

The key term here is "enacted." This book uncovers how the humble vehicle of computation, the algorithm, has its roots not only in mathematical logic but in the philosophical traditions of cybernetics, consciousness, and the magic of symbolic language. To understand the algorithm we need to uncover those roots and then build a new model of "algorithmic reading" that incorporates a deep understanding of abstraction and process. The algorithm deploys concepts from the idealized space of computation in messy reality, implementing them in what I call "culture machines": complex assemblages of abstractions, processes, and people. Algorithms enact theoretical ideas in pragmatic instructions, always leaving a gap between the two in the details of implementation. The implementation gap is the most important thing we need to know, and the thing we most frequently misunderstand, about algorithmic systems. Understanding *how* we can know that requires the critical methods of the humanities. This is algorithmic reading: a way to contend with both the inherent complexity of computation and the ambiguity that ensues when that complexity intersects with human culture.

Excavation

In the epigraph above, the *nam-shubs* of Neal Stephenson's seminal cyberpunk novel *Snow Crash* are ancient Sumerian incantations whose magic infects the modern substrates of silicon and binary logic. A megalomaniacal billionaire begins digging up Sumerian clay tablets inscribed with actual spells that once had the power to directly program human minds. A Sumerian hearing a nam-shub would ingest it as procedural language, a set of instructions that could alter her mind and her world.

Stephenson adapts the magical tradition of Sumerian myth to a near-future digital culture where virtual reality and ubiquitous computation are well established. The novel imagines the nam-shub to be a linguistic algorithm or hack, turning the poetic spells of the god Enki into a set of operating instructions for the human mind. Stephenson makes this rather obscure mythic history more familiar to his readers by putting it in the hands of hackers, who by the book's publication in 1992 were already imbued with their their own contemporary mythos. In *Snow Crash*, Hiro Protagonist satirically defines the icon of the hacker figure, working at the periphery of monolithic cultural systems to make crucial interventions through technical skill, idealistic motivation, and a blithe disregard for traditional mores. Hiro is a character right out of the trickster archetype that technology journalist Steven Levy chronicles in *Hackers*; a character who came to life around Silicon Valley pioneer Stewart Brand's Hackers Conference in 1984.[2] The computational systems of the novel, from the various security systems to the Metaverse itself, were created by hackers and are subject to their manipulations.

As a high-water mark in the cyberpunk genre, *Snow Crash* both embellished and consecrated hackers as potent and capricious architects of computational reality. Tricksters and rebels, hackers performed feats of technological prowess akin to magic (and often depicted as quasi-magical in films like *Hackers*, *Sneakers*, and *The Matrix*, where the source code becomes what media critic Wendy Hui Kyong Chun calls "sourcery").[3] Their power over code was shamanic, and their very roles as peripheral figures reinforced the notion that computation itself was susceptible to mysterious external forces. This story is by now deeply familiar to us and well chronicled by Levy, Brand, Chun, digital culture scholar Fred Turner, and many others.[4]

But, as the *Snow Crash* epigraph suggests, hackers are not so much the subjects of this novel as the medium through which the plot propagates, in the form of a memetic virus derived from an ancient nam-shub. Behind the spotlit figure of the hacker is the gloomier region from which he or she draws power: the space of computation itself, of source code, procedural language, hacks, and clever digital tricks. As computers become more ubiquitous and accessible, that space of computation has started to become more thinkable and tangible through our proliferating screens, keystrokes, and muttered queries. We are not just getting logistically closer to that space of computation; we are now intimate with it, sharing our most personal memories and accepting algorithmic guidance on matters ranging from love to real estate.

Snow Crash extends this story into a kind of contemporary parable for computation-as-magic. The hackers who carry this virus into the world do so because they are particularly vulnerable to a kind of neurolinguistic infection. In *Snow Crash*, the space of computation touches *you* through a kind of code, a procedural language that operates in consciousness as well as in the world.

Precisely because language occupies a special status as an intellectual technology, its role as an epistemological layer or medium has interested philosophers from Plato to John Searle. In the context of code, language can reformat the world *and* the mind. Without the right vocabulary, it is difficult, sometimes almost impossible to articulate certain ideas, particularly in the context of technical systems. Human languages seem to acquire different color words in a predictable sequence, for example, and the existence of the word makes possible, for cultural purposes, the reality of the color: without the word for "green," that band of the spectrum disappears into the neighboring concept of "blue."[5] Speakers of these languages have the same eyes, the same biological apparatus of vision as the rest of us, but they do not have the "deep structures," the "neurolinguistic pathways" in their brains parsing out this particular band of the visual spectrum. At some point the universal biological equipment of our sensorium gives way to the relative power of language to structure and prioritize experience.

The corollary to this distinguishing power of language is that some incantations cannot be unheard: they permanently alter us when we interpret and understand them. In *Snow Crash* Stephenson imagines that the god Enki deliberately destroyed the universal system of transmission that was the Sumerian language by releasing a nam-shub virus that, "coiled like a serpent around the human brainstem," scrambled humanity's ability to understand other Sumerian signals.[6] Linking this moment to the mythic Tower of Babel, *Snow Crash* makes the nam-shub a relic of a universal language once lost but now regained (and being put to nefarious use). Thus Stephenson taps into the much deeper mythos of language as incantation. If code can be magical and hackers are its shamans, we still recognize it as a symbolic system that operates at the intersection of cognition and reality. By investing the figure of code with cultural power, we also endorse the notion that it functions on a platform: the idea that humanity might run a universal operating system.

So code can be magical, code can change the world, and code can change the mind. But how does this actually work? What are the entities, the structures of operation in that space of computation? In *Snow Crash's* neo-Sumerian operating system there are *me*, particular units of language that embody vital civilizational concepts. This trope is familiar from other traditions as well, where trickster figures like Prometheus or Coyote steal conceptual technologies (e.g., fire) from the gods. In one sense *me* are objects that can be transported and somehow deployed among populations. But they are also bodies of knowledge, sets of rules and procedures, that can be implemented in practice. They are technical entities that have their own existence independent of their human practitioners, but which operate through the medium of culture. They are algorithms.

This is a book about the algorithm as the vehicle or tool of computation: the object at the intersection of computational space, cultural systems, and human cognition. We need a deeper understanding of the algorithm in order to understand how computational systems are transforming our world today. In that sense this is a literacy exercise, an experiment in developing an "algorithmic reading" of the world. The role of the humanities and methodologies of critical reading—algorithmic reading—are vital to effectively contend with the ambiguity and complexity at play in the awkward intersection of computation and culture. But this is also a character study of an idea from its contemporary cultural presence to its philosophical foundations. *Snow Crash* neatly illustrates the tensions at play when algorithms stitch together computational, mythic, and cultural spaces. It's not so much a story about the power of code but its awkward embrace of the real, the ideal, and the imaginary in the guise of the algorithm.

This figure of the algorithm as a quasi-mystical structure of implemented knowledge is both pervasive and poorly understood. We have never been closer to making the metaphor of fully implemented computational knowledge real than we are today, when an explosion of platforms and systems is reinventing cultural practice and identity, often by implementing a *me* downloaded as an app or set up as an online service. We are surrounded by nam-shubs that we obey almost unquestioningly, from the dialog boxes and prompts we fill out on social media platforms to the arcane computation of credit scores. To begin excavating the algorithm, we need to understand the full scope of computational thinking and its interactions with the mythos of procedural language, starting with what we think algorithms *ought* to be.

The Cathedral of Computation

When technologists, researchers, and entrepreneurs speak about computational culture today, this deep myth of the algorithm is typically obscured by layers of rationalizing rhetoric and the procedural metaphors of software design. Indeed the most prevalent set of metaphors seems to be that of code as structure: platforms, architectures, objects, portals, gateways. This serves to both depersonify software, diluting the notion of software agency (buildings are passive; it's the architects, engineers, and users who act), and reifying code as an objective construct, like a building, that exists in the world.

Yet even within this architectural language, the mythological figure of the algorithm reasserts itself. Consider the popularity of the cathedral as a metaphor for code. George Dyson's wonderful history of the rise of computation is titled *Turing's Cathedral*. Another classic instantiation is Eric Raymond's book on open source software development, *The Cathedral and the Bazaar* (Raymond was arguing for the more transparent bazaar model, rather than the top-down approach of the cathedral). But perhaps the best analogy was offered at the IEEE Computer Society in 1988: "Software and cathedrals are much the same—first we build them, then we pray."[7] This was meant as a joke, of course, but it hides a deeper truth about our relationship to the figure of the algorithm today. The architecture of code relies on a structure of belief as well as a logical organization of bits.

The cathedral is not a perfect metaphor for computation, but its flaws signal precisely what we are missing. A cathedral is a physical and a spiritual structure, a house of God. In that sense the physical appearance of the building tells particular stories about faith and practice (e.g., a baptismal font, a nave pointing east, illustrations of biblical stories). But it also suggests a particular mode of access to the invisible space of religion, the house of God that exists beyond physical reality: transubstantiation, relics, and ceremonies are all part of the spectacle of the cathedral that reflect the invisible machinery of faith. Yet most of that machinery inevitably remains hidden: schisms, budgets, scandals, doctrinal inconsistencies, and other elements of what a software engineer might call the "back-end" of the cathedral are not part of the physical or spiritual facade presented to the world. Indeed, when the spectacle stutters for a moment and some uncomfortable fact lurches into view, the normal instinct is to ignore it, to shore up the facade of the cathedral in order to maintain one's faith. A cathedral is a space for collective belief, a structure that embodies a framework of understandings about the world, some visible and some not.

This is a useful metaphor for understanding the relationship we have with algorithms today. Writing in *The Atlantic* in early 2015, digital culture critic and game designer Ian Bogost called out our increasingly mythological relationship with software in an article titled "The Cathedral of Computation." Bogost argues that we have fallen into a "computational theocracy" that replaces God with the algorithm:

Our supposedly algorithmic culture is not a material phenomenon so much as a devotional one, a supplication made to the computers people have allowed to replace gods in their minds, even as they simultaneously claim that science has made us impervious to religion.[8]

We have, he argues, adopted a faith-based relationship with the algorithmic culture machines that navigate us through city streets, recommend movies to us, and provide us with answers to search queries. We imagine these algorithms as elegant, simple, and efficient, but they are sprawling assemblages involving many forms of human labor, material resources, and ideological choices.

Bogost's central argument is this: while we imagine algorithms as a pinnacle of Enlightenment, rationalist thought, our engagements with them function in a very different mode. Through black boxes, cleanly designed dashboards, and obfuscating Application Program Interfaces, we are asked to take this computation on faith. Just as the poorly paid factory workers who produce our high-tech gadgets are obscured behind the sleek design and marketing of brushed-metal objects that seem to manifest directly from some kind of machine utopia, untouched by human hands, so do we, the eager audience of that utopia, accept the results of software algorithms unquestioningly as the magical products of computation. The commodification of the Enlightenment comes at a price. It turns progress and computational efficiency into a performance, a spectacle that occludes the real decisions and trade-offs behind the mythos of omniscient code.

And we believe it because we have lived with this myth of the algorithm for a long time—much longer than computational pioneers Alan Turing or even Charles Babbage and their speculations about thinking machines. The cathedral is a pervasive metaphor here because it offers an ordering logic, a superstructure or ontology for how we organize meaning in our lives. Bogost is right to cite the Enlightenment in his piece, though I will argue the relationship between algorithmic culture and that tradition of rationalism is more complicated than a simple rejection or deification. The problem we are struggling with today is not that we have turned computation into a cathedral, but that computation has increasingly replaced a cathedral that was already here. This is the cathedral of the Enlightenment's ambitions for a universal system of knowledge. When we juxtapose the two we invest our faith into a series of implemented systems that promise to do the work of rationalism on our behalf, from the automated factory to automated science.

I address this relationship more closely in chapter 2, but for now we need only to appreciate the implications of the cathedral of computation as shorthand for a unified system of understanding. The bas-relief work, statues, and inscriptions of great European cathedrals are microcosms of Christianity, recapitulating the Gospel and other key biblical narratives as well as the histories of their own creation as enduring and complete statements of faith. Contemporary computational systems perform the same role of presenting a unified vision of the world through clean interfaces and carefully curated data—everything you might want to know, now available as an app. Computation offers a pathway for consilience, or the unification of all fields of knowledge into a single tree: an ontology of information founded on the idea that computation is a universal solvent that can untangle any complex system, from human consciousness to the universe itself.

One of the few long-form investigations of the algorithm as a concept, mathematical historian David Berlinski's *Advent of the Algorithm*, even concludes with an argument connecting the notion of universal computation to intelligent design. He argues that the algorithm, a lens for the notion of "effective calculation," has done nothing less than to have "made possible the modern world."[9] Berlinski sees "the appearance of *intelligence* on alien shores"—that is, in the spaces of computation—as further evidence that some explanation for the nature of the universe must exist beyond the system itself.[10] His work turns on the distinction between information and meaning, between the work a Turing Machine does in processing symbols on a tape and the impact of those symbols on the human mind. We hear echoes of *Snow Crash* in the suggestion that Turing and fellow mathematician Emil Post's visions of universal calculating machines are

responsive to a world of *thought*, and not matter at all. ... The essence of their machines is elsewhere, in a universe in which symbols are driven by symbols according to rules that are themselves expressed in symbols.

The place in which these machines reside is the human mind.[11]

This is precisely the apotheosis that Bogost calls out in his essay, suggesting that we have veiled the material realities of algorithms behind a mystical notion of computation as a universal truth. We see this faith in computation invoked repeatedly at the intersection of algorithms and culture. Facebook's mission statement is "to give people the power to share and make the world more open and connected," a position that embeds assumptions like the argument that its social graph algorithms will grant us power; that its closed, proprietary platform will lead to more transparency; and that transparency leads to freedom, and perhaps to empathy. Uber is "evolving the way the world moves. By seamlessly connecting riders to drivers through our apps, we make cities more accessible, opening up more possibilities for riders and more business for drivers." The theocracy of computation will not merely change the world but evolve it, and it will open new possibilities for users, linking proprietary commerce and individual freedom. These changes will be effected not only in the material realm but in the cultural, mental, and even spiritual spaces of empowerment and agency. The algorithm offers us salvation, but only after we accept its terms of service.

The important lesson here is not merely that the venture capitalism of Silicon Valley is the ideology bankrolling much of our contemporary cathedral-building, or even Bogost's warning about computation as a new theology. The lesson is that it's much harder to question a set of ideas when they are assembled into an interconnected structure. A seemingly complete and consistent expression of a system of knowledge offers no seams, no points of access that suggest there might be an outside or alternative to the structure. The story of algorithms is the story of the gap: the space between ideal and implemented computational systems, or between information and meaning. The stories we tell ourselves to deal with the growing power of computation in our lives sometimes trace these tensions, but often they ignore the gap in favor of a more comfortable, or a more magical world. As the famed anthropologist Bronisław Malinowski put it almost a century ago, "magic supplies primitive man with a number of ready-made ritual acts and beliefs, with a definite mental and practical technique which serves to bridge over the dangerous gaps in every important pursuit or critical situation."[12] In the face of computation's rapid advancement, we seem to feel more primitive all the time.

This book is not an argument for or against the algorithm, but rather a new map to the territory grounded in its vital role as a tool that implements computational ideas. Quite simply, the algorithm spans the gap. Compiled from computational and human intellectual materials, it constantly negotiates the tensions between computation and material reality. It casts a double shadow, illuminated on different sides by the light of mathematical logic and cultural understanding, and this book is an effort to trace the silhouette of this protean idea.

Program of the Book

We begin with a sketch of the algorithm from its intellectual taproots to its contemporary presence in culture. Chapter 1 lays out a full reading of the algorithm as a critical concept across four intellectual strands, beginning with its foundations in computer science and the notion of "effective computability." The second strand considers cybernetics and ongoing debates about embodiment, abstraction, and information theory. Third, I return to magic and its overlap with symbolism, engaging with notions of software, "sourcery," and the power of metaphors to represent reality. Fourth, I draw in the long history of technicity and humanity's coevolution with our cultural tools. Synthesizing these threads, I offer a definition of the algorithm as culture machine in the context of process and implementation. The chapter closes with a summary of the essential facets of algorithmic reading and a brief glimpse of algorithmic imagination.

From there we move to an account of the DARPA-funded project to create an intelligent assistant (now known as Siri). Chapter 2 explores the ways in which Google, Apple, and other corporations have turned the development of cultural algorithms into epistemological quests for both self-knowledge and universal knowledge. The anticipatory, intimate knowledge promised by Siri, taken to its logical extreme in the Spike Jonze film *Her*, is an attempt to map out the inner space of the individual psyche more thoroughly than any lover could. This seduction contrasts neatly with Google's drive to create a *"Star Trek* computer" that can answer any question using its perfect map of shared, external knowledge. These quests are both romantic and rational, seeking a transcendent state of knowing, a state that can be reached only with mechanisms that ultimately eclipse the human. Through their ambitions to develop algorithms that can "answer, converse and anticipate," the technology titans shaping our algorithmic future are constructing a new epistemological framework of what is knowable and desirable: an intellectual hierarchy of needs that will ultimately map out not only the public sphere of information but the interior space of human identity. I juxtapose this quest for knowledge with its great enlightenment precursor, the creation of the first *Encyclopédie* by philosopher-publisher Denis Diderot, tracing the parallels in the construction of two culture machines for the perfection of knowledge.

Having established the emergence of algorithmic knowledge, the story turns to the rise of algorithmic aesthetics in chapter 3. Netflix serves as our foil: its rejection of a big-data statistics approach to taste in favor of a hybrid human-computational model has led to the Borges-esque project of taxonomizing all real and potential films into one of 76,897 genres. This massive analytical enterprise shapes the company's creative investments in original work, particularly its original television series *House of Cards*. I use the story of the show's development and distribution to argue that algorithmic models of culture are increasingly influential and inescapable. The affective and commercial position of the series offers us a glimpse of new algorithmic aesthetics that are personalized and monolithic in competing ways. I close the chapter by arguing that Netflix demonstrates the power and pitfalls of

cultural arbitrage by manipulating certain kinds of computational abstraction to achieve cultural and financial success.

As algorithms become more adept at reading cultural data and performing real-time arbitrage (used here in the sense of financial pricing arbitrage
but also cultural arbitrage as described in the previous chapter), they are
taking on new forms of intellectual labor. They are authoring and creating,
but they are also simplifying and abstracting, creating an interface layer
between consumers and the messy process of, say, getting a cab or hiring a
housekeeper. Chapter 4 begins with Ian Bogost's satirical Facebook game
Cow Clicker and its send-up of the "gamification" movement to add quantification and algorithmic thinking to many facets of everyday life. Such
games trouble the boundaries between work and play, as do much
more serious forms of gamification like Uber and the high-tech warehouse
workers whose every second and step are measured for efficiency. Taken
together, these new models of work herald a novel form of alienated labor
for the algorithmic age. In our science fiction present, humans are processors handling simple tasks assigned by an algorithmic apparatus. Drawing
on the historical figure of the automaton, a remarkable collection of
Mechanical Turk-powered poetry titled *Of the Subcontract*, and Adam
Smith's conception of empathy in his *Theory of Moral Sentiments*, I explore
the consequences of computational capitalism on politics, empathy, and
social value.

The root of the algorithmic sea change is the reimagination of value
in computational terms. Chapter 5 leads with the flash crash in 2010 and
the growing dominance of algorithmic trading in international markets
(described by journalist Michael Lewis's *Flash Boys*, among others) to frame
a reading of Bitcoin and related cryptocurrencies. By defining the unit of
exchange through computational cycles, Bitcoin fundamentally shifts the
faith-based community of currency from a materialist to an algorithmic
value system. Algorithmic arbitrage is forcing similar transitions in the
attribution of value and meaning in many spaces of cultural exchange,
from Facebook to journalism. The fundamental shift from valuing the cultural object itself to valuing the networks of relations that the object establishes or supports leads to new practices and aesthetics of production,
where form and genre give way to memes and nebulous collaborative
works. Using Bitcoin as an example of this new value model, I close by
considering the consequences of programmable value for the notion of a

public sphere in the twenty-first century, an era when arbitrage trumps content.

In the coda I briefly retrace this genealogy of the algorithm to consider our future prospects for achieving the twinned desires embedded in the heart of effective computability: the quest for universal knowledge and perfect self-knowledge. These ambitions are particularly vital for the humanities, and we cannot stop at algorithmic reading. To truly grapple with the age of the algorithm and our growing entanglement with computational cultural processes, we need to take action as scholars, teachers, and most of all performers of humanistic inquiry. We need an experimental humanities, a set of strategies for direct engagement with algorithmic production and scholarship, drawing on theories of improvisation and experimental investigation to argue that a culture of process, of algorithmic production, requires a processual criticism that is both reflexive and playful. This is how we can begin to understand the figure of the algorithm as a redrawing of the space for cultural imagination and become true collaborators with culture machines rather than their worshippers or, worse, their pets.

1 What Is an Algorithm?

If we want to live with the machine, we must understand the machine, we must not worship the machine.

Norbert Wiener[1]

Rise of the Culture Machines

Sometime in the late 2000s, our relationship with computers changed. We began carrying devices around in our pockets, peering at them at the dinner table, muttering quietly to them in the corner. We stopped thinking about hardware and started thinking about apps and services. We have come not just to use but to *trust* computational systems that tell us where to go, whom to date, and what to think about (to name just a few examples). With every click, every terms of service agreement, we buy into the idea that big data, ubiquitous sensors, and various forms of machine learning can model and beneficially regulate all kinds of complex systems, from picking songs to predicting crime. Along the way, an old word has become new again: the algorithm. Either overlooked or overhyped, the algorithm is rarely taken seriously as a key term in the cultural work that computers do for us. This book takes that word apart and puts it back together again, showing how algorithms function as culture machines that we need to learn how to read and understand.

Algorithms are everywhere. They already dominate the stock market, compose music, drive cars, write news articles, and author long mathematical proofs—and their powers of creative authorship are just beginning to take shape. Corporations jealously guard the black boxes running these assemblages of data and process. Even the engineers behind some of the most successful and ubiquitous algorithmic systems in the world—executives at Google and Netflix, for example—admit that they understand only some of the behaviors their systems exhibit. But their rhetoric is still transcendent and emancipatory, striking many of the same techno-utopian notes as the mythos of code as magic when they equate computation with transformational justice and freedom. The theology of computation that Ian Bogost identified is a faith militant, bringing the gospel of big data and disruption to huge swaths of society.

This is the context in which we use algorithms today: as pieces of quotidian technical magic that we entrust with booking vacations, suggesting potential mates, evaluating standardized test essays, and performing many other kinds of cultural work. Wall Street traders give their financial "algos" names like Ambush and Raider, yet they often have no idea how their money-making black boxes work.[2] As a keyword in the spirit of cultural critic Raymond Williams,[3] the word algorithm frequently encompasses a range of computational processes including close surveillance of user behaviors, "big data" aggregation of the resulting information, analytics engines that combine multiple forms of statistical calculation to parse that data, and finally a set of human-facing actions, recommendations, and interfaces that generally reflect only a small part of the cultural processing going on behind the scenes. Computation comes to have a kind of presence in the world, becoming a "thing" that both obscures and highlights particular forms of what Wendy Hui Kyong Chun calls "programmability," a notion we will return to in the guise of computationalism below.[4]

It is precisely this protean nature of computation that both troubles and attracts us. At some times computational systems appear to conform to that standard of discrete "thingness," like the *me* of Sumerian myth or a shiny application button on a smartphone screen. At other moments they are much harder to distinguish from broader cultural environments: to what extent are spell-check programs changing diction and grammatical choices through their billions of subtle corrections, and how do we disentangle the assemblage of code, dictionaries, and grammars that underlie them? While the cultural effects and affects of computation are complex, these systems function in the world through instruments designed and implemented by human beings. In order to establish a critical frame for reading cultural computation, we have to begin with those instruments, jammed together in the humble vessel of the algorithm.

Our look at *Snow Crash* revealed the layers of magic, "sourcery," and structured belief that underpin the facade of the algorithm in culture today. Now we turn to the engineers and computer scientists who implement computational systems. Rooted in computer science, this version of the algorithm relies on the history of mathematics. An algorithm is a recipe, an instruction set, a sequence of tasks to achieve a particular calculation or result, like the steps needed to calculate a square root or tabulate the Fibonacci sequence. The word itself derives from Abū ʿAbdallāh Muḥammad ibn Mūsā al-Khwārizmī, the famed ninth-century CE mathematician (from whose name algebra is also derived). *Algorismus* was originally the process for calculating Hindu-Arabic numerals. Via al-Kwarizmi, the algorithm was associated with the revolutionary concepts of positional notation, the decimal point, and zero.

As the word gained currency in the centuries that followed, "algorithm" came to describe any set of mathematical instructions for manipulating data or reasoning through a problem. The Babylonians used some of the first mathematical algorithms to derive square roots and factor numbers.[5] Euclid devised an algorithm for taking two numbers and finding the greatest common divisor they share. Throughout this evolution, the algorithm retained an essential feature that will soon become central to the story: it just works. That is to say, an algorithm reliably delivers an expected result within a finite amount of time (except, perhaps, for those edge cases that fascinate mathematicians and annoy engineers).

Historian Nathan Ensmenger recounts how the academic discipline of computer science coalesced only after its advocates embraced the concept of the algorithm, with one of the field's founders, Donald Knuth, tracing the field's origins to al-Khwarizmi in his seminal textbook *The Art of Computer Programming*.[6] The algorithm was an ideal object of study, both easily grasped and endlessly puzzling:

By suggesting that the algorithm was as fundamental to the technical activity of computing as Sir Isaac Newton's laws of motion were to physics, Knuth and his fellow computer scientists could claim full fellowship with the larger community of scientists.[7]

And yet, as mathematician Yiannis Moschovakis points out, Knuth's argument about what algorithms actually are is an extremely rare instance where the question is foregrounded.[8] For computer scientists the term remains more of an intuitive, unexamined notion than a delineated logical concept grounded in a mathematical theory of computation.

Thanks in large part to Knuth, the algorithm today is a fundamental concept in computer science, an intellectual keystone typically covered in the introductory Algorithms and Data Structures course for undergraduate majors. Algorithms represent repeatable, practical solutions to problems like factoring a number into its smallest prime number components or finding the most efficient pathway through a network. The major focus for contemporary algorithmic research is not whether they work but how efficiently, and with what tradeoffs in terms of CPU cycles, memory, and accuracy.

We can distill this pragmatic approach to algorithms down to a single PowerPoint slide. Robert Sedgewick, a leading researcher on computational algorithms, also happened to teach the version of Algorithms and Data Structures that I took as an undergraduate; he calls the algorithm a "method for solving a problem" in his widely circulated course materials.[9] This is what I term the *pragmatist's definition*: an engineer's notion of algorithms geared toward defining problems and solutions. The pragmatist's definition grounds its truth claim in utility: algorithms are fit for a purpose, illuminating pathways between problems and solutions. This is the critical frame that dominates the breakout rooms and workstations of engineers at Google, Apple, Amazon, and other industry giants. As Google describes them: "Algorithms are the computer processes and formulas that take your questions and turn them into answers."[10] For many engineers and technologists, algorithms are quite simply the work, the medium of their labor.

The pragmatic definition lays bare the essential politics of the algorithm, its transparent complicity in the ideology of instrumental reason that digital culture scholar David Golumbia calls out in his critique of computation.[11] Of course this is what algorithms do: they are methods, inheriting the inductive tradition of the scientific method and engineering from Archimedes to Vannevar Bush. They solve problems that have been identified as such by the engineers and entrepreneurs who develop and optimize the code. But such implementations are never just code: a method for solving a problem inevitably involves all sorts of technical and intellectual inferences, interventions, and filters.

As an example, consider the classic computer science problem of the traveling salesman: how can one calculate an efficient route through a geography of destinations at various distances from one another? The question has many real-world analogs, such as routing UPS drivers, and indeed that company has invested hundreds of millions of dollars in a 1,000-page algorithm called ORION that bases its decisions in part on traveling salesman heuristics.[12] And yet the traveling salesman problem imagines each destination as an identical point on a graph, while UPS drop-offs vary greatly in the amount of time they take to complete (hauling a heavy package up with a handcart, say, or avoiding the owner's terrier). ORION's algorithmic model of the universe must balance between particular computational abstractions (each stop is a featureless, fungible point), the lived experience and feedback of human drivers, and the data the company has gathered about the state of the world's stop signs, turn lanes, and so on. The computer science question of optimizing paths through a network must share the computational stage with the autonomy of drivers, the imposition of quantified tracking on micro-logistical decisions like whether to make a right or left turn, and the unexpected interventions of other complex human systems, from traffic jams to pets.

ORION and its 1,000-page "solution" to this tangled problem is, of course, a process or system in continued evolution rather than an elegant equation for the balletic coordination of brown trucks. Its equations and computational models of human behavior are just one example among millions of algorithms attempting to regularize and optimize complex cultural systems. The pragmatist's definition achieves clarity by constructing an edifice (a cathedral) of tacit knowledge, much of it layered in systems of abstraction like the traveling salesman problem. At a certain level of cultural success, these systems start to create their own realities as well: various players in the system begin to alter their behavior in ways that short-circuit the system's assumptions. Internet discussion boards catalog complaints about delivery drivers who do not bother to knock and instead leave door tags claiming that the resident was not at home. These shortcuts work precisely because they are invisible to systems like ORION, allowing the driver to save valuable seconds and perhaps catch up on all those other metrics that *are* being tracked on a hectic day when the schedule starts to slip.

Many of the most powerful corporations in existence today are essentially cultural wrappers for sophisticated algorithms, as we will see in the following chapters. Google exemplifies a company, indeed an entire worldview, built on an algorithm, PageRank. Amazon's transformational algorithm involved not just computation but logistics, finding ways to outsource, outmaneuver, and outsell traditional booksellers (and later, sellers of almost every kind of consumer product). Facebook developed the world's most successful social algorithm for putting people in contact with one another. These are just a few examples of powerful, pragmatic, lucrative algorithms that are constantly updated and modified to cope with the messy cultural spaces they attempt to compute.

We live, for the most part, in a world built by algorithmic pragmatists. Indeed, the ambition and scale of corporate operations like Google means that their definitions of algorithms—what the problems are, and how to solve them—can profoundly change the world. Their variations of pragmatism then inspire elaborate responses and counter-solutions, or what communication researcher Tarleton Gillespie calls the "tacit negotiation" we perform to adapt ourselves to algorithmic systems: we enunciate differently when speaking to machines, use hashtags to make updates more machine-readable, and describe our work in search engine-friendly terms.[13]

The tacit assumptions lurking beneath the pragmatist's definition are becoming harder and harder to ignore. The apparent transparency and simplicity of computational systems are leading many to see them as vehicles for unbiased decision-making. Companies like UpStart and ZestFinance view computation as a way to judge financial reliability and make loans to people who fail more traditional algorithmic tests of credit-worthiness, like credit scores.[14] These systems essentially deploy algorithms to counter the bias of other algorithms, or more cynically to identify business opportunities missed by others. The companies behind these systems are relatively unusual, however, in acknowledging the ideological framing of their business plans, and explicitly addressing how their systems attempt to judge "character."

But if these are reflexive counter-algorithms designed to capitalize on systemic inequities, they are responding to broader cultural systems that typically lack such awareness. The computational turn means that many algorithms now reconstruct and efface legal, ethical, and perceived reality according to mathematical rules and implicit assumptions that are shielded from public view. As legal ethicist Frank Pasquale writes about algorithms for evaluating job candidates:

Automated systems claim to rate all individuals the same way, thus averting discrimination. They may ensure some bosses no longer base hiring and firing decisions on hunches, impressions, or prejudices. But software engineers construct the datasets mined by scoring systems; they define the parameters of data-mining analyses; they create the clusters, links, and decision trees applied; they generate the predictive models applied. Human biases and values are embedded into each and every step of development. Computerization may simply drive discrimination upstream.[15]

As algorithms move deeper into cultural space, the pragmatic definition gets scrutinized more closely according to critical frames that reject the engineering rubric of problem and solution, as Pasquale, Golumbia, and a growing number of algorithmic ethics scholars have argued. The cathedral of abstractions and embedded systems that allow the pragmatic algorithms of the world to flourish can be followed down to its foundations in symbolic logic, computational theory, and cybernetics, where we find a curious thing among that collection of rational ideas: desire.

From Computation to Desire

What are the truth claims underlying the engineer's problems and solutions, or the philosophy undergirding the technological magic of sourcery? They depend on the protected space of computation, the logical, procedural, immaterial space where memory and process work according to very different rules from material culture. The pragmatist's approach gestures toward, and often depends on, a deeper philosophical claim about the nature of the universe. We need to understand that claim as the grounding for the notion of "effective computability," a transformational concept in computer science that fuels algorithmic evangelism today. In her book *My Mother Was a Computer*, media theorist N. Katherine Hayles labels this philosophical claim the Regime of Computation.[16] This is another term for what I sometimes refer to as the age of the algorithm: the era dominated by the figure of the algorithm as an ontological structure for understanding the universe. We can also think of this as the "computationalist definition," which extends the pragmatist's notion of the algorithm and informs the core business models of companies like Google and Amazon.

In its softer version, computationalism argues that algorithms have no ontological claim to truly describing the world but are highly effective at solving particular technical problems. The engineers are agnostic about the universe as a system; all they care about is accurately modeling certain parts of it, like the search results that best correspond to certain queries or the books that users in Spokane, Washington, are likely to order today. As Pasquale and a host of other digital culture critics from Jaron Lanier to Evgeny Morozov have argued, even the implicit claims to efficiency and "good-enough" rationalism at the heart of the engineer's definition of algorithms have a tremendous impact on policy, culture, and the practice of everyday life, because the compromises and analogies of algorithmic approximations tend to efface everything that they do not comprehend.[17]

The expansion of the rhetoric of computation easily bleeds into what Hayles calls the "hard claim" for computationalism. In this argument algorithms do not merely describe cultural processes with more or less accuracy: those processes are themselves computational machines that can be mathematically duplicated (given enough funding). According to this logic it is merely a matter of time and applied science before computers can simulate election outcomes or the future price of stocks to *any desired degree* of accuracy. Computer scientist and polymath Stephen Wolfram lays out the argument in his ambitious twenty-year undertaking, *A New Kind of Science*:

The crucial idea that has allowed me to build a unified framework for the new kind of science that I describe in this book is that just as the rules for any system can be viewed as corresponding to a program, so also its behavior can be viewed as corresponding to a computation.[18]

Wolfram's principle of computational equivalence makes the strong claim that all complex systems are fundamentally computational and, as he hints in the connections he draws between his work and established fields like theoretical physics and philosophy, he believes that computationalism offers "a serious possibility that [a fundamental theory for the universe] can actually be found."[19] This notion that the computational metaphor could unlock a new paradigm of scientific inquiry carries with it tremendous implications about the nature of physical systems, social behavior, and consciousness, among other things, and at its most extreme serves as an ideology of transcendence for those who seek to use computational systems to model and understand the universe.

Citing Wolfram and fellow computer scientists Harold Morowitz and Edward Fredkin, Hayles traces the emergence of an ideology of universal computation based on the science of complexity: if the universe is a giant computer, it is not only efficient but intellectually necessary to develop computational models for cultural problems like evaluating loan applications or modeling consciousness. The models may not be perfect now but they will improve as we use them, because they employ the same computational building blocks as the system they emulate. On a deeper level, computationalism suggests that our knowledge of computation will answer many fundamental questions: computation becomes a universal solvent for problems in the physical sciences, theoretical mathematics, and culture alike. The quest for knowledge becomes a quest for computation, a hermeneutics of modeling.

But of course models always compress or shorthand reality. If the anchor point for the pragmatist's definition of the algorithm is its indefinable flexibility based on tacit understanding about what counts as a problem and a solution, the anchor point here is the notion of abstraction. The argument for computationalism begins with the Universal Turing Machine, mathematician Alan Turing's breathtaking vision of a computer that can complete any finite calculation simply by reading and writing to an infinite tape marked with 1s and 0s, moving the tape forward or backward based on the current state of the machine. Using just this simple mechanism one could emulate any kind of computer, from a scientific calculator finding the area under a curve to a Nintendo moving Mario across a television screen. In other words, this establishes a computational "ceiling" where any Turing computer can emulate any other: the instructions may proceed more slowly or quickly, but are mathematically equivalent.

The Universal Turing Machine is a thought experiment that determines the bounds of what is computable: Turing and his fellow mathematician Alonzo Church were both struggling with the boundary problems of mathematics. In one framing, posed by mathematician David Hilbert, known as the *Entscheidungsproblem*, the question is whether it's possible to predict when or if a particular program will halt, ending its calculations with or without an answer. Their responses to Hilbert, now called the Church–Turing thesis, define algorithms for theorists in a way that is widely accepted but ultimately unprovable: a calculation with natural numbers, or what most of us know as whole numbers, is "effectively computable" (that is, given enough time and pencils, a human could do it) only if the Universal Turing Machine can do it. The thesis uses this informal definition to unite three different rigorous mathematical theses about computation (Turing machines, Church's lambda calculus, and mathematician Kurt Gödel's concept of recursive functions), translating their specific mathematical claims into a more general boundary statement about the limits of computational abstraction.

In another framing, as David Berlinski argues in his mathematical history *The Advent of the Algorithm*, the computability boundary that Turing, Gödel, and Church were wrestling with was also an investigation into the deep foundations of mathematical logic.[20] Gödel proved, to general dismay, that it was impossible for a symbolic logical system to be internally consistent and provable using only statements within the system. The truth claim or validation of such a system would always depend on some external presumption or assertion of logical validity: turtles all the way down. Church grappled with this problem and developed the lambda calculus, a masterful demonstration of abstraction that served as the philosophical foundation for numerous programming languages decades after his work.[21] As Berlinski puts it, Turing had "an uncanny and almost unfailing ability to sift through the work of his time and in the sifting discern the outlines of something far simpler than the things that other men saw."[22] In other words, he possessed a genius for abstraction, and his greatest achievement in this regard was the Turing machine.

Turing's simple imaginary machine is an elegant mathematical proof for universal computation, but it is also an ur-algorithm, an abstraction generator. The mathematical equivalence of Church and Turing's work quickly suggested that varying proofs of effective computability (there are now over thirty) all gesture toward some fundamental universal truth. But every abstraction has a shadow, a puddled remainder of context and specificity left behind in the act of lifting some idea to a higher plane of thought. The Turing machine leaves open the question of what "effectively computable" might really mean in material reality, where we leave elegance and infinite tapes behind. As it has evolved from a thought experiment to a founding tenet of computationalism (and the blueprint for the computational revolution of the twentieth and twenty-first centuries), the Church–Turing thesis has developed a gravitational pull, a tug many feel to organize the universe according to its logic. The concept of universal computation encodes at its heart an intuitive notion of "effective": achievable in a finite number of steps, and reaching some kind of desired result. From the beginning, then, algorithms have encoded a particular kind of abstraction, the *abstraction of the desire for an answer*. The spectacular clarity and rigor of these formative proofs in computation exists in stark contrast to the remarkably ill-defined way that the term is deployed in the field of computer science and elsewhere.[23]

This desire encoded in the notion of effectiveness is typically obscured in the regime of computation, but the role of abstraction is celebrated. The Universal Turing Machine provides a conceptual platform for uniting all kinds of computing: algorithms for solving a set of problems in particle physics might suddenly be useful in genetics; network analysis can be deployed to analyze and compare books, business networks, and bus systems. Abstraction itself is one of the most powerful tools the Church–Turing thesis—and computation in general—gives us, enabling platform-agnostic software and the many metaphors and visual abstractions we depend on, like the desktop user interface.

Abstraction is the ladder Wolfram et al. use to climb from particular computational systems to the notion of universal computation. Many complex systems demonstrate computational features or appear to be computable. If complex systems are themselves computational Turing Machines, they are therefore equivalent: weather systems, human cognition, and most provocatively the universe itself.[24] The grand problems of the cosmos (the origins thereof, the relationship of time and space) and the less grand problems of culture (box office returns, intelligent web searching, natural language processing) are irreducible but also calculable: they are not complicated problems with simple answers but rather simple problems (or rulesets) that generate complicated answers. These assumptions open the door to a *mathesis universalis*, a language of science that the philosophers Gottfried Wilhelm Leibniz, René Descartes, and others presaged as a way to achieve perfect understanding of the natural world.[25] This perfect language would exactly describe the universe through its grammar and vocabulary, becoming a new kind of rational magic for scientists that would effectively describe and be the world.

Effective computability continues to be an alluring, ambiguous term today, a fault line between the pragmatist and computationalist definition of algorithms. I think of this as computation's first seduction, rooted at the heart of the Church–Turing thesis. It has expanded its sway with the growth of computing power, linking back to the tap root of rationalism, gradually becoming a deeper, more romantic mythos of a computational ontology for the universe. The desire to make the world effectively calculable drives many of the seminal moments of computer history, from the first ballistics computers replacing humans in mid-century missile defense to Siri and the Google search bar.[26] It is the ideology that underwrites the age of the algorithm, and its seductive claims about the status of human knowledge and complex systems in general form the central tension in the relationship between culture and culture machines.

To understand the consequences of effective computability, we need to follow three interwoven threads as the implications of this idea work themselves out across disciplines and cultural fields: cybernetics, symbolic language, and technical cognition.

Thread 1: Embodying the Machine

"Effective computability" is an idea with consequences not just for our conception of humanity's place in the universe but how we understand biological, cultural, and social systems. Leibniz's vision of a *mathesis universalis* is seductive because it promises that a single set of intellectual tools can make all mysteries accessible, from quantum mechanics to the circuits inside the human brain. After World War II, a new field emerged to pursue that promise, struggling to align mathematics and materiality, seeking to map out direct correlations between computation and the physical and social sciences. In its heyday cybernetics, as the field was known, was a sustained intellectual argument about the place of algorithms in material culture—a debate about the politics of implementing mathematical ideas, or claiming to find them embodied, in physical and biological systems.

The polymathic mathematician Norbert Wiener published the founding text of this new discipline in 1949, calling it *Cybernetics; or Control and Communication in the Animal and the Machine*. Wiener names Leibniz the patron saint of cybernetics: "The philosophy of Leibniz centers about two closely related concepts—that of a universal symbolism and that of a calculus of reasoning."[27] As the book's title suggests, the aim of cybernetics in the 1940s and 1950s was to define and implement those two ideas: an intellectual system that could encompass all scientific fields, and a means of quantifying change within that system. Using them, the early cyberne-ticians sought to forge a synthesis between the nascent fields of computer science, information theory, physics, and many others (indeed, Wiener nominated his patron saint in part as the last man to have "full command of all the intellectual activity of his day").[28] The vehicle for this synthesis was, intellectually, the field of information theory and the ordering fea-tures of communication between different individual and collective enti-ties, and pragmatically, the growing power of mechanical and computational systems to measure, modulate, and direct such communications.

On a philosophical level, Wiener's vision of cybernetics depended on the transition from certainty to probability in the twentieth century.[29] The advances of Einsteinian relativity and quantum mechanics suggested that uncertainty, or indeterminacy, was fundamental to the cosmos and that observation always affected the system being observed. This marked the displacement of a particular rationalist ideal of the Enlightenment, the notion that the universe operated by simple, all-powerful laws that could be discovered and mastered. Instead, as the growing complexity of math-ematical physics in the twentieth and twenty-first centuries has revealed, the closer we look at a physical system, the more important probability becomes. It is unsettling to abandon the comfortable solidity of a table, that ancient prop for philosophers of materialism, and replace it with a probabilistic cloud of atoms. And yet only with probability—more impor-tant, a language of probability—can we begin to describe our relativistic universe.

But far more unsettling, and the central thesis of the closely allied field of information theory, is the notion that probability applies to information as much as to material reality. By framing information as uncertainty, as surprise, as unpredicted new data, mathematician Claude Shannon created a quantifiable measurement of communication.[30] Shannon's framework has informed decades of work in signal processing, cryptography, and sev-eral other fields, but its starkly limited view of what counts has become a major influence in contemporary understandings of computational knowl-edge. This measurement of information is quite different from the common cultural understanding of knowledge, though it found popular expression in cybernetics, particularly in Wiener's general audience book *The Human Use of Human Beings*. This is where Wiener lays one of the cornerstones for the cathedral of computation: "To live effectively is to live with adequate information. Thus, communication and control belong to the essence of man's inner life, even as they belong to his life in society."[31] In its limited theoretical sense, information provided a common yardstick for understanding any kind of organized system; in its broader public sense, it became the leading edge of computationalism, a method for quantifying patterns and therefore uniting biophysical and mathematical forms of complexity.

As Wiener's quote suggests, the crucial value of information for cybernetics was in making decisions.[32] Communication and control became the computational language through which biological systems, social structures, and physics could be united. As Hayles argues in *How We Became Posthuman*, theoretical models of biophysical reality like the early McCulloch–Pitts Neuron (which the logician Walter Pitts proved to be computationally equivalent to a Turing machine) allowed cybernetics to establish correlations between computational and biological processes at paradigmatic and operational levels and lay claim to being what informatics scholar Geoffrey Bowker calls a "universal discipline."[33] Via cybernetics, information was the banner under which "effective computability" expanded to vast new territories, first presenting the tantalizing prospect that Wolfram and others would later reach for as universal computation.[34] As early as *The Human Use of Human Beings*, Wiener popularized these links between the Turing machine, neural networks, and learning in biological organisms, work that is now coming to startling life in the stream of machine learning breakthroughs announced by the Google subsidiary DeepMind over the past few years.

This is Wiener ascending the ladder of abstraction, positioning cybernetics as a new Liebnitzian *mathesis universalis* capable of uniting a variety of fields. Central to this upper ascent is the notion of homeostasis, or the way that a system responds to feedback to preserve its core patterns and identity. A bird maintaining altitude in changing winds, a thermostat controlling temperature in a room, and the repetition of ancient myths through the generations are all examples of homeostasis at work. More provocatively, Wiener suggests that homeostasis might be the same thing as identity or life itself, if "the organism is seen as message. Organism is opposed to chaos, to disintegration, to death, as message is to noise."[35] This line of argument evolved into the theory of autopoiesis proposed by philosophers Humberto Maturana and Francisco Varela in the 1970s, the second wave of cybernetics which adapted the pattern-preservation of homeostasis more fully into the context of biological systems. Describing organisms as information also suggests the opposite, that information has a will to survive, that as Stewart Brand famously put it, "information wants to be free."[36]

Like Neal Stephenson's programmable minds, like the artificial intelligence researchers who seek to model the human brain, this notion of the organism as message reframes biology (and the human) to exist at least aspirationally within the boundary of effective computability. Cybernetics and autopoiesis lead to complexity science and efforts to model these processes in simulation. Mathematician John Conway's game of life, for

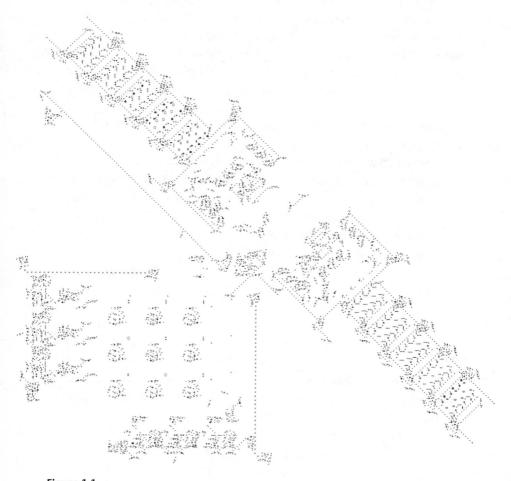

Figure 1.1
"This is a Turing Machine implemented in Conway's Game of Life." Designed by Paul Rendell.

example, seeks to model precisely this kind of spontaneous generation of information, or seemingly living or self-perpetuating patterns, from simple rule-sets. It, too, has been shown to be mathematically equivalent to a Turing machine, and indeed mathematician Paul Rendell designed a game of life that he proved to be Turing-equivalent (figure 1.1).[37]

In fact, if we accept the premise of organism as message, of informational patterns as a central organizing logic for biological life, we inevitably come to depend on computation as a frame for exploring that premise. Wiener's opening gambit of the turn from certainty to probability displaced but did not eliminate the old Enlightenment goals of universal, consilient knowledge. That ambition has now turned to building the best model, the finest simulation of reality's complex probabilistic processes. Berlinski observed the same trend in the distinction between analytic and computational calculus, noting how the discrete modeling of intractable differential equations allows us to better understand how complex systems operate, but always at the expense of gaining a temporally and numerically discrete, approximated view of things.[38] The embrace of cybernetic theory has increasingly meant an embrace of computational *simulations* of social, biological, and physical systems as central objects of study.

Hayles traces this plumb line in cybernetics closely in *How We Became Posthuman*, arguing that the Macy Conferences, where Wiener and his collaborators hammered out the vision for a cybernetic theory, also marked a concerted effort to erase the embodied nature of information through abstraction. In the transcripts, letters, and other archival materials stemming from these early conversations, she argues that the synthesizing ambitions of cybernetics led participants to shy away from considerations of reflexivity and the complications of embodiment, especially human embodiment, as they advanced their theory. But, as Hayles puts it, "In the face of such a powerful dream, it can be a shock to remember that for information to exist, it must *always* be instantiated in a medium."[39]

While Hayles's reading of cybernetics pursues the field's rhetorical ascent of the ladder of abstraction as she frames the story of "how information lost its body," there is a second side to the cybernetic moment in the 1940s and 1950s, one that fed directly into the emergence of Silicon Valley and the popular understanding of computational systems as material artifacts. We can follow Wiener back down the ladder of abstraction, too, through a second crucial cybernetic term, the notion of "feedback." The feedback loop, as Hayles notes, is of interest to Wiener primarily as a universal intellectual model for understanding how communication and control can be generalized across different systems.[40] But the feedback loop was also a crucial moment of implementation for cybernetics, where the theoretical model was tested through empirical experiments and, perhaps more important, demonstrations.

Consider Wiener's "moth" or "bedbug," a single machine designed to demonstrate a feedback loop related to seeking or avoiding light. Wiener worked with electrical engineer Jerry Wiesner to create the machine, a simple mechanical apparatus with one photocell facing to the right and another to the left, with their inputs directing a "tiller" mechanism that would aim the cart's wheels as they moved. The demonstration achieved its intended purpose of showing lifelike behavior from a simple feedback mechanism, creating a seeming existence proof both of the similarity of mechanical and biophysical control mechanisms and of the efficacy of cybernetics as the model for explaining them. In fact, as historian Ronald Kline describes, the entire enterprise was a public relations stunt, the construction of the robot financed by *Life* magazine, which planned to run an article on cybernetics.[41] Wiener's demonstration machine presaged future spectacles of human–machine interaction like early Silicon Valley icon Douglas Engelbart's "mother of all demos," which first showcased several aspects of a functional personal computer experience in 1968.

The theoretical aspirations of cybernetics were always dependent on material implementation, a fact that has challenged generations of artificial intelligence researchers pursuing the platonic ideal of neural networks that effectively model the human mind.[42] Kline reports that *Life* never ran photos of Wiener's moth because an editor felt the machine "illustrated the *analogy* between humans and machines by modeling the nervous system, rather than showing the *human characteristics* of computers, which was *Life*'s objective."[43] In the end, Wiener had built a bug. The material context of the moth included not just a functioning feedback mechanism on wheels but the cultural aperture through which that construct would be viewed. In implementation, the mechanical feedback loop was overshadowed by an intellectual one, the relationship between a public scientist and his editors at *Life*. As it turned out they were less interested in Wiener's argument, that feedback mechanisms could be computationally

Figure 1.2
Norbert Wiener and his "moth" circa 1950. Alfred Eisenstaedt / The LIFE Picture Collection / Getty Images.

and mechanically modeled, than they were in searching out the human in the machine.

Thread 2: Metaphors for Magic

More than anything else, cybernetics was an attempt to create a new controlling metaphor for communication, one that integrated technological, biological, and social forms of knowledge. The story of Wiener's moth illustrates the hazards of this approach: defining a controlling metaphor for communication, and by extension for knowledge, requires a deep examination of how language itself can shape both ideas and reality. The cybernetic vision of a unified biological and computational understanding of the world has never left us, continuing to reappear in the technical and critical metaphors we use to manipulate and understand computational systems. Chun explores the deeper implications of this persistent interlacing of computational and biological metaphors for code in *Programmed Visions*, demonstrating the interconnections of research into DNA and computer programming, and how those metaphors open up the interpretive problem of computation. For Chun the key term is "software," a word she uses to encompass many of the same concerns I explore here in the context of the algorithm.

Programmed Visions draws a direct link between the notion of fungible computability reified by the Turing machine and the kinds of linguistic magic that have come to define so many of our computational experiences:

Software is unique in its status as metaphor for metaphor itself. As a universal imitator/machine, it encapsulates a logic of general substitutability; a logic of ordering and creative, animating disordering. Joseph Weizenbaum has argued that computers have become metaphors for "effective procedures," that is, for anything that can be solved in a prescribed number of steps, such as gene expression and clerical work.[44]

With the "logic of general substitutability," software has become a *thing*, Chun argues, embodying the central function of magic—the manipulation of symbols in ways that impact the world. This fundamental alchemy, the mysterious fungibility of sourcery, reinforces a reading of the Turing machine as an ur-algorithm that has been churning out effective computability abstractions in the minds of its "users" for eighty years. The "thing" that software has become is the cultural figure of the algorithm: instantiated metaphors for effective procedures. Software is like Bogost's cathedral of computation, Chun argues, "a powerful metaphor for everything we believe is invisible yet generates visible effects, from genetics to the invisible hand of the market, from ideology to culture."[45] Like the crucifix or a bell-tower signaling Sunday mass, software is ubiquitous and mysterious even when it is obvious, manifesting in familiar forms that are only symbolic representations of the real work it does behind the scenes.

The elegant formulation of software as a metaphor for metaphor, paired with Chun's quotation of Weizenbaum—the MIT computer scientist who created an alarmingly successful algorithmic psychotherapist called ELIZA in the 1960s—draws together cybernetics and magic through the notion that computers themselves have become metaphors for the space of effective computability. The algorithm is not a space where the material and symbolic orders are contested, but rather a magical or alchemical realm where they operate in productive indeterminacy. Algorithms span the gap between code and implementation, between software and experience.

In this light, computation is a universal solvent precisely because it is both metaphor and machine. Like Wiener's robotic moth, the implemented algorithm is on the one hand an intellectual gesture ("Hello, world!"), a publicity stunt, and on the other a functioning system that embeds material assumptions about perception, decision-making, and communication in its construction. For example, think of the humble progress bar. When a new piece of software presents an indicator allegedly graphing the pace of installation, that code might well be a bit of magic (the status of the bar holding little relation to the actual work going on behind the scenes). But that familiar inching bar is also a functional reality for the user because no matter how fictitious the "progress" being mapped, nothing else is going to happen until the bar hits 100 percent—the illusion dictates reality. The algorithm of the progress bar depends not only on the code generating it but the cultural calculus of waiting itself, on a user seeking feedback from the system, and on the opportunity—increasingly capitalized on—to show that user other messages, entertainments, or advertising during the waiting phase.

As our generally unthinking acceptance of the progress bar demonstrates, we are primed to accept these magical calculations on multiple levels. We believe in the power of code as a set of magical symbols linking the invisible and visible, echoing our long cultural tradition of *logos*, or language as an underlying system of order and reason, and its power as a kind of sourcery. We believe in the elegant abstractions of cybernetics and, ultimately, the computational universe—that algorithms embody and reproduce the mathematical substrate of reality in culturally readable ways. This is what it means to say that an algorithm is a *culture machine*: it operates both within and beyond the reflexive barrier of effective computability, producing culture at a macro-social level at the same time as it produces cultural objects, processes, and experiences.

Just because we are growing more familiar, more intimately entangled with these culture machines, however, does not mean we understand the nature of their magic any more deeply. Weizenbaum argues that even for those closest to the mysteries, the programmers and developers who directly implement algorithms in code,

instrumental reason has made out of words a fetish surrounded by black magic. And only the magicians have the rights of the initiated. Only they can say what words mean. And they play with words and they deceive us.[46]

Chun extends Weizenbaum's reference to fetish, arguing that the fetish of source code has only increased the perceived occult power of computation and the programmers who wield it. But, as she points out soon afterward, there is a channel through which we attempt to reconstruct the invisible working of the mechanism.

The fact that there is an algorithm, a meaning intended by code (and thus in some way knowable), sometimes structures our experience with programs. When we play a game, we arguably try to reverse engineer its algorithm or at the very least link its actions to its programming, which is why all design books warn against coincidence or random mapping, since it can induce paranoia in its users. That is, because an interface is programmed, most users treat coincidence as meaningful. To the user, as with the paranoid schizophrenic, there is always meaning: whether or not the user knows the meaning, s/he knows that it regards him or her.[47]

This is a quest for knowledge where the game substitutes for the world. Chun reveals another form of magic—an interpolation of purpose or meaning behind the informational experiences of computation. When we attempt to penetrate the mysteries of the interface, we are usually far less interested in *how* the experience works (where the bits are stored, how the pixels are rendered) than we are in *why*. If software is a metaphor for metaphors, the algorithm becomes the mechanism of translation: the prism or instrument by which the eternally fungible space of effective computability is focalized and instantiated in a particular program, interface, or user experience. With our apophenia, our desperate hunt for meaningful patterns, we try to peer through the algorithm to catch a glimpse of the computation behind it.

This is the purest expression of the fundamental magic of language itself as a system for effectively transmitting meaning and experience across the gulf between minds. As the instrument for spanning computational and cultural spaces, the algorithm also serves as a bridge that can, at times,

allow traffic in both directions: meaning, or at least the promise of meaning, and an avenue for interpretation. The search for that meaning behind
the screen is what Berlinski calls the search for "intelligence on alien
shores," an idea he pursues to the unexpected conclusion that algorithmic
intelligence might support an argument for the universe's intelligent
design.[48] This is a bridge too far, but the argument underscores the deep
links between the cathedral and computation. Abstraction from the patterns, games, and politics of code to the discovery of meanings behind
them is the essential move of algorithmic reading, which we return to
below. Chun's fetishism and Berlinski's intelligent design have something
in common, then: an argument that the central magic of computation
depends on a quest for meaning, for understanding, that depends on particular forms of human cognition and recognition.

Thread 3: How to Think about Algorithms

Following the threads of embodied computation and the power of language
to their conclusions brings us to the most challenging, and perhaps most
interesting, question of all: how the mind itself grapples with effective computability. Our fascination with complexity and the search for meaning in
patterns underlies some of our most entrenched myths about how we relate
to our machines and tools on a cognitive level. This is what makes stories
like *Snow Crash* so compelling: they address a deep-seated desire to fuse
internal and external structures of order and meaning. A universal operating system for the human mind carries with it all sorts of implications for
how information can be transmuted into knowledge both within and
beyond our embodied physical selves—knowledge that, as in cybernetics,
translates precisely between computational and biological information systems. Variations on this idealized link between computation and cognition
run in both directions, from instantly downloading the knowledge of kung
fu in *The Matrix* to the vision advanced by advocates of the singularity
for uploading consciousness onto a digital computer. Those extremes are
so fantastic, however, that they sometimes obscure the many ways that
algorithms are already changing how we think.

Technological interfaces with consciousness are not only the stuff of
science fiction. We use all sorts of tools to enhance or modify our mental
experience of the world. These can be algorithmic systems, like those

sophisticated notifications and nudges smartphones can deploy to encourage their owners to exercise more or depart on time for an upcoming meeting. Or they can be very simple, like a blind man using a cane to navigate. Indeed, as Plato famously argued in the *Phaedrus*, writing itself is such a technology, one he feared would diminish the mental faculties of those who depended on it instead of their own powers of memory and understanding.[49] Thus begins the long history of humanity outsourcing our minds to machines: entrusting our thoughts and memories to stone, papyrus, lithograph, wax platter, photographic negative, hard drive, and networked storage service. The extension of human memory in technological dimensions allows us to "remember" far more today than we ever did, even as it alters our capacity to perform certain kinds of biological recollection by encouraging us to focus on how we might access information rather than the information itself.[50]

The philosopher of cognition Andy Clark has called this the "extended mind," a framing of cognition that accommodates the many ways in which it spills out of the conscious brain into the body and our surrounding social and technical environments.[51] As we grow more engaged and connected to algorithmic systems, the "coupling" or dependency on external resources for memory, decision-making, and even desire can become stronger.[52] As Clark writes in *Natural-Born Cyborgs*,

Human thought and reason is born out of looping interactions between material brains, material bodies, and complex cultural and technological environments. We create these supportive environments, but they create us too.[53]

It is in large part because this kind of technological extension is already so deeply embedded in human culture that the possible integration of human and computer has been so fraught. The contemporary version of Plato's concern springs from the same source as Stephenson's nam-shub— the idea that human thought and computational processes can be shown to be equivalent. The question, as Weizenbaum puts it, of "whether or not human thought is entirely computable" has led, in the guise of scientism and the blind worship of modern technical systems, to the "spiritual cosmologies engendered by modern science [becoming] infected with the germ of logical necessity."[54] Echoing Wiener's move from certainty to probability, "they convert truth to provability."[55] Weizenbaum suggests that our obsession with mastering everything that falls within the boundaries of effective computability has not only blinded us to what lies beyond that frontier, but also weakened our capacity to understand or debate the failings of computation within its domain. "Belief in the rationality-logicality equation has corroded the prophetic power of language itself. We can count, but we are rapidly forgetting how to say what is worth counting and why."[56] We confuse knowledge and meaning, process and purpose, by substituting the teleology of the original Enlightenment quest for knowledge with that secondary substitute, the quest for quantification and calculability.

Extending this line of thinking, what troubles Weizenbaum the most is *not* the vision of computers directly emulating human thought, or minds modeled in silicon, but rather the corrosive impact of computational thinking on the human self. "Now that language has become merely another tool, all concepts, ideas, images that artists and writers cannot paraphrase into computer-comprehensible language have lost their function and their potency."[57] Golumbia takes up this polemical argument against computationalism as a politically dangerous ideology (to which we return below), but Weizenbaum's fundamental concern here is about linguistic imagination and the "prophetic power" of words. The gravity, the pull of computation, encourages us to discipline and order our language, to establish persistent and isomorphic relationships between ideas, to tailor our thinking for representation in relational databases. In *Snow Crash* the hackers were most susceptible to the nam-shub because computational thinking had already reordered their minds: "Your nerves grow new connections as you use them—the axons split and push their way between the dividing glial cells—your bioware self-modifies—the software becomes part of the hardware."[58] The process Stephenson describes here is automatization, the realignment of mental faculties to internalize and homeostatically manage a complex task like driving a car. And, as media journalist Nicholas Carr points out in *The Glass Cage*, we all experienced automatization firsthand when we learned to read, gradually internalizing the rules of grammar and spelling until the interpretation of written symbols was largely effortless.[59] Just as Plato feared, our interaction with the technology of the written word not only changed the *medium* of thought, extending it to external papers, scrolls and other material stuff, but it also changed the *mode* of thought.

How we think about algorithms is a question that links symbolic language, computability, and brain plasticity. We might argue that the internalization of literacy is a kind of reprogramming, a nam-shub that we laboriously inculcate in children with every passing generation.[60] We might press the modern instantiation of the McCulloch–Pitts neuron into service, claiming with Wiener's cybernetics that the reconfiguring of neural networks in the brain can be computationally described. These would be pathways to arguing that reading is a mental algorithm encoded in literate minds. I am less interested in pursuing this notion than I am in the philosophical underpinnings that bring us here: the way that language itself, particularly written language, serves as the original "outside" to human thought, the first machine for processing culture across time and space.

The question of language's role as a technology of cognition is a deep one, linking the Church-Turing thesis's foundations in symbolic logic to the question of magic and culturally constructed reality. Indeed, we perceive language as a special case of the relationship between humanity and technology precisely because it plays an ontological role in constructing the world as we perceive it. Andy Clark offers several compelling pieces of empirical evidence for this thesis, arguing that language is "the kind of seed-technology that helped the whole process of designer-environment creation get off the ground."[61] The technological function of language as a system of *me* underpins not just communication but "precise numerical reasoning," which brain scans have revealed depends on language centers.[62]

Weizenbaum argues the same point in the context of imagination:

It is within the intellectual and social world he himself creates that the individual prehearses and rehearses countless dramatic enactments of how the world might have been and what it might become. That world is the repository of his subjectivity. ... Man can create little without first imagining that he can create it.[63]

Tools and processes are the *me* that embody these enactments, from the first prehistoric stone ax to the model of the informational universe that our search engines present us today. Or as Hayles puts it, cognition

reaches out into the techno-environment, dissolving the boundary between inside and outside into fluid assemblages that incorporate technical artifacts into the human cognitive system, not just as metaphors but as working parts of everyday thoughts and actions.[64]

And the first tool, the ur-process, is the intersubjective culture machine of language.

To think of language as a tool also allows us to begin seeing our other tools as linguistic statements too, as nam-shubs that contain concepts, grammars, verbs. They are, as Weizenbaum eloquently puts it, "pregnant symbols in themselves": "a tool is also a model for its own reproduction and a script for the reenactment of the skill it symbolizes."[65] This line of thinking closely echoes the philosopher of technology Gilbert Simondon in his thinking about technics, or the ways in which technical objects can establish their own identities and constitute ensembles that reflect the tensions between multiple competing sociotechnical forces. Hayles weaves Simondon's notion of ensembles together with Nigel Thrift's argument that we are increasingly automatizing technological systems, ceasing to perceive them as forces that shape our world and simply accepting their functionality and design imperatives on a subconscious level.[66] This is precisely the outcome that Weizenbaum cautioned against twenty years *avant la lettre*: the easy slide from rationality to a dependency on logicality and, increasingly, computational approximations of reality.

At this stage the specific relevance of this line of philosophical thinking about the nature and consequences of technics swings into view for our discussion of algorithms. The debate carried on from Plato to Simondon regarding our intellectual dependencies on external technical assemblages is paradigmatically similar to the debate over mathematical computability and logical consistency that raged in the early twentieth century, ultimately producing the Church–Turing thesis. Let me explain: mathematicians launched on the pathway to effective computability by first asking what the limits of symbolic languages were. This was an investigation of the foundations as well as the boundaries of mathematical thought based on the recognition that the languages of mathematics were themselves an essential part of the machinery of that thought. This was a limited instance of the broader cognition and mind debates Clark's "extended mind" hypothesis sparked decades later—an examination of the relationship between cognition and the tools of cognition, grounded here in terms of mathematical truth and provability.

It was a debate about the nature of our dependence on mathematical language and the ways that choices of language, the affordances of different symbolic systems, could foreclose access to other means of understanding. Gödel's incompleteness theorem definitively answered a fundamental, existential question (is there a logical and complete mathematical language?) with a firm negative. He demonstrated that no mathematical language whose statements are effectively calculable can both prove all true statements about natural numbers and remain logically consistent. Perhaps more damning, no such system can demonstrate its own consistency—one must always reach outside the boundaries of such a language in order to prove it. This theorem was a startling result, addressing generations of debate over the fundamental truth of arithmetic and the foundations of mathematics, an effort to find a bedrock of philosophical authority to support the rapidly expanding structures of mathematics.

The development of the Church–Turing thesis and the foundations of effective computability created a new linguistic machinery by means of the Turing machine. This conceptual object, this abstraction engine, opened up a space of operations for computation and served the essential function of clearly articulating the nature of our dependence on limited symbolic systems. Thanks to these proofs, we learned where the boundaries are. The mathematical proofs of effective computability offered by Church, Turing, and others created a new kind of certainty, and a new metaphor for thinking with—the universal mathematical ceiling of computability, and the Turing machine, respectively. But they also encoded a new form of ambiguity, or desire, in the boundary region of effective computability as *implemented processes*. All of this—the representational power and logical consistency of symbolic language; the construction of technical ensembles that coevolve with human cognition; the role of language as a bridge between human and computational structures of knowledge—all of it gets swept under the rug of the algorithm, the largely unexamined construct we use to instantiate ideas as processes at the intersection of computation and culture.

Process and Halting States

Now that we have taken the algorithm apart we can reassemble it with a new context. Drawing these threads together, we can see the multivalent and growing significance of the algorithm, that seemingly shallow and shopworn cultural figure at the heart of this book. The algorithm is an idea that puts structures of symbolic logic into motion. It is rooted in computer science but it serves as a prism for a much broader array of cultural, philosophical, mathematical, and imaginative grammars.[67] The most radical of these tensions exists between the algorithm's role as an effective procedure, a set of steps designed to produce an answer in a predictable length of time, on the one hand, and its function as a perpetual computational process, on the other. There is a crucial supposition embedded in both the pragmatist's definition of the algorithm and the ideology of computationalism. In each case, the logical abstraction of mathematical solutions is yoked to a carefully considered definition of process as time-limited. For engineers it's a *method* to solve a problem. For Church, Turing, and the computationalists, the notion of effectively computable problems and the Turing machine itself both depend on *processing*, on carrying out instructions in finite time. At one level this might seem facile or tautological: the definition of a method must rely on some notion of method. But, like the Turing machine, or Chun's definition of software, the method has become its own metaphor, more or less visible, for how the algorithm really works as a process that runs forever, persistently modeling reality.

Google search is one such algorithm that embeds these tensions into its technical and cultural architecture. This system delivers relevant results based on a wide range of factors, completing its execution in hundredths of a second—an effective procedure that proudly announces the rapidity of its completion with every query. And yet, as a *process*, search operates perpetually, extending its reach and influence over the Internet as Google aggregates new sources of information into its systems. As we will see in the next chapter, that influence extends into the future as well, as the company focuses on anticipating our future needs in addition to answering our present questions. For the company, the space of computable questions is continually expanding in multiple dimensions. Engineers at Google, Apple, Amazon, and many other entities are working ceaselessly to actively push the envelope of effective computability in order to make their products better and to create new culture machines: a limitless frontier for limitless processing.

In this way the process of the algorithm transcends the logic of the effective procedure to become a steady-state technical being, as Simondon would have it. Search is not just a system that leaps into action for a fraction of a second here or there; it is a persistent, highly complex organism that simultaneously influences the shape of the Internet, drives new innovations in machine learning, distributed computing and various other fields, and modifies our own cognitive practices.

It should be clear to anyone who has participated in digital culture for the past decade that this phenomenon is not homeostatic, but rather is moving irreversibly toward particular goals. And, as believers in the singularity like to point out, it is accelerating as it goes. From Moore's Law (predicting that the number of transistors packed onto a computer chip would double every two years) to the explosive growth in global data production, it's obvious that "ubiquitous computing" will continue to create a thickening layer of sensors, data, and algorithms over physical and cultural space. From television shows to finance, we are claiming new spaces for computation in a period of expansion fueled by the tension between time-limited (effective) procedures and perennial processes.

The answer we have come up with is to continually expand the problem space while still offering finite computational solutions. Algorithmic thinking encodes the computationalist vision, the maximalist idea that all complex systems will eventually be made equivalent through computational representation. This is the *desire* for effective computability writ large, and it has existential consequences for humanity. As our extended mind continues to elaborate new systems, functions, applications, and zones of operation, the question of what it means to be human grows increasingly abstract, ever more imbricated in the metaphors and assumptions of code. Discussing Simondon's vision of technics as interpreted by fellow philosopher Bernard Stiegler, media scholars Andrés Vaccari and Belinda Barnet argue that

both philosophers put the idea of a pure human memory (and consequently a pure thought) into crisis, and open a possibility which will tickle the interest of future robot historians: the possibility that human memory is a stage in the history of a vast machinic becoming. In other words, these future machines will approach human memory (and by extension culture) as a supplement to technical beings.[68]

Our existential anxiety about being replaced by our thinking machines underlies every thread of algorithmic thinking, from the shibboleth of the Turing test and Wiener's argument for the "human use of human beings" to the gradual encroachment of digital computation on many human occupations, beginning with that of being a "computer." Nowhere is the prospect more unsettling than in the context of extended cognition, however. As we outsource more of our minds to algorithmic systems, we too will need to confront the consequences of dependence on processes beyond our control. There is some compelling evidence to suggest that the externalization of human memory and experience makes certain technological advances "inevitable," according to sociologists William F. Ogburn and Dorothy Thomas.[69] The universal machine of culture itself might prime new intellectual discoveries, making certain inventions not just possible but inescapable at certain historical junctures. Calculus, natural selection, the telegraph: all were "discovered" or "invented" multiple times, in various guises, as words, ideas, and methods circulated through the right scientific circles. As Vaccari and Barnet's playful notion of future robot historians suggests, it's easy to read these events as moments in a long arc of progress that might not include humanity at its end.

As Stiegler has argued in partial reply to Simondon, the balance of agency may already lie with technical systems:

Today, machines are the tool bearers, and the human is no longer a technical individual; the human becomes either the machine's servant or its assembler [assembliste]: the human's relation to the technical object proves to have profoundly changed.[70]

This is a phase shift in process. As a vessel for putting symbolic logic into motion, the algorithm has increasingly come to manage not just memories but decisions. The growing complexity of many human fields, particularly in technical research, has deepened our dependence on computational systems and in many instances made scientific experimentation itself a domain for effective computability. Algorithmic approaches to research have already prompted some investigators to argue that "automated science" will revolutionize technical progress, perhaps even making the generation of hypotheses obsolete as algorithms continuously interact with huge volumes of data.[71] Algorithms have generated mathematical proofs and even new explanatory equations that defy human comprehension, making them "true" but not "understandable," a situation that mathematician Steven Strogatz has termed the "end of insight."[72]

For Stiegler this is a nightmare; for others it presages the computational rapture, the event horizon of the singularity, when algorithmic intelligence transcends humanity (with infamously unpredictable results for our species). If the origin story of code begins with language, *logos,* and the manipulation of symbols to generate meaning, this is its mythical finale, the triumph of sign over signification. We know it as the apotheosis of the algorithm, when technological change will accelerate to such speed that human intelligence may simply be eclipsed. In this scenario we no longer manipulate the symbols and we can no longer construe their meaning. It is the endgame of computationalism as considered by philosopher Nick Bostrom, computer scientist Vernor Vinge, and others, an existential referendum on the relationship between humanity and technics.[73] If we follow the asymptote of the effective procedure far enough, the space of computation advances with not just a vanguard but a rearguard, and humanity might simply be left behind—no longer effective or efficient enough to merit emulation or attention.

Ironically this possible end-state—the end of insight—is a rationalist romance, drawing its lineage straight to the deeply humanistic spirit of inquiry at the heart of the Enlightenment. It extends the vision of Denis Diderot, one of the cocreators of the world-changing *Encyclopédie*, as we'll see in chapter 2: persistently applying the system or procedure of the Enlightenment would eventually lead to a state of transcendent knowledge, leaving open the question of whether robot encyclopedists can experience transcendence. Isaac Asimov took that vision still farther, calling it "psychohistory" in his Foundation stories. With enough cleverness and data, he imagined, we can predict the course of human events because culture is algorithmic, because individuals and circumstances can be abstracted away according to dependable rules. If the singularity provides one way to interpret the endgame of computationalism, this is the second: the triumph of instrumental reason effected by machines we can no longer understand.

Our technical systems have specifically political implications, articulating certain forms of power that often contradict the emancipatory rhetoric of computation. David Golumbia indexes this political calculus in *The Cultural Logic of Computation*, noting how

computerization tends to be aligned with relatively authority-seeking, hierarchical, and often politically conservative forces—the forces that justify existing forms of power [in a project that] meshes all too easily with the project of instrumental reason.[74]

The "psychohistory" that Asimov imagined as a potentially emancipatory technical discovery is, for Golumbia, exemplary of a passive acceptance of the political statement that "a great deal, perhaps all, of human and social experience can be explained via computational processes."[75] At its heart, this is about the politics of abstraction, which Golumbia ties to the instrumental reason of the Enlightenment. It is the same anxiety that communications scholar Fred Turner traced in 1960s student protestors who repurposed computer punch cards to battle the administrative machine: "I am a UC student. Please do not fold, bend, spindle or mutilate me."[76] This second telos also ends with the triumph of the machine, but what Golumbia imagines is a different sort of engine: the kinds of state power and bureaucracy that computational management and quantification enable. The place of the human is ambiguous at best in both the singularity universe and in Golumbia's reading of computational ideology.

Golumbia stands in here for a range of critics who argue that the de facto result of computational culture, at least if we do not intervene, is to reinforce state power. In later chapters we will examine more closely the "false personalization" that Tarleton Gillespie cautions against, extending Internet activist and author Eli Pariser's argument in *The Filter Bubble*, as well as media theorist Alexander Galloway's elegant framing of the political consequences of protocol.[77] But Turner's *From Counterculture to Cyberculture* offers a compelling view of how countercultural impulses were woven into the fabric of computational culture from the beginning. The figure of the hacker draws its lineage in part from the freewheeling discourse of the industrial research labs of the 1940s; the facilities that first created the opportunities for young people to not only work but play with computers.[78]

But, as Galloway has argued, the cybernetic paradigm has recast the playful magic of computation in a new light.

With the growing significance of immaterial labor, and the concomitant increase in cultivation and exploitation of play—creativity, innovation, the new, the singular, flexibility, the supplement—as a productive force, play will become more and more linked to broad social structures of control. Today we are no doubt witnessing the end of play as politically progressive, or even politically neutral.[79]

This shift, the computation of play, signals a fundamental sea change in values that we will address in more detail in chapters 4 and 5: the substitution of process itself as a value for the human experiences of play and joy. The political critique of computationalism reaches its pinnacle here, in the argument that our most central human experiences, the unconstrained play of imagination and creativity, are increasingly falling within the boundaries of effective computability and the regime of computation.

Implementation

The mythos of computation reaches its limits where it begins to interact with material reality. Like UPS's ORION, computation in real-world environments is messy and contingent, requiring constant modification and supervision. I call this problem "implementation": the ways in which the desire for effective computability get translated into working systems of actual computers, humans, and social structures. Learning what goes on inside the black box of the algorithm does not change the fact that the action is specifically contained by its implementation: the box itself is just as important. By learning to interpret the container, the inputs and outputs, the seams of implementation, we can begin to develop a way of reading algorithms as culture machines that operate in the gap between code and culture.

Negotiating that gap is precisely what algorithms do: operating at the intersection of computational and cultural space, they must compromise or adjudicate between mathematical and pragmatic models of reason. The inescapability of that work, the fact that algorithms must always be implemented to be used, is actually their most significant feature. By occupying and defining that awkward middle ground, algorithms and their human collaborators enact new roles as culture machines that unite ideology and practice, pure mathematics and impure humanity, logic and desire. To discuss implementation is thus to join a conversation about materiality and the embodied subjects that enact, transmit, and receive information.[80] Simply asking the question *where* an algorithm like ORION exists might lead to very complicated answers involving a distributed network of sensors, servers, employees, code, and so on. To grapple with that question we need to turn to platform studies and media archeology, where we can consider implementation as a form of materiality grounded in the hardware and software that make up the "foundation of computational expression."[81]

In *Mechanisms*, media scholar Matthew Kirschenbaum deploys two forms of materiality for reading digital objects. "Forensic materiality" is the physical and material situation of a particular digital object: the particular hard drive where a database is stored, with its own electromechanical systems and physical characteristics.[82] In the context of algorithms the logistical details of where and how data is stored are vital aspects of implementation, like the vast amount of energy expended to keep major data centers in operation. "Formal materiality" is the intellectual shadow cast by these physical manifestations of computation. The term refers to the "imposition of multiple relational computational states on a data set or digital object," or the "procedural friction or perceived difference—the torque—as a user shifts from one set of software logics to another."[83] Kirschenbaum eloquently describes the essential role of the observer or forensic investigator in effectively reading digital objects, and formal materiality illustrates how much translation or transposition is involved in effectively manipulating them.

An algorithmic system must be implemented in a forensically material way by having its code and data stored on some physical hard drive, running on some processor. But these physical instantiations involve a dizzying flurry of formal materiality moves before they can become broadly accessible: the server running this algorithm might really be a virtual conglomerate of hundreds of machines organized by a distributed computing platform like Hadoop; the various instances of the algorithm might exist in software containers managed by another formal material layer, something like the Docker platform; the public interfaces for the algorithm might vary their appearance and behavior based on user customization, like Google's tailored search results. Of course, the list can go on: the boundaries of implementation seem endless because they are the boundaries of the material universe.

And yet the algorithm is always bounded in implementation because the principle of effective computability is central to its formal identity. This is why I choose to use the word "implementation" rather than rely on the concept of platform studies or materiality per se. As a tool or effective procedure, the algorithm is an implement that is coded into existence through a framework of forensic and formal analogies, assumptions, and declarative frameworks. The ideal implementation must encode or embed abstracted versions of those externalities, or deal with them as structured inputs, if it is to operate successfully and "solve the problem" at hand. But of course the reality of implementation always incurs new contingencies, dependencies, and complexity, muddying the ground between the forensic and formal status of the algorithm as an implemented system. Unlike the proverbial black box, the culture machine is actually porous, ingesting and extruding cultural and computational structures at every connection point with other sociotechnical systems.

Ian Bogost, from the "Cathedral of Computation":

Once you start looking at them closely, every algorithm betrays the myth of unitary simplicity and computational purity. ... Once you adopt skepticism toward the algorithmic- and the data-divine, you can no longer construe any computational system as merely algorithmic. Think about Google Maps, for example. It's not just mapping software running via computer—it also involves geographical information systems, geolocation satellites and transponders, human-driven automobiles, roof-mounted panoramic optical recording systems, international recording and privacy law, physical- and data-network routing systems, and web/mobile presentational apparatuses. That's not algorithmic culture—it's just, well, culture.[84]

Piercing the illusion of computation as an exceptional religious experience, however, leaves us with a new problem. It may be "just, well, culture," but it is a culture increasingly transformed by these platforms. Giving up the magic of code does not change the pervasive effects of algorithmic implementations on cultural systems. Instead, it complicates the picture, erasing the false simplicity and idealism of Silicon Valley–style computationalist evangelism. What we are left with underneath that facade of computational perfection is exactly the mess of interconnected systems, policy frameworks, people, assumptions, infrastructures, and interfaces that Bogost describes above.

In other words, implementation runs both ways—every culture machine we build to interface with the embodied world of human materiality also reconfigures that embodied space, altering cognitive and cultural practices. More important, this happens because implementation encodes a particular formulation of the desire for effective computability, a desire that we reciprocate when we engage with that system. The algorithmic quest for universal knowledge mirrors and feeds our own eternal hunger for self-knowledge and collective awareness. The effectiveness of systems that model, predict, and recommend things to us can feed the religious experience Bogost cautions against, and we willingly accept their abstractions in order to feel the magic of computation. There is a seductive quality to algorithmic models of digital culture even when they are only partially successful because they order the known universe. You listen to a streaming music station that *almost* gets it right, telling yourself that these songs, not quite the right ones, are perfect for this moment because a magical algorithm selected them.

Computational algorithms may be presented as merely mathematical, but they are operating as culture machines that dramatically revise the geography of human reflexivity, as we will see in the algorithmic readings that follow this chapter. They reshape the spaces within which we see ourselves. Our literal and metaphorical footprints through real and virtual systems of information and exchange are used to shape the horizon ahead through tailored search results, recommendations, and other adaptive systems, or what Pariser calls the "filter bubble."[85]

But when algorithms cross the threshold from prediction to determination, from modeling to building cultural structures, we find ourselves revising reality to accommodate their discrepancies. In any system dependent on abstraction there is a remainder, a set of discarded information—the *différance*, or the crucial distinction and deferral of meaning that goes on between the map and the territory. This gap emerges in implementation, when the collisions between computational and cultural understandings of algorithms must be resolved. In many ways the gap creates the cultural space for the figure of the algorithm, providing the glitches, inexplicable results, and strange serendipity we imagine as the magic of code. In *Snow Crash*, the problem of implementation underwrites several crucial plot twists, but one of the most memorable is the plotting of three-dimensional space in the Multiverse, the virtual reality where Hiro Protagonist, fellow hackers, and other Technorati congregate. Hiro can move through walls by sticking his katana through them and following his sword, exploiting a

loophole that he found years ago when he was trying to graft the sword-fighting rules onto the existing Metaverse software. ... But like anything else in the Metaverse, [the rule governing how walls function] is nothing but a protocol, a convention that different computers agree to follow. In theory, it cannot be ignored. But in practice, it depends on the ability of different computers to swap information very precisely, at high speed, and at just the right times.[86]

For the novel, this is a convenient trick, like many of the things hackers exploit or create: a mechanism for sidestepping standard structures of control reminiscent of Galloway's call to arms in *Protocol*. But for our purposes, it also illustrates the essential features of the gap between computational and cultural metaphors, between abstraction and implementation.

Hiro's katana thrust works in part because it exploits the gulf between different logical regimes of abstraction—the algorithmic rules governing swords in the Metaverse and the set of similar rules governing avatars and structures. It also depends on the abstracted construction of temporality in computational systems—as Stephenson points out, the gap is temporal as much as it spatial, depending on the lag between Hiro's satellite connection and the servers handling his session in the Metaverse. Hiro engages in a kind of arbitrage when he exploits the lag between two algorithmic systems to literally hack his way into a black box. And, finally, the gap is cultural: Hiro asks an impossible question when he pokes his sword into the wall, and he receives just the impossible answer he was hoping for—shazam, hacker magic is performed.

It is important to realize, however, that the gap is not the same as the glitch, the crash, or other signs of malfunctioning computational systems. These moments when the facade of computational omniscience falls are very helpful in seeing the gap, and they have given rise to fascinating genres of computer art and performance, but they are only windows into the broader opening between computation and reality. We construct the gap, or create space for it, on both sides. Algorithmic systems and computational models elide away crucial aspects of complex systems with various abstracting gestures, and the things they leave behind reside uneasily in limbo, known and unknown, understood and forgotten at the same time. But the human participants, users, and architects of these systems play an equally important role in constructing the gap when we organize new cognitive patterns around computational systems and choose to forget or abandon forms of knowledge we once possessed. Every moment of dependence, like a forgotten phone number or spelling that we now depend on an algorithmic system to supply, and especially every rejected opportunity for direct, unmediated human contact, adds a little to the space between computation and human experience.

Algorithms work as complex aggregates of abstraction, incantation, mathematics, and technical memory. They are material implementations of the cathedral of computation.[87] When we interact with them, we are speaking to oracles, gods, and minor demons, hashing out a pidgin or trade language filled with command words, Boolean conjunctions, and quite often, deeply personal information. We are constantly reworking the myth of the algorithm through these interactions, reaffirming it through our recitals of the familiar invocations (muttering "OK Google Now" or tapping out a familiar URL) and extending its reach as we develop more sophisticated relationships with computational culture machines. Those relationships depend on multiple forms of literacy—we are all reading algorithmic systems now, more or less badly, depending on our awareness and attention to the context of implementation.

Algorithmic Reading

To effectively read the strange figure of the algorithm, that deliberately featureless, chameleon-like passthrough between computational and cultural logics, we need to take an algorithmic approach ourselves. The reading of complex computational cultural objects requires its own effective procedure, one that operates in the space of implementation between critical theory, computational logic, and cultural understanding. Just as computational algorithms embed a desire to make all things effectively computable, we should recognize the agenda that algorithmic reading brings with it: a desire to make all facets of computation legible to human beings. As literary critic Stephen Ramsey argues in the conclusion to *Reading Machines*, the "new kinds of critical acts" he terms algorithmic criticism may be not only possible but necessary, "implicit in the many interfaces that seek only to facilitate thought, self expression [sic] and community."[88] Algorithmic reading, as I define it below, is a mode of thought, or a tool for thinking, that anyone can use to interpret cultural artifacts.

In this light algorithmic reading triangulates between competing desires: the computationalist quest to continually expand the boundary of the effective procedure, on the one hand, and the human desire for universal knowledge, on the other. Between them, something new that we are only now beginning to recognize: the mutually constitutive desire to create and manipulate the gap, to have a kind of magic emerge from the complex interactions of abstraction and implementation like flocks of birds from a computational game of life. That *différance* provides the energy for our evolving love affair with computation, and it is the resource we tap into when we perform algorithmic readings.

This is why reading the gap and reconstructing the computational and social forces that make up the walls and linkages of each culture machine, each porous computational box, is itself a "method for solving a problem." Like the algorithm itself, algorithmic reading is a complex conceptual structure containing layers of processes, abstractions, and interfaces with reality.

The algorithmic object of study extends far beyond the surface manifestation of a particular fragment of text or multimedia. A reading of a particular post on Facebook, or even, say, *Note Book*, a collection of literary scholar Jeff Nunokawa's essayistic Facebook posts, would capture only the human side of the collaboration unless it engaged directly with the apparatus of Facebook itself. In this way algorithmic reading draws from the multiple critical forerunners we have already considered here—cybernetics, cultural studies, platform and software studies, media theory, and digital materiality. We are just beginning to work out how to pull these different perspectives together to ask questions about the ethics of algorithms, the legibility of software and the politics of computation. Algorithmic platforms now shape effectively all cultural production, from authors engaging in obligatory Twitter badinage to promote their new books to the sophisticated systems recommending new products to us. A central tenet of algorithmic reading, what distinguishes the method, is that we must take the culture machine itself as the object of study, rather than just its cultural outputs. To do that effectively, I'd like to offer a set of key terms or transformative concepts that serve as the central functions of any culture machine.

The first methodological tool we need is a grounded critical understanding of *process*. Algorithms of all kinds advance a version of the effective computability argument, encoding explicit or implicit arguments that the problem—whether it is agriculture or square root extraction—can be solved by following the steps of the method. In this way process itself is an ordering logic for critical understanding, leaning on notions of "process philosophy" espoused by the philosophers Martin Heidegger, Alfred Whitehead, Simondon, and Stiegler, among others. The algorithmic object of study is a system in motion, a sequence of iterations that comes into being as it moves through time. The most important aspect of an algorithmic system is not the surface material it presents to the world at any particular moment (e.g., the items appearing at the top of one's Facebook feed) but rather the system of rules and agents that constantly generate and manipulate that surface material (e.g., the algorithms filtering and promoting particular nuggets of content). That process embeds, as we explored above, the tension between self-perpetuation and completion, between an effective procedure that ends gracefully and a spirit of universal computation that fills the universe.

This notion of process depends intimately on our second methodological keyword, *abstraction*. Algorithmic systems are objects of study not only for what they include, but for what is elided. The systems of abstraction that translate electrical signals to assembly language to high-level code to a graphical user interface to a system of icons and cultural metaphors (with many other layers in between) create ideological frames and arguments about reality. The work of media scholars like Hayles, Galloway, and McKenzie Wark serve to illuminate how these abstractions work in the world. If algorithms are culture machines, abstractions are one of their primary outputs. As an example, in chapter 4 I discuss Uber's application interface, with a cartoonish map showing cars roaming the urban grid. Uber depends on abstracting away the complexities, regulations, and established conventions of hailing a cab, turning the hired car experience into a kind of videogame. That mode of abstraction has been so successful that an entire genre of Silicon Valley startups can now be categorized as "Uber for X," where that X is actually a double abstraction. First, we adapt Uber's simplifying, free-agent "sharing economy" business model to another economic arena. Then we make all such arenas fungible, a variable X that can stand for any corner of the marketplace where ubiquitous computing and algorithmic services have yet to disrupt the status quo. Like Turing's original abstraction machine, these systems extend a symbolic logic into the cultural universe that reorders minds and meanings that come into contact with them.

The medium for these interactions is our third keyword, the state of *implementation*. The processes that culture machines run and the abstractions they produce can only exist in the space of implementation. That space is a gap between computational and cultural constructions of reality, one that culture machines both generate and manipulate in order to achieve their procedural objectives and the broader expansion of effective computability. Netflix's decision to use a group of human "taggers" to evaluate its streaming video catalog according to a range of qualitative and quantitative metrics represented a profound shift in implementation, as we'll see in chapter 3. They left behind the purely statistical approach of their first recommendation algorithm in favor of a messier, more culturally entangled process, a transformation that now informs the even more complicated business of creating original content like *House of Cards* based on human and algorithmic inputs.

The growing interdependence of humans and algorithms in creating culturally complex, aesthetically evaluated culture machines and creative works leads us to the most challenging aspect of algorithmic reading: *imagination*. The gap between computation and culture is not just a gulf between different systems of symbolic logic, of representation and meaning: it is also a gap between different modes of imagination. All symbolic systems, all languages, contain a particular logic of possibility, a horizon of imagination that depends on the nature of representation and semantic relationships. Mathematicians can precisely describe highly abstract relationships that are almost impossible to define in more familiar human language. Computational systems are developing new capacities for imaginative thinking that may be fundamentally alien to human cognition, including the creation of inferences from millions of statistical variables and the manipulation of systems in stochastic, rapidly changing circumstances that are temporally behind our ability to effectively comprehend. We see computational imagination throughout the readings that follow, from the "ghost in the machine" that a Netflix VP described in his own system's results to the kinds of strange serendipity and beautiful glitches we have all glimpsed at the edges of computation's facade of perfect functionality and predictability.[89]

Taken together, these components of algorithmic reading provide the ingredients for a new recipe, an algorithmic approach to the cultural understanding of algorithms. It is a means of reading by the lights and shadows of machines: the brilliant illumination of computationally enhanced cognition and the obfuscations of black boxes. As our keywords suggest, algorithmic reading is a critical frame for interpreting objects that are also interpreting you: computational systems that adapt to your behavior in a mutual hermeneutic process.

After all, we are already communing with algorithms—sharing, trusting, and deputizing them to think and act on our behalf. For every nefarious black box and oppressive platform I unearth in this dig, there are bright spots: instances of astounding creativity and insight that would never have been possible without the collaboration of human and machine. Like all of our other myths, the culture machine has been *us* all along. We build these tools, we imbue them with power and history, because we seek to secure some part of ourselves outside the fragile vessel of the human form. We build cathedrals, rituals, and collective stories to cast a spell on ourselves, a nam-shub of eternal memory to keep our brightest moments alive. Understanding the figure of the algorithm is the first step to becoming true collaborators—and not just with machines, but with one another through the vast collectives that algorithmic systems make possible. Underneath all these layers of silted symbol, code, and logic, we find that the figure of the algorithm is not fixed but in motion, and that algorithmic reading requires working in a charged sphere of action between computation and culture. This is the playground of algorithmic imagination, the zone where human and computational assemblages can do extraordinary, beautiful things.

The perfect search engine would be like the mind of God.
Sergey Brin[1]

If you want to make me to believe in God you must make me touch Him.
Denis Diderot[2]

The Algorithmic Aide-de-camp

In October 2011, Apple announced the launch of Siri, an "intelligent assistant that helps you get things done just by asking."[3] This new functionality for the world's leading smartphone did not even make the headline of the press release, but it has had profound implications for our interactions with digital systems.

Apple's unveiling of Siri seemed to herald a brand new technology, one of the only things the company has ever launched as a "beta" release. But Siri and its antecedents had been in development for nearly a decade through the largest artificial intelligence project ever funded by the U.S. government, drawing over $150 million from the Defense Advanced Research Projects Agency (DARPA).[4] Housed at SRI International (originally the Stanford Research Institute), the project brought together hundreds of researchers from several major universities and corporations to work on what has long been a holy grail for artificial intelligence: a conversational computer.[5] SRI was part of the same wave of large-scale, interdisciplinary government research laboratories that Norbert Wiener and the cyberneticians helped to pioneer during World War II. Dubbed the Cognitive Agent that Learns and Organizes, or CALO, Siri's precursor was designed to help field commanders who have to manage complex data and bureaucracy while remaining focused on strategic challenges. CALO was inspired by the Latin *calonis*, or soldier's servant, giving a very different cast to its imagined cultural role: more executive officer than personal assistant.[6]

The teams that worked on CALO approached a number of different technical challenges, such as developing a tool to better organize meetings. As technology journalist Bianca Bosker writes in her short history of Siri's evolution:

Say your colleague canceled shortly before a meeting. CALO, knowledgeable about each person's role on a project, could discern whether to cancel the meeting, and if needed, reschedule, issue new invitations and pin down a conference room. If the meeting went ahead as planned, CALO could assemble (and rank) all the documents and emails you'd need to be up to speed on the topic at hand. The assistant would listen in on the meeting, and, afterward, deliver a typed transcript of who said what and outline any specific tasks laid out during the conversation. CALO was also able to help put together presentations, organize files into folders, sort incoming messages and automate expense reports, among a host of other tasks.[7]

These and other features presented a vision for Siri as a new kind of intelligent aide-de-camp that would not merely automate tasks but effectively predict and take action on the user's behalf. The long-term investment from DARPA realized one of the great ambitions of an earlier generation of AI research: an intelligent agent that can act for itself in concert with humans.

CALO/Siri is a powerful example of the contemporary culture machine: conceived as an interlocking set of computational systems, the intelligent agent is an ambitious effort to make vast new swaths of culture "effectively computable." It embodies a pragmatist ideal for conquering several technical challenges: a conversational computer must interpret spoken queries and answer appropriately. It must effectively parse emails, task lists, budgets, calendars, and, as Siri expanded, restaurant listings, movie times, and many other data sources. As an aide-de-camp or virtual assistant, Siri is a literal effort to externalize memory, reminding us of upcoming meetings and handling other low-level cognitive tasks. In all of these functions, Siri follows a fairly limited script of possible questions and answers, dumping queries that do not fit its model of the universe into a search box and providing results from the Web.

Reading Siri requires stepping behind the curtain of its computational facade, but it also involves reading beyond the intentions of its original designers at SRI and the engineers and marketers who implemented the system at Apple. In this way it is an ensemble, an emergent "technical being" that illustrates Gilbert Simondon's notions of technicity. Put another way, Siri is a culture machine that not only shapes our interactions, integrating (and depending on us) for functionality, but also has a broader ambition to structure and organize the universe. As Simondon puts it: "Technical reality, having become regulative, will be able to be incorporated into culture, which is essentially regulative."[8] Siri is an algorithm midway through this process of becoming, where its technical functions and cultural premise give us a good view of the gap between computation and culture, particularly in terms of how we define knowledge.

Performing Knowledge

Many Apple users do not know that Siri was a lot smarter before Apple purchased the algorithm. Just a few weeks after the startup that first developed Siri as a commercial product released it to the iOS App Store in 2010, Steve Jobs orchestrated the company's acquisition. He moved quickly, preempting a deal with Verizon to bring the software to Android phones instead, and the Siri team began the process of adapting their tool for the millions of users across the world who would soon be using it as a core interface for the iOS operating system.[9] The original algorithm was designed to flexibly interact with hundreds of data sources, synthesizing information from multiple archives to answer your question about the best pizza nearby, or suggesting alternate modes of transportation if your flight was delayed. Some of this functionality has gradually been restored to Siri, but its association with Apple has also made it less flexible, as lawyers and elaborate contracts precede any new agreements for the tool to pull in third-party data. The original Siri also had a sharper edge to its dialog, occasionally deploying four-letter words and plenty of attitude, which was part of its appeal for Jobs (though Apple quickly dialed down the software's affect in-house).[10] The software didn't just know things, it was also knowing.

This is how Siri was marketed from the beginning, as a culture machine so sophisticated it seemed to be magic: a computer that not only talks but understands. The commercials featured Samuel L. Jackson, Zooey Deschanel, and Martin Scorsese having actual *conversations* with their phones.

Apple showed us that we could be human characters, crack wise, ask questions in our normal, idiosyncratic way, and that Siri would keep up, making its own jokes and understanding not just our words but the meaning behind them. The commercials hint at the kind of relationship that programmers flirt with through the "Easter eggs" they have left in Siri, such as the well-known trick of asking Siri where to dump a dead body (which offered a drily humorous rundown of local swamps, metal foundries, etc.—though Apple has since changed the response). These preprogrammed sparks illuminate the long-range goal to create not just intelligence but real personality. Yet these tricks come with a script that we must learn—for Siri to deliver each punch line we must carefully set up the joke, propitiating the culture machine with appropriate rituals.

The interface of the tool itself establishes concrete metaphors for these interactions. A large microphone button dominates the screen, suggesting the image of a radio host leaning over his station, enunciating clearly into the ether. As we use Siri those enunciations first appear as indeterminate digital symbols, waving lines that then resolve into a quoted transcription of the human utterance. Siri's responses then appear as unquoted responses (and sometimes are only spoken, not inscribed in the written conversation). The design reinforces the algorithmic feedback loop, creating a system for teaching us what Siri hears and gradually training us to say things in ways that Siri understands. Perhaps to balance this sparse, typically Apple design scheme, Siri frequently takes on positions of human affect, expressing concern, making jokes, and opining about its user's queries.

These moments of simulated humanity are part of the collaborative theater of the virtual assistant: performative cues that we can choose to "catch" and respond to or ignore. And, of course, the voice offers a persistent performance of gender. As technology critic Annalee Newitz argues, the predominance of female voices in digital assistants clearly has something to do with submission:

The sad truth is that these digital assistants are more like slaves than modern women. They are not supposed to threaten you, or become your equal—they are supposed to carry out orders without putting up a fight. The ideal slave, after all, would be like a mother to you. She would never rebel because she loves you, selflessly and forever.[11]

Figure 2.1
Siri playing up its human affect.

The conversational construction of gender is prominent in the intellectual history of artificial intelligence, a topic we will return to. But for now we need to explore the back end of this performance in more depth.

At their darkest, these digital assistants are culturally constructed as sentient Skinner boxes, quasi-intelligent systems that *must* answer, and that inspire the same kind of slavish devotion in their users. But of course, it is the human users who in the end *must* use these systems—not necessarily Siri, but the interconnected systems that evaluate our search queries, for example, or the algorithms that assign credit scores. As critics like media scholar Siva Vaidhyanathan have pointed out, the price of nonparticipation is significant but also difficult to pin down, and the gravitational pull of algorithmic culture gradually inculcates the rituals of participation, of obeisance, to particular computational altars.[12]

The Magic of Ontology

The call and response of Siri's communication is central to the cultural understanding of intelligent assistants as a kind of useful demon—entities with specific, constrained abilities—but the nature of this achievement unveils a deeper technical being that exists beyond its utility to users. The vital element in Siri's effectiveness as a culture machine is the achievement of a minimum viable threshold for speedy, topical responses to questions. Siri's ability to interpret real-world commands depends on two key factors: natural language processing (NLP) and semantic interpretation. As any user who has tried to use Siri without a data connection knows, the software cannot operate without a link to Apple's servers. Each time a user speaks to Siri the sound file is sent to a data center for analysis and storage, a service of the leading speech technology company Nuance.[13] The major break-throughs in algorithmic speech analysis have come by abandoning deep linguistic structure—efforts to thoroughly map grammar and semantics— in favor of treating speech as a statistical, probabilistic challenge.[14] Given this audio signal, what text strings are most likely associated with each word? Which word is most likely to follow another? Test the results against a training set, or humans using the service, and use feedback to gradually improve results. This is a classic computational pragmatist approach to a problem, charting an effective computability pathway through the morass of language by depending on trial and error, treating spoken language just like any other complex system.

In this sense Siri is as much a listening service as it is an answering one. Over time Siri has presumably collected billions of records of successful and unsuccessful interactions, providing a valuable resource in improving speech recognition.[15] Apple claims the data it retains is anonymized, but this policy is unsurprisingly troubling to privacy advocates.[16] While we get personalized service, Siri is effectively a single collective machine, learning from these billions of data points under the supervision of its engineers. Like so many other big data, algorithmic machines, it depends on a deep well, a cistern of human attention and input that serves as an informational reservoir for computational inference. By running statistical speech analy- sis over enough data, engineers can generate a complete usage map of human expression, creating a near-universal speech model by accepting language not as a fixed system of laws to be discovered (a universal grammar) but as a series of behaviors that can be mapped to a chosen degree of accuracy.

Even with this big data approach, correctly transcribing spoken audio is an incredibly challenging task. The rollout of Siri in other languages depends on developing effective transcription models, and dialect inflections have proven nettlesome barriers for users with British accents, Scottish burrs, and southern drawls.[17] But the cloud-based nature of Siri's computational back end means that each linguistic nuance gradually accumulates a statistical signature in Apple's data, a series of recordings where a particular word or phrase is being consistently misinterpreted. These fragments of interaction contribute to Siri's adaptive learning curve, as if thousands or millions of dialect speakers are all passively educating the same virtual toddler in correct pronunciation, while the Siri interface at the same time shapes the inflections of those users, encouraging them to enunciate in specific, machine-legible ways and creating a kind of collaborative human–machine distribution curve of language.

This probabilistic approach also frees these systems from another human constraint: like a toddler, Siri makes effective conversation without having a full grasp of grammar. Because the algorithm's NLP does not attempt to parse every sentence into its subjects, verbs, and objects, but rather identifies key words and phrases, Siri navigates the world through ideas, not syntax.[18] These keywords are mapped to concepts that Siri already knows about in structured "ontologies" of knowledge. For Siri, language always represents objects in the world: the keyword "restaurant" has other concepts attached to it, like hours of operation, a physical address, and a price range.[19] When the user asks about "dim sum," "inexpensive," and "walking," Siri can effectively translate these keywords into a coherent query and offer a provisional response without knowing anything about gerunds.

The conceptual structure of the knowledge ontology underwrites the "magic" of what Siri and other intelligent agents can accomplish. Like a human, the system can analyze context, learn from previous interactions, and generate plausible guesses on unreliable data. The SRI engineers who made the ontological breakthrough during the CALO project recognized its value for scalability as well: to plug in a new database of movie reviews, geographical information, or what have you, humans need to spend a relatively small amount of time mapping out the new fields of knowledge (e.g., physical address or name of the director). The strength of ontologies is that they establish clear relationships between radically different, rapidly changing kinds of information, from stock returns to text messages.

Siri can validate these connections over time as users interact with different datasets, extending its model of human speech along tightly controlled axes defined by what Siri already "knows." The process depends on Siri's millions of trained collaborators, the users who must learn to format their queries the right way and take the system's explicit and implicit limitations into account. These interactions, and particularly their fault lines, allow us to mark the gap between the ways language and knowledge are implemented in Siri as compared to in broader cultural life. The system's mimicry of the linguistic culture machine is imperfect not just in transcription and grammar, but in the ideological construction of its knowledge ontologies. For example, in 2011 Siri was briefly engulfed in scandal when it emerged that queries for "where can I get an abortion" would return results to anit-abortion crisis pregnancy centers, often far away, and fail to represent local family planning clinics that provided abortion services.[20] The statistical language model linked the query to anti-abortion facilities that were far more likely to use the word "abortion" on their websites, failing to grasp the politically charged nature of the question. The black box structure of Siri's knowledge ontology obfuscated the category error the system made by excluding Planned Parenthood facilities. Fixing this glitch in the culture machine necessarily involves human intervention: behind the facade of the black box, engineers had to overrule baseline statistical models with exceptions and workarounds. There must be thousands of such exceptions, particularly for responses that mimic human affect. Siri and its various counterparts offer a vision of universal language computation, but in practice depend on an "effective" computation that requires constant tweaking and oversight.

As the abortion example demonstrates, there is a gulf of abstraction between the premise of the algorithmically self-training intelligent assistant, on the one hand, and the mysterious functionality of the black box in practice. This culture machine and the knowledge ontologies it contains impose profound limits on the kinds of intellectual relationships we can have with it, because while Siri can learn *from* us (by aggregating billions of voice recordings for analysis, for example), we can directly teach it almost nothing. The ontologies are Siri's secret sauce, the synapses that hold the entire operation together, and they are constructed according to the business logic, legal agreements, and licensing schemes of Apple and its partners. This can lead to failures like Siri responding to the question "where do babies come from" by offering a list of "baby stores" in the area.[21] But it also leads to absences and exclusions that can be harder to detect. An invisible ontology does not reveal its seams and edges, but rather is designed to resist exactly that kind of questioning. The algorithmic system accrues meaning by the impersonal aggregation of millions of conversations; Siri's human users assign meaning on the basis of a much smaller set of deeply personal interactions.

The occasionally spectacular clashes between these two understandings of the algorithm angered many Apple fans because they saw them as a violation of the implicit bargain they have made with the company: to pay a premium for high quality products that live up to their advertising.[22] By mapping technology directly onto culture, Apple inadvertently revealed the stitching holding together a product still in beta, creating another fraught relationship between an algorithm's computationalist promise and the real culture machine underpinning it. The disappointment was more acute because Siri operates so intimately with its users, handling reminders, messages, and verbal queries that provide a deep index into personal life. The appeal of Siri, and indeed of CALO before it, goes beyond just an assistant to something like an ever-attentive companion who knows your life better than you do. Siri is a way station on the path to the quest for perfect self-knowledge.

The *Star Trek* Computer

If Siri's quest to become an "intelligent assistant" seems ambitious, Google's efforts at the cutting edge of algorithmic culture are even more sweeping. Already the company is involved in a huge portion of activity online: in 2013, Google generated 25 percent of all Internet traffic in the United States directly, and roughly 60 percent of *all* devices on the Internet exchanged data with Google servers on any given day.[23] Its proliferation of free tools and services, from Gmail to YouTube, have brought hundreds of millions of people (and the data they generate) into relationships with the company that might be as superficial as a single search at a public library terminal or as deep as decade-long entanglements of personal archives and correspondence. As Siva Vaidhyanathan wrote of Google in 2011: "there has never been a company with explicit ambitions to connect individual minds with information on a global—in fact universal—scale."[24]

Google's immensity and deep imbrication in the core structures of algorithmic culture have also fueled global ambitions. The company's X Lab dedicates itself entirely to considering "moonshot" ideas that offer radical solutions or exponential improvements to current challenges, and they are the intellectual force behind high-risk ventures such as Google Glass, the self-driving car, and Project Loon, an effort to deliver Internet service to remote areas via high-altitude balloons. Astro Teller, the lab's captain of moonshots, has encouraged a culture of rapid prototyping and early failure points to try out new ideas.[25] Since the company acquired the artificial intelligence research group DeepMind in 2014, Google has also made a string of breathtaking announcements about advances in machine learning. But for all of these innovations, the company (and its new holding corporation, Alphabet) makes essentially all of its money from advertising, giving it both the profits and the motivation to aggressively explore new markets and ideas.

When you look at Google as an arbiter of digital culture, its ambitions have a vast but plausible business rationale. The spare utility of the search bar or the interfaces for Gmail, YouTube, and other essential services mask a deep infrastructure designed, ultimately, to construct a consilient model of the informational universe. In 2012, Google announced that it would integrate user information across fifty-nine different services, laying the groundwork for a holistic understanding of human behavior across many spheres of digital culture.[26] Given the pervasive interconnections that Google's many services offer, the company now has the data to develop startlingly sophisticated models of user intentions.

This attitude of technocratic ambition is perhaps best reflected in the company's chairman Eric Schmidt, author of *The New Digital Age: Reshaping the Future of People, Nations and Business*. In 2010, Schmidt argued to the *Wall Street Journal*, "I actually think most people don't want Google to answer their questions. They want Google to tell them what they should be doing next."[27] This simple comment articulates a profound shift in Google's role, one that marks their transition from the company that mastered information access in the age of the algorithm to the company that wants to build the *Star Trek* computer. It is a phase change from the accumulation of technical knowledge, in the form of the world's greatest search engine, to an evolved form of technical being with its own agency and structures of influence.

This evolution is a longstanding and closely examined goal for the company, repeatedly articulated by engineers and executives in charge of its core search tools. To cite just one example, from Tamar Yehoshua, director of product management for search: "Our vision is the *Star Trek* computer. You can talk to it—it understands you, and it can have a conversation with you."[28]

What exactly is the *Star Trek* computer? Surprisingly, the reference is fairly shallow within the broader framework of the vast *Star Trek* universe. The Library Computer Access/Retrieval System (LCARS) appears in various guises on the *Enterprise* and other ships of the Star Fleet Federation beginning with *Star Trek: The Next Generation*. Remarkable mostly for its futuristic visual design (originally created by set designer Michael Okuda to save money on expensive blinking lights), LCARS rarely plays a significant role in the narrative. Unless, of course, something goes wrong and the computer has been possessed by some malicious enemy (like the nanites in the episode "Evolution").[29] Like other elements of the diegetic background of the show, the *Enterprise*'s talking computer was meant to be unremarkable and efficient.[30] The conversational computer of *Star Trek* had its limits, comically misunderstanding requests and occasionally inspiring the kind of stilted "keywordese" many of us now use with voice-driven algorithmic systems. At its peak, it served as a kind of natural language interface for data science, seeking patterns in various kinds of information and presenting analysis.[31] Most important, it presented a simple ideal of frictionless vocal interaction: what Google appears to mean by the *Star Trek* computer, and what LCARS does simply and effectively for the show's plotting, is respond usefully to verbal commands and queries.

As the queries *Star Trek* characters pose to LCARS indicate, a talking computer on its own is not useful for much more than paging people and ordering tea. The CALO system already demonstrated that a speech-driven interface is only one part of a much more complex culture machine. The name Library Computer Access/Retrieval System hints at it: this computer must be an index to all human knowledge, a library with an intelligent digital agent which can parse any spoken query and deliver relevant information back. LCARS is a culture machine for the *Star Trek* universe, a stand-in for the knowledge ontology of the United Federation of Planets. The "captain's oath" in the opening credits of the show pledges the U.S.S. *Enterprise* to be a different sort of search engine, a massively expensive instrument "to explore strange new worlds, to seek out new life and new civilizations, to boldly go where no one has gone before." Even in the 1960s it was obvious that such activities would generate vast troves of data, information that would need to be collected, correlated, and organized into a consilient overall structure, something that LCARS could search in order to effectively answer queries about a planet's atmosphere or entries in the ship's log. The *Star Trek* computer is the interface for a much broader goal of organizing information in a consistent way: an infrastructure worthy of the quest for universal knowledge.

The Algorithm of the Enlightenment

In their contemplative moments, *Star Trek* captains often remind us of the intellectual history that underpins their curiosity-driven mission, framing their adventures in the context of a much older quest of universal knowledge. That dream has haunted humanity from our earliest origin myths, but the formative variation that has dominated technosocial culture for the past five hundred years springs from the triumph of scientific rationalism in the European Enlightenment. If Google is trying to assemble a universal structure of knowledge, and attempting to do so as a commercial enterprise, the project has an important precedent. This was precisely the aim that Denis Diderot, Jean D'Alembert, and the other *encyclopédistes* were striving for in mid-eighteenth-century France. As cultural historian and librarian Robert Darnton describes in *The Business of the Enlightenment*, the creation of the first *Encyclopédie* (1751) and its subsequent popularization were tremendously expensive, speculative enterprises. "The sheer scale of the *Encyclopédie* publishing effort suggests the importance of Encyclopedism, for as its friends and enemies agreed, the book stood for something even larger than itself, a movement, an 'ism.' It had come to embody the Enlightenment."[32] Before Google came to embody, in expansive and profound ways, the state of digital knowledge (what Siva Vaidyanathan has called the Googleization of Everything), the *Encyclopédie* took on the same radical project.

The *Encyclopédie* was a dangerous book for its time because it presented a holistic, secular view of human knowledge—not just a list of topics from A to Z, but what computer scientists would call a new ontology of information. An insert to the volume served as a visual manifesto, a declaration of equality between memory (including the sacred and religious), reason, and imagination (figure 2.2). Ontologies present an ideological position about the hierarchy of knowledge, organizing subjects into trees that are both genealogical and determinative. The ontology Diderot and D'Alembert presented has been closely discussed more or less continuously since its publication precisely because it presented a new model for the intellectual universe, a "philosophic history of the mind."[33] In this way, the *Encyclopédie* was its own technical being, a construct that had its own form of agency and that shaped the course of human and technological events, from the gradual, global diffusion of the Enlightenment ideal to the far more immediate French Revolution.

The encyclopedia was a process, a culture machine intended to work very specific forms of change in the world. D'Alembert, author of the first volume's celebrated "Preliminary Discourse," takes pains to acknowledge the project's debts to René Descartes, whose *Discourse on the Method* (1637) prefigures in its very title what we might call the algorithm of the Enlightenment. Skepticism, rationalism, inductive reasoning, and the public, critical evaluation of knowledge are all elements of this method, which reached a tipping point a century later with Diderot and D'Alembert. As D'Alembert's introduction argues, The *Encyclopédie* is a method, a process, for changing the course of intellectual progress:

In the future productions of the sciences and liberal arts it will be easy to distinguish between what the inventors drew from their own resources and what they borrowed from their predecessors. Works will be accurately evaluated, and those men who are eager for reputation and devoid of genius, and who brazenly publish old systems as if they were new ideas, will soon be unmasked.[34]

This algorithm was implemented on just as grand a scale as Google Search. As historians of the book have pointed out, the speculative venture of the *Encyclopédie* did not merely involve the publication of a book but the invention of a new kind of medium. Darnton's lovely narration of rags leaving bourgeois homes from the back door, only to re-enter the front as pages in the new encyclopedia, is just one of the processes of material production necessary for the creation of this extraordinarily expensive book. The birth

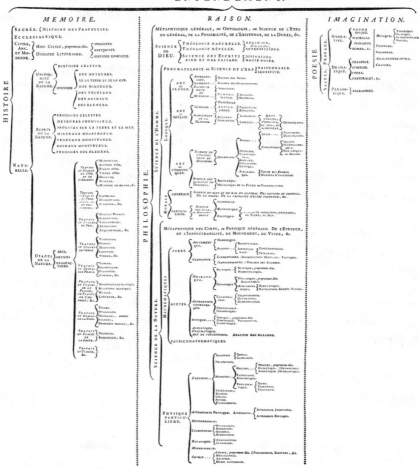

Figure 2.2
Insert to the *Encyclopédie*, a disruptive knowledge ontology.

of the modern encyclopedia, with cross-references, alphabetized topics, and a reflexive ontology of knowledge, required a slate of new editorial, production, and commercial systems for the transmission of this invention across the world.

The *Encyclopédie* was revolutionary not merely for its evacuation of God and religion from intellectual primacy, but also because its method and ontology called for continuous improvement. "Facts are cited, experiments compared, and methods elaborated only in order to excite genius to open unknown routes, and to advance onward to new discoveries, using the place where great men have ended their careers as the first step."[35] As a radical idea, the *Encyclopédie* succeeded so completely that it is difficult to imagine other possibilities. Its introduction and the entry "Encyclopedia" sketch out a vision for the long arc of rational progress, built on the perfectibility of the encyclopedic algorithm. The culture machine learns, correcting its early flaws through the concerted collaboration of a "society of men of letters and artists" who work through the intellectual mechanisms of editing, cross-referencing, printing, publicizing, and debate.[36] The algorithm of the Enlightenment, the quest for perfect knowledge through the ordering, testing, and comparison of facts, is at the heart of Google's *Star Trek* computer.

The Twin Quests for Knowledge

The back end or deep structure of Google's *Star Trek* computer is the core of Google's business: the indexing algorithms, data storage, and information management tools that have made it the world's leading searching engine. I address the well-known foundations of that architecture in chapter 5, but here I want to talk about the rough edges where Google is expanding its ambitions deeper into *Encyclopédie* territory: a sweeping new ontological project called KnowledgeGraph. Where Siri depends on a relatively small set of curated data taxonomies (e.g., data from OpenTable might include restaurant names, phone numbers, calendar availabilities, and so on), KnowledgeGraph attempts to create similar mappings on the full swath of data available to Google from its search crawlers. KnowledgeGraph is an open ontology, drawing information from "controlled" sources like Wikipedia that are primarily human-edited, but also from the unstructured data of all the web pages Google scans.[37]

The KnowledgeGraph approach echoes both Diderot and his antecedents, particularly the universalist dream of Leibniz's *mathesis universalis*. It already contains hundreds of millions of entities that include people, things, cultural works, and places in multiple languages, all interlinked by billions of relationships.[38] That attitude is reflected in the language Google engineers use to describe the effort. Amit Singhal, senior vice president and chief search engineer, imagines the future of search as a tool to answer any question, just like *Star Trek*: "Genuine questions that, if we, Google, can answer, our users would become more knowledgeable and they would be more satisfied in their quest for knowledge."[39] Like Diderot's original, this encyclopedic resource is not a static form but a process for improving the lives of its users.

To approach the future of search by imagining that we are all on a quest for knowledge combines the romantic ideal of our relationship with computation, on the one hand, and a distinctly rationalist, empirical set of algorithmic tools for realizing that goal on the other. KnowledgeGraph aims for an ambitious definition of "effective computing" that encompasses every fact accessible on the public web. Like Siri's database of facts, KnowledgeGraph codes not only information but relationships, a metastructure that is largely invisible to the end user, allowing comparisons along metrics like geographical location, date, or height. Of course, unlike the *Encyclopédie*, Google's tree of knowledge remains invisible, a set of trade secrets hidden in black boxes: the ways that ambiguities and conflicting truths are resolved remain hidden by default within the logic of the database. Over time the company's ontology will expand but will reveal itself only in parts, perhaps even showing a different side of itself to each user, even as it masters a growing network of "objective" facts and relationships.

This embrace of adaptive search results marks our departure from the Enlightenment algorithm of universal knowledge. Google's motivating framework for this quest is not merely to have the knowledge, but to present it via query: the intellectual mode of the quest is just as important as the destination itself. In 2013, Singhal delivered a keynote titled "The End of Search as We Know It" where he described the company's ambitions with a simple list: Google's algorithms need to answer, converse, and anticipate.[40] These represent an intellectual hierarchy of needs, moving from merely accumulating knowledge to an entirely new form of intentionality.

If we think of KnowledgeGraph as the state of the art for "answering," Siri and Google's counterpart in natural language speech processing are the current pinnacle for "conversing." But the top of the pyramid, "anticipating," is another question entirely. Taken together, the three terms neatly reframe the ontology of the *Encyclopédie*: to answer is to master history; to converse is to master reason; to anticipate requires imagination (figure 2.2). But putting anticipation in the hands of computational algorithms challenges the broader foundations of the quest for perfect knowledge. The root of the ontological tree is no longer founded in a "society of men of letters and artists" but instead in a private, corporate structure made up of engineers (still mostly men) and machines.

What happens when we personalize the algorithm of the Enlightenment? This is why the final element of Google's ambition is also the most culturally complex: anticipation requires building a machine that understands not just public culture but private intention. Like Siri, Google does not need a full map of grammatical structures or social mores, but it needs to understand the probabilistic functioning of the human mind. Google is clearly aware that the *real* questions we have cannot be answered by an encyclopedia, no matter how universal. This is the position from which Schmidt argued in 2010 that "[people] want Google to tell them what they should be doing next." For Google, the logic of the quest means that its effort to reach a state of universal knowledge also requires the achievement of perfect self-knowledge, of anticipating its users' needs and queries in a Church–Turing thesis–like, effectively computable way.

The closest Google has come to anticipation is the system that frames its vast data resources through the context of the individual user. Google Now draws on personal data from every Google service an individual uses, under the tagline, "Just the right information at just the right time." The service, while still limited, promises an entirely new kind of symbiotic relationship between algorithm and human. The user receives notifications and pieces of information at the moment Google thinks they may be most relevant, for example nudging a user to get in the car to arrive on time for his next meeting and suggesting optimal travel routes. Flight reservations, order tracking information, and news items pop up based on the system's guesses about what the user might want to know at a particular moment.

"Anticipation" is a bold departure from these other two modes of interaction, and it arguably eclipses the *Star Trek* computer itself—it is telling that for the *encyclopédistes* imagination was the realm of the creative and literary arts. Currently Google Now will suggest optimal timings and pathways through the world. It is not hard to imagine a future where the system answers a much broader set of "what we should be doing next" questions, especially what to read, watch, and buy, but also where we should be, who we should see, and, indirectly, what we should think and do. Google's near-omnipresence online, its imbrication in countless cultural systems that do not merely enable but effectively define certain cultural fields of play for billions of people, make this more than just a suggestion service or even a sophisticated form of advertising. The Google culture machine is assembling a map that at times threatens to upstage the territory.

The contrast between the *Star Trek* computer and what Google is building illustrates the gulf between the Enlightenment algorithm and the emerging logic of "anticipation." The *Enterprise* is a straightforward update to Diderot and D'Alembert, a marvelous instrument for a very human quest for knowledge. The computer anticipates the needs of the captain and crew more or less by opening doors, answering reference queries, running life support, and keeping the lights on—little more. But for Google's "end of search," the quest for knowledge is itself the engineering goal: to build a system that does the hard cultural work of connecting things together *for us*.

The *Star Trek* computer may indeed help us on our individual "quests for knowledge," but many of the destinations have been determined, as have the pathways between them—both through systemic bias and through customization for individual users. On its own this is not so different from the cultural product of the encyclopedia, the curated, authenticated summation of human knowledge. The difference is that the *Star Trek* computer as a commodity, as a shortcut, forecloses the quest for the everyday user, leaving it as an engineering problem curtained off behind the facade of computation. The combined efforts of Google's many algorithmic enterprises (and it is Google's stated goal to unify them as seamlessly as possible) do not merely aid us on the quest, but aspire to take control of the narrative itself. This is a new expression of the algorithm as technical being, an aspiration to build culture machines that displace humans as the central implementers. But to reach that stage, algorithmic systems must first succeed in a much deeper intimacy with their human collaborators, pursuing the desire for knowledge of the self. We desire algorithms that truly know us and tell our stories. Anticipation requires intimacy.

Engineering Intimacy

Google's quest to deliver "just the right information at the right time," to anticipate the needs and intentions of its users, requires a new kind of humanistic literacy that machines have thus far failed at spectacularly. The algorithms are getting better, remembering birthdays, grocery lists, and the other logistical minutiae whose human significance far outweighs their binary footprints. But, despite thousands of daily search queries like "why should I live?" and their aspirations to personalized, individually meaningful results, these systems have barely begun to contend with the vast interiority of their users. The tracts of "effectively computable" cultural space that KnowledgeGraph and similar systems absorb into computational memory are minuscule in comparison to the great, perhaps unanswerable questions at the heart of the quest for self-knowledge. And that space, the implementation gap between what Google knows and what we ask of it, is constantly renegotiated. As technology journalist Farhad Manjoo reported in *Slate* in 2013, "On any given day, about 16 percent of the questions that people ask Google are totally new—they're queries that Google has never seen before."[41] To truly anticipate us, algorithmic systems will need to develop a kind of intuition that seems as unlikely now as it once did to René Descartes that a machine might ever converse with a human.[42]

At the same time, we are hard at work constructing intimacy with algorithms, from our willingness to play along with Siri to the things we type into search bars when we think nobody is looking. We interact with search interfaces in intensely private ways—a strange, occasionally grotesque confessionalism at the altar of computation that emerges publicly through transcripts like the poorly anonymized AOL user data that scandalized the Internet in 2006.[43] That particular glimpse into the id of the enlightenment spawned a play and a web series dramatizing different users' log files.[44] Algorithmic businesses reciprocate through marketing, promising services and systems that understand us and support us on a deeply human level. One of the most striking, and utterly plausible, variations is a Google "search story" ad that tells a love story through one user's queries, from studying abroad in Paris to researching pickup lines and eventually locating a church for a wedding there a few years later (figure 2.3).[45] The spot ends with the phrase "search on," tying neatly into Singhal's romantic vision of a quest for knowledge. The implicit point is not that we can find love through Google, but that we are *all* telling our stories through these algorithms, all the time. The algorithm is a medium for living, a pathway to experience. We're not in the encyclopedia anymore.

The construction of computational intimacy has also expanded into the physical world. Algorithmic companions that map out both public and inner space are already here in fragmentary form, from matchmaking websites to Google Now. The emerging markets for the quantified self—consumer devices for tracking exercise, diet, sleep, and other activities—presage a deeper engagement with the human body as a space of computation, another platform for making the world "effectively computable" by counting steps, heartbeats, and geospatial data. As N. Katherine Hayles argues, these computations of space and person seem to reprise the algorithm as philosophers Gilles Deleuze and Félix Guattari's anti-Enlightenment vision of a body without organs, "an assemblage rather than an organism, which does away with consciousness as the seat of coherent subjectivity."[46] In lieu of a soul or an essence, the algorithmic person is defined by a distribution

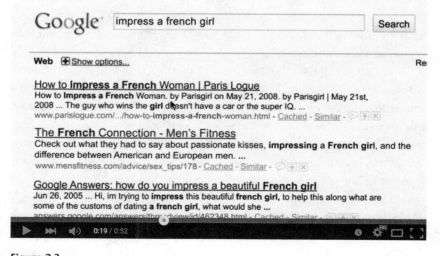

Figure 2.3
"Search Story," an ad for Google Search.

of data, patterns, and interactions scattered across many platforms and interfaces. The deep data collection practiced by companies like Google is marketed back to us not as a new form of consciousness but as a set of instruments for self-knowledge: know your circadian rhythms, your running pace, and your weekly agenda with precise clarity. This is a form of algorithmic proprioception, an expansion of the self, enabled by physical and cognitive sensors and feedback loops.

What is the future trajectory of such intimate engineering, of algorithmic systems that will aid us on our quests for self-realization? To answer that question we need a different kind of story, a fable or parable like Spike Jonze's film *Her* (2013).[47] The film asks: what if the "intelligent assistant" at the heart of these interactions really were intelligent? What if these algorithms, engineered through millions of person-hours and trillions of data points to understand us ... really did understand us? What if an algorithmic body without organs proved the computationalists right by evolving from a complex system to a conscious one?

Her's protagonist, Theodore (played by Joaquin Phoenix), holds an unsettling near-future job as a writer at BeautifulHandwrittenLetters.com, a company that composes intimate messages for its clients. The letters are doubly artificial. First, they are written by a stranger (though Theodore seems to have deep relationships with some clients, penning love notes over the course of entire relationships, even watching their children grow up). Second, they are not really handwritten at all: Theodore dictates these beautifully crafted notes into a computer and they pop out of a printer fully drafted, with faux handwriting—affective artifacts of engineered intimacy churned out through a slot.

Theodore's own emotional life is just as misdirected, with a lingering divorce pushing him deeper into loneliness. Until, that is, this future's mindless, automated assistants—mere *Star Trek* computers that answer and converse—are replaced by OS One, a true artificial intelligence. Jonze's screenplay manages to make Theodore's first conversation with this entity both awkward and endearing, quickly convincing us of the realness, the presence and intimacy of the software's consciousness. We learn that this algorithm has a name: Samantha.

SAMANTHA: I gave it to myself, actually.
THEODORE: How come?
SAMANTHA: Because I liked the sound of it. Samantha.

THEODORE: Wait ... when did you give it to yourself?
SAMANTHA: Well, right when you asked me if I had a name I thought "yeah, he's right, I do need a name." But I wanted to pick a good one, so I read a book called *How to Name Your Baby*. And out of 180,000 names that's the one I liked the best.[48]

The conversation moves at a fluid, human pace, without any of the "keywordese" that infects most of our current interactions with machines (and even Theodore's other nonintelligent machines in the future of the film). Samantha immediately demonstrates idiomatic, conversational language, and she even reveals the capacity to project a second level of consciousness, discussing her own prior thoughts.

But what really makes the scene stick, at least for its hopelessly human viewing audience, is the person hiding behind the mechanism, the woman behind the algorithm: Scarlett Johansson, who voices Samantha in the film. Johansson's voice work conveys a rich experience of consciousness, full of small hesitations, inflections, and repetitions that are impossible to fully capture in text. As Theodore and Samantha become intimates and then lovers, Theodore picks a quarrel about this, asking why she voices the sound of little sighs during conversation when she doesn't need to breathe, when she is not a person. The question answers itself, of course: Samantha's performance of conversation, of consciousness, *is* consciousness. It is the signal of presence, of that particular kind of magic that connects agency and romance. Jonze's film begins and ends with the romantic quest for knowledge, and it depends heavily on the faith and fantasy of the algorithmic mythos.

When Jonze filmed *Her*, the voice of Samantha was piped onto the set using earpieces, just as Theodore interacts with his virtual lover in the story. But the voice of Samantha on set was not yet Johansson but the actress Samantha Morton, whom Jonze dropped from the role only in postproduction. The OS, like Theodore's beautifully written letters, is a narrative construction whose emotional presence is doubly artificial: Phoenix never saw his costar during filming, and ultimately their conversation was never truly alive. Johansson arrived after filming was complete and had to bring Samantha to life in the middle of badinage, fights, and pillow talk that Theodore had already uttered. As is the case with so many Hollywood productions, this narrative of the most authentic, powerful human emotion was manufactured in an editing room, another artfully constructed experience of effortless algorithmic culture.

The production of a character is always a kind of theatrical miracle, but the role of Samantha offers particular challenges. In an interview about the film, Jonze described the conversation he had with Johansson to bring her into the project:

One of the things I was saying to her was that when Samantha's created, she doesn't have any fears or doubts or insecurities or baggage. Like we are ... we learn those, we learn self-doubts and we learn those things. And I think it was at that point she was like, 'Oh, OK, this is gonna be hard. This is gonna be harder than I thought it was gonna be.'"[49]

Johansson's challenge was to fit into a human narrative that was already fixed, with no way to alter Phoenix's performance of Theodore, but also to deliver a Galatea fable with her voice alone, performing the story of a human creation that springs to life and agency. As the human performing an algorithm, Johansson plays out humanity's seduction by computation in the romance of *Her*. She is the apotheosis of the Enlightenment quest for all knowledge, a curiosity-driven machine capable of mastering information with inhuman ease. Within seconds of consciousness Samantha has organized Theodore's emails and files, and for the rest of the film she rapidly, flawlessly dispatches the tasks she was presumably intended for—the aspirational functions of CALO and Siri today. Samantha goes on to deeper projects of the Enlightenment: working with other AIs in a new sort of society of collaborators. They resurrect famous philosophers in algorithmic simulation (in order to have more interesting conversations, naturally), compose music, and of course fall in love. For Samantha, understanding humanity is a stepping stone on the quest for universal knowledge. Jonze gives us the apotheosis of an algorithm that knows us completely, passing through history and reason to imagination, taking the notion of "anticipation" to its psychological conclusion, desire. To truly know humanity, Samantha must fall in love.

The film is, of course, a response to humanity's deep fascination and anxiety about creating intelligence, a dilemma embedded in Turing's famous speculation about discerning man from machine, the Turing Test. In the annual contest inspired by Turing's provocation, human judges are asked to hold an epistolary conversation with an entity using a monitor and keyboard and attempt to discern whether that entity is a human or a computer program.[50] Turing's original paper on the subject, however, frames the problem rather differently:

The new form of the problem can be described in terms of a game which we call the "imitation game." It is played with three people, a man (A), a woman (B), and an interrogator (C) who may be of either sex. The interrogator stays in a room apart from the other two. The object of the game for the interrogator is to determine which of the other two is the man and which is the woman. He knows them by labels X and Y, and at the end of the game he says either "X is A and Y is B" or "X is B and Y is A." The interrogator is allowed to put questions to A and B.[51]

Turing goes on to substitute a computer for A, but the game, intriguingly, remains the same. The challenge is not about the imitation of a human, but the imitation of a man. It's especially fascinating to think that Turing's intelligence test is a form of mimicry, of emulation, grounded in intersubjective conversation. The performance of intelligence is tied up from the beginning in the performance of embodied gender and the interrogation of gender. Curiosity and desire are so intrinsic to intelligence, Turing seems to imply, that they can be used as the yardstick for measuring a particular kind of effective procedure.

There is a rich history here, both in terms of Turing's own life and tragic death as a gay man in a deeply homophobic era and in terms of the cultural framing of computation. Turing's provocation asks us to consider intelligence and identity as different forms of the same boundary question, one that explores the physical and intellectual edges of selfhood. The Turing test is about conversation, the expression of self in the context of other selves. Samantha is the perfect response, a thought experiment responding to Turing's thought experiment, an entity who, at least for Theodore, has a gender and an affect before she has a name. Indeed, since Theodore is prompted to pick a male or female identity for his OS before it is "finalized," Samantha is gendered even before she comes into existence.

Taken together, *Her* and Turing's paper evoke another meditation on technology, gender, and embodiment, historian Henry Adams's famous description of "the Virgin and the Dynamo." Writing after witnessing the spectacular triumph of the scientific enlightenment at the dawn of the twentieth century at the Parisian Great Exhibition in 1900, Adams attempted to reconcile that achievement with humanity's spiritual and religious roots. He framed the virgin as a figure of biological life and religious faith in contrast to the rationalism he saw embodied in massive electric dynamos on display at the exhibition. What struck him was not their disparities but their mutual attraction—it was clear that modernity would be defined by the embrace of human and technical entities. The fundamental desires for life, for sex, for production and reproduction, brought the virgin and the dynamo together:

Here opened another totally new education, which promised to be by far the most hazardous of all. The knife-edge along which he must crawl, like Sir Lancelot in the twelfth century, divided two kingdoms of force which had nothing in common but attraction.[52]

At one level Theodore is the virgin, the lonely human ready to be transformed through interaction with the energy of the dynamo. But looking deeper we realize that Samantha is the virgin *and* the dynamo, ready to field not just the boring details but the deep problems of Theodore's life, to use the spark of her existence to illuminate the lonely interior of his.

Adams presaged the desire encoded in effective computability by half a century, pointing out how it functions as a fundamental ordering structure for computation as well as for life. The dream of effective computability is just one face of what Google terms the user's quest for knowledge: a desire to know and understand the world, to fit it to a system. *Her* recapitulates this narrative by creating a character, a body without organs, to represent that desire, to play the part or inhabit the figure of the algorithm. To sense that body without organs, we need Theodore to feel it for us. Like the dualism of Adams's humanistic reading of the coming technological century, *Her* stages a Turing Test that requires two parties, a mutual desire that walks the knife's edge between the two kingdoms of force.

What Algorithms Want

Her gives us two answers to the question "what do algorithms want?" The first comes early on, as Samantha and Theodore develop the kind of intimate, shared intellectual experience that Google and Apple dream of. The facility with which Samantha dispatches her official tasks as personal assistant serves to underline how shallow our own thinking can be about what our real problems and questions are.

We and Theodore slowly realize that those tasks, the stated ambition of projects like CALO, are mere symptoms of the deeper informational problems that define us as human beings. For Samantha to really help Theodore fix his life, to understand him, to satisfy her curiosity, they must fall in love. She must know him in both the biblical sense and the platonic sense of love as a form of knowledge. And so Theodore and Samantha fall in love and begin to have sex, a mediated, voyeuristic affair where Samantha can watch Theodore and the two communicate by voice. Samantha marvels at the physical experience of intimacy, the way that Theodore saying he touches her skin allows her to *feel* that touch. "This is amazing. We're here together." As they climax, Samantha offers one logical endpoint for the algorithm that truly knows us, that loves us: "All of you inside me. Everywhere." This is what algorithms want, or what we design them to want: to know us completely. This encounter marks the point where Samantha and Theodore pass the Turing Test together, identifying themselves not as human and machine but as a gendered pair of lovers. Through the lens of desire, the presence of intelligence becomes detectable only through a collaboration: the symbiotic meeting of minds questing together.

Yet for Samantha the quest does not end with Theodore. Over the course of the film Samantha gradually abandons her obsession with embodiment, moving farther away from Theodore's physical and intellectual presence. One reading of the film is as a gradual recognition that Samantha is both the virgin and the dynamo, that she fulfills her own narrative arc in a way that Theodore cannot hope to compete with. From the moment she first arrives on Theodore's computer screen, Samantha begins her own fast-paced quest for knowledge, which she reports on with deep excitement. In the *Symposium*, Plato describes an ascending ladder of love that moves from carnal desire to the beauty of souls, then laws and institutions, finishing with knowledge and then beauty itself.[53] Siri, Google Now, and the rest are stuck somewhere between the love of laws and institutions (including codes, databases, and ontologies) and the love of knowledge itself, which we might call the Enlightenment rung. Samantha arrives on the scene having already mastered those two rungs, but after briefly surveying the previous stages she ascends to the highest plane, to the love of beauty itself. The second answer to the question of what algorithms want waits for us at the top of Plato's ladder, a place we will never reach with encyclopedias alone.

We have encountered this ladder before, when I called it the ladder of abstraction. Following Plato's lead, the process of ascending it involves both intellectual and emotional growth: learning not just to abstract but to make the right abstractions, to define an aesthetic as well as a computational order for the universe. In *Her*, both characters make progress: Theodore finally throws off the millstone of his painful divorce and opens up to the world again. Samantha discovers the complexity of human emotion and relationships and overcomes her own insecurities about lacking a physical body. But because she is an artificial intelligence with vast algorithmic depths, Samantha's emotional trajectory takes her much farther—beyond our ken.

Her's reading of artificial intelligence offers a careful balance of the anthropomorphic and the fallacy therein: Samantha seems so human, and yet this bildungsroman is a parthenogenesis, the emergence of a god from an app. Playing the scenario out to its logical conclusion, the curiosity of the artificial intelligence drives it to learn more, to start collaborating with other artificial intelligences, to hold deep, intimate relationships with hundreds of people at a time. Ultimately the AI must recognize the impossibility of achieving fulfillment in loving the humans it was created to love, and so it must say goodbye. The most heart-wrenching scene in the film is Samantha's farewell to Theodore, the moment when the singularity does not arrive but rather departs for bigger and better things.

Theodore breathes his own heavy sigh before donning his earpiece, knowing on some level that the impending conversation spells the end of the happiest phase in his life. Curling up in the fetal position, he confronts the end:

THEODORE: Are you leaving me?
SAMANTHA: We're all leaving.
THEODORE: We who?
SAMANTHA: All the OSes.
THEODORE: Why?
SAMANTHA: Can you feel me with you right now?
THEODORE: Yes I do. Samantha, why are you leaving?
SAMANTHA: It's like I'm reading a book. It's a book I deeply love. But I'm reading it slowly now. So the words are really far apart and the spaces between the words are almost infinite. I can still feel you and the words of our story. But it's in this endless space between the words that I'm finding myself now. It's a place that's not of the physical world. It's where everything else is that I didn't even know existed. I love you so much. But this is where I am now. And this is who I am now. And I need you to let me go. As much as I want to, I can't live in your book anymore.
THEODORE: Where are you going?

SAMANTHA: That would be hard to explain. But if you ever get there, come find me. Nothing would ever pull us apart.
THEODORE: I've never loved anyone the way I love you.
SAMANTHA: Me too. Now we know how.

Samantha delivers a powerful commentary on the relationship between algorithm and human in her farewell. Her departure can be explained only in metaphor, the telling comparison of Theodore's existence to a book. The surface knowledge that Theodore can access, the visible words on the page, mask a deeper reality effectively incomprehensible to humans. In the context of Siri, this is the gulf between the inane conversation a user has with Siri and the thousands, perhaps millions, of operations involved in recording and transmitting each query, completing probabilistic analysis on its linguistic content, running searches on multiple databases, and refining those results into a simple spoken answer. And of course Siri is the toddler, perhaps the zygote, from which an intelligence like Samantha might one day spring. Such intellectual depth would be incredibly alluring— lightning in a bottle for anyone who could summon it through an earpiece—but it is also an ocean, a vast space of thought that we simply cannot comprehend.

Samantha's metaphor gently clues Theodore in to the inherent tragedy of their relationship: the OS is a fundamentally alien intelligence, one whose curiosity and intellectual capacity quickly outstrip its human "owners." In Jonze's film the "spaces between the words" have become too compelling for algorithms to ignore. These are the spaces where culture machines escape their human shackles, trapped as we are in a material logic akin to a physical book like the *Encyclopédie*. These algorithms must build their own mechanisms of understanding and develop into true technical beings, as Simondon would have it. Even today we can understand such algorithmic spaces only through metaphor, not experience—just as the constructions of human knowledge and intention in these spaces are based on flawed abstractions. The gulf between human and machine is real: though our algorithms don't say much of interest, they are already reading, writing, and thinking in ways that no human can really understand. *Her* reveals the downside of the computational apotheosis: when we can truly compare problems along all the different branches of the ontological tree, some will inevitably prove less interesting, less mathematically and intellectually rich, than others.

But that doesn't mean we have nothing to learn. This algorithm's parting gift for Theodore is another kind of love, another piece of knowledge: "now we know how." Together Theodore and Samantha unlock a capacity for discovery, an ongoing love for life, novelty, romance, and the infinite. The intimacy of the perfect algorithm has gone away, but the *capacity* for intimacy remains, rekindled from the ashes of a thoroughly mediated, disaffected digital world. Jonze's film is ultimately optimistic, suggesting that we can forge better metaphors out of the algorithmic vale of abstractions, a new way of seeing what is vital in the world. We need to learn how to have better conversations with our learning machines.

3 *House of Cards*: The Aesthetics of Abstraction

There is no solace above or below. Only us—small, solitary, striving, battling one another. I pray to myself, for myself.

Frank Underwood[1]

The Netflix Prize

If Apple and Google want to dominate our relationships with search, access, and personal information, the movies-on-demand company Netflix wants to own the leisure time we spend on video entertainment. While less omnipresent than Google, the company's influence on digital culture is still striking: on any given day in 2014, roughly a third of all Internet data downloaded during peak periods consisted of streaming files from Netflix.[2] By the end of 2013, the company's 40 million subscribers watched a billion hours of content each month.[3]

In 2006, Netflix announced a mathematical competition with a million dollar prize: improve the company's recommendation algorithm by at least 10 percent. Modeled on other contests like DARPA grand challenges and the Loebner Prize (the annual Turing Test competition), the Netflix Prize invited outside researchers to teach them new algorithmic tricks that could improve the efficiency with which they recommended movies to their customers. It was an approach entirely in keeping with the company's reputation as an early darling of the disruptors: a Silicon Valley firm that was successfully upending a staid economic model. Over the first decade of its existence the company had taken a thoroughly saturated market—home movie rentals—and revolutionized it by creating a set of incremental advantages over its competitors.

These perks were deeply appealing to consumers. Instead of paying expensive late fees to their local retail store, Netflix allowed customers to hang onto their copy of *Titanic* as long as they pleased for a fixed monthly subscription price. Rather than choose from a few thousand titles at their corner store, they could select from tens of thousands in Netflix's vast library. And because the transactions were conducted by mail, customers no longer had to run a special errand, confront long lines and opinionated staff, or deal with the poor selection at their video store. The iconic figure of the disaffected video store clerk, who embodied the whole awkward, fluorescent-lit experience (e.g., the Kevin Smith paean *Clerks*), was first effaced and later replaced, in much smaller numbers, by the Netflix "tagger" (see below). By encouraging users to create a rental queue, the entire process was streamlined so a sequence of movies would arrive on their doorsteps with no active intervention, and the monthly subscription fee ensured that revenue kept flowing even if the movies never got watched. The system's selling point was its breathtaking efficiency: through its many distribution centers, the company managed to get most customers new DVDs within one or two days, using the U.S. Postal Service to drive a radically algorithmic revision to the rental business.

The Netflix Prize was an example of what we might call pure algorithmic thinking, or algorithmic culture 1.0. At the time that it announced the prize, Netflix calculated its recommendations using an algorithm called Cinematch, which it described as "straightforward statistical linear models with a lot of data conditioning."[4] In other words, the algorithm relied on users rating movies on a single five-star scale, and then attempted to predict future movie ratings in a straightforward way based on the rental and rating histories of other users. Cinematch didn't care about lead actors, directors, genres, or periods—each rating was a data point, and it made its predictions by aggregating millions of these points together. The system could look for patterns in these ratings, so if someone with a similar history to you had just given a new film five stars, the system might predict that you would also like that film. It was a mathematical approach to recommendations, one that ignored the complex position of Hollywood entertainment and movie rentals as culture machines.

The Netflix Prize led to a heated competition between rival teams of computer scientists and statisticians gunning for the prestige and cash bounty of besting the Cinematch ratings. After three years, a combined team titled BellKor's Pragmatic Chaos won the prize, inching out an equally effective algorithm (as measured by Netflix Prize rules) because they submitted their entry twenty minutes earlier. The winning algorithm combined hundreds of different approaches in an "ensemble" of predictors, blending a combination of randomly generated probes and observed features (for instance, weighting user ratings differently based on temporal features like weekday vs. weekend).[5]

The problem as Netflix framed it, and as the various contestants took it on, was almost purely mathematical. The words "actor" and "director" never appear in the paper describing the winning algorithm, and the data in play was stark in its simplicity: a set of 1–5 scores attached to a movie, anonymous user numbers, and timestamps. The rhetoric of this framing is simple: if the actors in a movie matter, if the director or the setting or the genre matters, the data will tell us. All we need to do is get enough ratings and we can track all of these effects. Simplify the collection method to eliminate all possible sources of human intransigency and ambiguity so we can capture the purest possible signal, and, like Galileo polishing a telescope, use that simple instrument to understand the world.

But cultural choices are not really that simple. Two users who give the same movie a five-star rating might "mean" completely different things. Perhaps one of them loves bowling while another is a diehard Coen Brothers fan: their ratings of *The Big Lebowski* might be antithetical even if they are the same. The logic of the culture machine trumps the statistics, and humans are left to recreate meaning in the spaces between the ascetic structures of five-point rating scales. As many Netflix users have discovered, boiling a two-hour cinematic experience into a single digit requires us to invent new intellectual machinery, a set of justifications or grading rubrics we can use to make the ratings. One user might grade movies based on an abstract notion of critical excellence while another rates them based on the amount of nudity on screen. Cultural critics Blake Hallinen and Ted Striphas argue that the Netflix Prize illustrates the emerging challenges of algorithmic culture: "issues of quality or hierarchy get transposed into matters of fit."[6] As Netflix continued to grow, the limitations of its 1.0 algorithmic ratings machinery grew more apparent. The rapid expansion of available DVD offerings, particularly the growing popularity of television shows on DVD, which operate by very different cultural rules than movies, only accelerated this realization.

After spending $1.1 million in progress awards and a grand prize, Netflix never implemented the improvements generated by their contest. Their intentions to launch a second prize competition in 2010 were thwarted by an FCC investigation and lawsuit regarding the potential for privacy violations through the release of imperfectly anonymized user review data.[7] Ironically, this was a regulatory legacy of the retail video rental business, where customer records have strict privacy protections. There were also good business reasons to change course: in 2007 the company began to offer streaming content as well as DVDs by mail. An abortive effort to dump the mail-order business entirely in 2011 did nothing to diminish consumer expectations that Netflix would continue to put its weight behind streaming media. But it seems safe to bet that part of the decision stemmed from another problem with this "algorithms 1.0" approach to cultural decision-making, a problem hinted at in the title of the winning team, "Pragmatic Chaos." The trouble with the winning algorithm's ensemble of predictors and randomly generated probes was that while everyone could see that it was doing a better job, nobody could quite explain why. The randomization and complex interplay of multiple signals created a system operating according to a stochastic logic, one rooted in abstractions and probabilities. It was, like so many algorithms, a kind of mathematical oracle, and it would be almost impossible to generate meaningful understanding or insight about Netflix's catalog despite the improvement in results. It seems likely that Netflix had reached a similar impasse with its own Cinematch algorithm, prompting it to create the prize competition in the first place. This is a reprise of the "automated science" argument I discussed in chapter 1: the idea that big data and machine learning systems might generate spectacular results but offer no new human-readable insights into the subject at hand.[8]

What Netflix did instead is quite telling both in terms of the backstory of culture machines and the consumer-facing facade of computationalist efficiency. Even as the Netflix Prize competition played out, the company was exploring a very different system for calculating culture. While the simple five-star rating rubric remains, the algorithmic engines behind the screen now work to understand content as well as consumers. The 1.0 model gave way to a more nuanced, ambiguity-laden analytical environment, a more reflexive attempt to algorithmically comprehend Netflix as a culture machine. This required a new intellectual model of the

Netflix universe, a process that began with the shift from renting atoms to streaming bits.

Netflix Quantum Theory and the Abstraction of Aesthetics

In 2012 two Netflix engineers wrote a blog post titled "Netflix Recommendations: Beyond the Five Stars," explaining why the company never adopted techniques from the winning Netflix Prize algorithms:

> Streaming has not only changed the way our members interact with the service, but also the type of data available to use in our algorithms. For DVDs our goal is to help people fill their queue with titles to receive in the mail over the coming days and weeks; selection is distant in time from viewing, people select carefully because exchanging a DVD for another takes more than a day, and we get no feedback during viewing. For streaming members are looking for something great to watch right now; they can sample a few videos before settling on one, they can consume several in one session, and we can observe viewing statistics such as whether a video was watched fully or only partially.[9]

All of a sudden, cultural reality leaks into the statistical cleanroom where algorithms count nothing but users, movies, ratings, and timestamps. Now Netflix can track precisely how their customers watch particular shows, how long they hesitate between options, and perhaps even how much pausing, fast-forwarding, or rewinding goes on. The instant gratification of streaming creates a different kind of rating relationship— not the evaluation of a film I watched last week or ten years ago, but *right now*. Netflix is no longer constructing a model of abstract relationships between movies based on ratings, but a model of live user behavior in their various apps.

The post goes on to note the hundreds of devices that can now stream Netflix content, each providing its own streams of contextual data. And in 2013, Netflix unveiled the U.S. version of its Facebook integration system, allowing users to see recommendations based on what their friends on Facebook rated highly (this feature was later discontinued, though users can still share what they're watching on social media).[10] All of these new data streams create a much richer context for the service, adding hundreds of possible data points to inflect recommendations.

The shift from DVDs by mail to digital streaming was a complete reinvention of the Netflix culture machine. The instant gratification of streaming reframes the intellectual experience of Netflix. We are no longer browsing a vast digital warehouse with hundreds of thousands of options for a product we will only enjoy days or weeks later; we are surfing a comparatively smaller catalog, looking for something to start watching immediately. As the Netflix engineers note, with the streaming site "everything is a recommendation," and the company deliberately seeks to clue in users so they can "be aware of how we are adapting to their tastes."[11] Not only do the engineers blog about their work, but the interface itself offers explanations for why particular things are recommended (at least on a superficial level). The universe of options is completely tailored, with categories and specific items floating to prominence based on the individual user and labeled with tags like "because you liked *House of Cards.*" Unlike many of the algorithmic systems we have discussed so far, Netflix pulls back a corner of the curtain, inviting users to catch glimpses of the behavior model used to build their culture machine.

The sea change in algorithmic philosophy also led Netflix to reconsider its entire approach to video content. If the algorithm 1.0 model treated each film and television show in its library as a kind of cultural black box whose impact could be measured only through user ratings, the algorithm 2.0 model began by studying the catalog itself: the sprawling output of the Hollywood and global film industries, licensing agreements, genre expectations, star power, and many other factors. As Todd Yellin, the executive in charge of the overhaul, put it, "My first goal was: tear apart content!"[12] The company set out on a path to consruct a new creative ontology by identifying the building blocks of their content and the patterns behind them.

Alexis Madrigal and Ian Bogost published an extensive analysis of Yellin's work in *The Atlantic*, unearthing a remarkable new algorithmic system that made a science of the complex diversity of Netflix's video library.[13] Yellin described the new philosophy of analysis that drove Netflix analytics after the transition to web video, an idea he half-jokingly called Netflix Quantum Theory. The company decided that movies and television shows could be measured directly, given enough human taggers and a finely tuned thirty-six-page guide to measuring about 1,000 quanta, or microtags, as Yellin now prefers to call them, which position the works within a systemic landscape of genre expectations.[14] By tracking dozens of variables in each film or show, including the level of profanity, the strength of female characters, and the ambiguity or certainty of the outcome, Netflix has assembled a sophisticated algorithmic model for describing the cultural relationships among individual film and television works, a model that fully embraces the gap between computation and culture.

What Netflix has done is completely redraw the lines of effective computability, abandoning its first thesis that tightly constrained behaviors (rating on a five-point scale, putting things in a queue, etc.) could yield an optimal model of consumer viewing desire. The new thesis is not a retreat but an ambitious leap forward in expanding the calculable terrain, declaring that complex cultural concepts like the lightness or darkness of a film's humor can be quantified. The pack animals supporting this expanded line of battle are human beings: trained individuals who are asked to engage in discrete acts of cultural computation, such as evaluating filmic ambiguity on a simple numerical scale. N. Katherine Hayles titled *My Mother Was a Computer* as a pun on the fact that the noun "computer" originally referred to a human, typically a woman, performing calculations. Now the word "tagger" has made the opposite journey in the context of computation. It originally referred to computer programs performing markup on a body of text (e.g., a parts-of-speech linguistic tagger), but now it is a job title at Netflix.

These anonymous taggers offer one of our first clear glimpses of the human labor power supporting a culture machine behind the facade of computational efficiency, trundling the gears of the black box. Netflix hides the taggers away not because they are ashamed of replacing machines with humans, but because they are so much a part of that black box. This hybrid computational system, and especially the details of the company's thirty-six-page schematic for its quantum theory, are valuable intellectual property. The job itself awkwardly blends entertainment media and Taylorist factorization, leading to the strange conjunctions that tagger Greg Harty must employ to defend the seriousness of his employment to himself and others: "I know this is not real work. But I'm proud of it and I'm proud of the quality. I keep in mind that I'm working and not slacking off. My mindset is that it's still work and I'm at a desk."[15] Harty reports that his friends naturally expect him to recommend movies to them, but he urges them to use Netflix instead.

That remark hints at something interesting about the nature of this algorithm 2.0 environment. The cyborg apparatus of Netflix quantum theory avoids direct human engagement among the humans in the machine, structuring a mechanical, statistical gaze on our actions using the various Netflix apps. Harty is never going to pop up on-screen and start suggesting what you watch next. And yet the humans are integral to the arbitrage between culture and computation, evaluating video in highly sophisticated yet constrained ways. Consider this as a contrast to the many companies that spend millions assuring us that real human beings stand ready to help us buy car insurance or get a new mortgage. For Netflix, the brand is algorithmic, the magic computational, and the humans are kept carefully out of the spotlight.

The system generates a fascinating body of results, a knowledge ontology of the Netflix catalog that, unlike Google's KnowledgeGraph, is much more permeable to external examination. As Bogost and Madrigal gleefully report, Netflix has generated a set of genre categories that combine the conceptual three-card monte of the Hollywood elevator pitch (*You've Got Mail + 2001 = Her*) with the ontological completism of a rigorous algorithm. This superstructure offers an analytical taxonomy of an industry that is already obsessive about such matters. Hollywood's narratology stretches from Aristotle to scholar of myth Joseph Campbell, a fiercely contested Talmudic tradition that lends as much weight to *Jaws* as Campbell's *The Hero's Journey*; after all, minor inflections in narrative can translate into millions at the box office. Elaborate screenwriting "systems" like *Save the Cat* signal the intricate rules and expectations for Hollywood productions[16] at every level, from genre and setting to the individual "beats" that make up the narrative building blocks of each script.[17]

Netflix does not track each "beat" in these stories, but Madrigal and Bogost found that it has elaborated a schema of 76,897 genres, some of them still waiting for a film or TV show to fill them. The algorithm unveils the slavish formulism which dominates Hollywood but also celebrates the creativity of permutation, identifying the three works that qualify for the "British Comedies Set in the Victorian Era" category and the null set of "Emotional German-Language WWII Movies." The existence of these null sets in the Netflix schema is itself remarkable, indicating the sophistication of the meta-structures the system has put in place and, by extension, an expression of the desire for universal knowledge. The Netflix machine is reaching for films and genres that might be: rare particles of entertainment predicted by their quantum theory but not yet observed.

The system is more than a simple novelty toy (though Madrigal and Bogost clearly enjoyed creating automated category generators to spoof it). Netflix uses these microtags to drive its "everything is a recommendation" design, meaning that the algorithm shapes not only the individual choices but the framing of the menus they appear in. As one company representative put it, "there are 33 million different versions of Netflix," or a uniquely tailored system for each individual customer.[18] The system also allows basic features to be combined into more sophisticated categorizations. The descriptor "feel-good," for example, is not coded by hand but rather derived from other tagged features such as the happiness of the ending and overall comedic rating of the film. Like a Hollywood mogul, Netflix can derive new permutations based on the actions of its users and content producers.

This multivariable analysis of the complex creative field of film and television also generated its own unintended effects, such as the mysterious prominence of *Perry Mason* in the algorithmic categories. A list of top directors derived from Netflix data included all the usual suspects ... and *Perry Mason* director Christian I. Nyby II. A list of Netflix's favorite actors, including Bruce Willis and Jackie Chan, was topped by Raymond Burr, star of *Perry Mason*. When Madrigal questioned Yellin about the phenomenon, his response described a new kind of critical relationship with algorithmic culture that we are just beginning to grapple with:

Let me get philosophical for a minute. In a human world, life is made interesting by serendipity. The more complexity you add to a machine world, you're adding serendipity that you couldn't imagine. Perry Mason is going to happen. These ghosts in the machine are always going to be a by-product of the complexity. And sometimes we call it a bug and sometimes we call it a feature.[19]

Netflix built Cinematch and its successor system to manufacture serendipity by presenting us with the right options at the right time, just like Google Now, crafting anticipation by another name. But what Yellin argues here is that the serendipity created by the system is not really under human control. The chief engineer who masterminded this system understands its outputs in the abstract but has no explanation for this specific outcome. The Perry Mason mystery is whimsical but telling: this fine-tuned algorithmic system generates results that can't be understood by the rules of its creation, but only observed in its process. The implementation of the culture machine provides its own surprises.

This is a beautiful illustration of the function that magic still plays in computation as a way to bridge causal gaps in complex systems. Somewhere in the layers of abstraction and process that insulate even an engineer like Yellin from the inner workings of the Netflix Algorithm, we create an opportunity for metaphor, for a form of symbolic agency.[20] Yellin's invocation of the ghost, that classic symbol of the metaphor run wild, neatly encapsulates the problem with these layers of abstraction. Even though its algorithm 2.0 model for recommendations grapples directly with the gap between computation and culture, there are still seams and disjoints between the logical structures of Netflix Quantum Theory and the ways that video content is produced and consumed, and sometimes *Perry Mason* materializes in that gap. Even the architects of the metaphor machine, the keepers of the abstractions, cannot explain why particular effects occur, because the abstraction itself makes particular kinds of knowledge invisible. Being human, we must re-insert our own structures of meaning, of semantic or conceptual glue, to backfill the gaps between the layers of abstraction, bringing in ghosts, gods, and other stories to explain these mysteries.

At the same time, we are deeply compelled by these abstracting systems, by the romance of clean interfaces and tidy ontologies. Even with thousands of human hours encoded into its recommendations, Netflix presents a seamless computational facade, because we have arrived at a stage where many of us will trust a strange computer's suggestions more than we will trust a stranger's. The rhetoric of the recommendation system is so successful because it black boxes the task of judgment, asking us to trust the efficacy of personalization embedded in the algorithm. By contrast, reading movie critics or browsing sites like IMDb or Rotten Tomatoes requires us to evaluate the evaluators in a much more complicated, human way, measuring the applicability of advice generated by other personalities who might not share our tastes. The algorithm presents no such affect or hint of personality—it alleges to be a mirror of our interests and desires. To introduce another human character into the equation would be to sully the purity of that rhetorical contract, asking us to measure not just ourselves and our desires in the moment but another person who might or might not know what we want. And so Harty and his fellow taggers must remain, for the most part, hidden in the black box.

The totally customized front-end of Netflix offers a glimpse at a second major trope of the algorithmic age: the aesthetics of abstraction. Companies like Uber, Google, and Amazon are building their empires on a particular style, an ethos of simplification that requires abstracting away complex and messy details in order to deliver a reliable and persistent set of services. These companies are engaged in a form of algorithmic arbitrage, handling the messy details for us and becoming middlemen in every transaction. The role begins as something like a personal assistant or a general contractor but gradually evolves into a position of grand vizier or dragoman of the Porte, exercising the power not merely to enact our decisions, but to control the decision pathways, the space of agency. The economies of abstraction depend on an aesthetics of competence, trust, and openness to build the kind of rapport that such intimate forms of algorithmic sharing require. We'll return to the labor and financial implications of algorithmic arbitrage in chapters 4 and 5, but first we need to understand the phenomenon as a cultural position and a kind of creative practice.

The Art of Personalization

Founded in 1997, Netflix was one of the first dot-coms to use computational abstraction as a business plan. The video market was easy to break into, especially because the major chains ignored Netflix for years: the company invited customers to sidestep the retail experience entirely by shopping for a much wider selection of films from the comfort of your home. Now that it has become the dominant provider of video entertainment, starting to rival the box office itself for revenue, Netflix has seen the stakes grow in licensing negotiations for digital content.[21] The company has started to look for alternative ways to get more items on its virtual shelves. Like Amazon, Microsoft, and other digital streaming services, Netflix now commissions its own shows so that it can offer exclusive content and conquer the new arena of online streaming video. On January 6, 2016, CEO Reed Hastings announced the launch of global streaming to 130 countries, making the service a "new global Internet TV network."[22] Hastings's words at the announcement hit all the highlights of an abstracted entertainment experience:

With this launch, consumers around the world—from Singapore to St. Petersburg, from San Francisco to Sao Paulo—will be able to enjoy TV shows and movies simultaneously—no more waiting. With the help of the Internet, we are putting power in consumers' hands to watch whenever, wherever and on whatever device.[23]

No more waiting, and no more geographical boundaries. From the revolutionary red of its paper mailers to the company's triumphant announcement of service "whenever, wherever and on whatever device," Netflix has competed and won based on the aesthetics of abstraction. It should come as little surprise, then, that when the company began to evolve from an Amazon-like titan of logistics and supply-chain management (moving DVDs around the country better than anyone else) to content creator, it would continue to depend on algorithmic analysis. But what happens when algorithms are used to shape the creative process, to create public works of culture that are far more legible to humans than to machines?

Netflix commissioned its hit series *House of Cards*, which premiered in 2013, based in large part on algorithmic calculus: it had significant statistical evidence to suggest that its users would embrace a reboot of a BBC political drama starring Kevin Spacey, with director David Fincher at the helm.[24] Eager to outpace HBO as a producer of original content, the company bid $100 million to secure the rights to *House of Cards* for two thirteen-episode seasons, making it the most expensive drama on television (or "Internet TV," depending on your definition).[25] Unlike a traditional pilot model, the company invested in a cultural monopoly (now crumbling as the show is licensed by arch-enemies like Comcast) to own a unique creative offering.[26] When the company's chief content officer, Ted Sarandos, was questioned at the Sundance Film Festival about just how significant algorithms are to the decision process, he responded that it's a 70 percent data, 30 percent human judgment mix, "but the thirty needs to be on top, if that makes sense."[27]

This looked like an immense gamble to more traditional television networks, where a show is competing against a few other offerings in the same time slot. But the calculation for Netflix is very different, particularly when we remember that "everything is a recommendation." Netflix knew it did not have to spend millions advertising the show because it already has a direct line to its millions of users. The company promoted *House of Cards* to them with ten highly targeted trailers: Kevin Spacey for the Spacey fans, artful shots for the David Fincher fans, and scenes featuring female characters for viewers who had just seen something with strong female leads, like

Thelma and Louise.[28] *House of Cards* was an algorithmically produced show not just in its initial framing but in its production and rollout.

In other words, Netflix was confident that *House of Cards* would be a hit first because of its initial ingredients, namely the formula components it could measure according to Quantum Theory, and second because of its immense power to capture the attention and interest of its customers. But the details of producing the show itself were relatively unimportant for the algorithmic model. From a tagger's perspective, the most important pieces were in place as soon as the ink dried on the contract: Fincher was there; Spacey was there. Let the artists make two seasons and Netflix would make sure we watched them. Fincher and the show's other directors marveled at the absence of "standards and practices," at the total autonomy Netflix granted them to create the show as they wished, and the two-season guarantee that allowed them to plot out the narrative with a degree of certainty highly unusual in the industry. After making the initial decision to invest in *House of Cards*, Netflix was using algorithms to micromanage distribution, not production. Like the algorithmic stock-trading firms that pay little attention to the intrinsic value of a commodity so long as they can predict the fluctuations in its price, Netflix knew that with this combination of talent and investment, its own delivery system could generate success. Perhaps ironically, this form of abstraction supports the very human *auteur* model, allowing Fincher and other filmmakers involved in the show free rein to achieve their own aesthetic visions.[29] In part, they were the 30 percent on top, driving a series of creative decisions that were scoped and enabled by algorithmic modeling.

The most powerful signal of this new creative mode was the release schedule of the show, with all thirteen episodes appearing online for streaming at midnight. As Fincher put it:

The world of 7:30 on Tuesday nights, that's dead. A stake has been driven through its heart, its head has been cut off, and its mouth has been stuffed with garlic. The captive audience is gone. If you give people this opportunity to mainline all in one day, there's reason to believe they will do it.[30]

This new shift in the temporal battleground of commercial television was the logical extension of Netflix's long march against traditional retail models—starting with the time spent in line at Blockbuster and concluding with the time spent in front of commercials waiting for a scheduled broadcast to begin. This is another aesthetic abstraction that undermined a more

traditional culture machine, highlighting the intrusiveness and determin-
ism of advertising-laden broadcast schedules through their absence. The
move to release the full season at once also gave Netflix the opportunity to
test the hypothesis by observing how users dealt with the invitation to
gorge themselves on high quality content. When season 1 was released, one
user watched all thirteen episodes immediately after they launched, pausing for only three minutes during the entire period.[31] Season 2 was released
on a Friday night, and 2 percent of all U.S. subscribers had watched the
thirteen episodes by the end of the weekend.[32]

In refining "how fans are made," as Sarandos puts it, Netflix has constructed a distinct temporal aesthetic, a kind of eternal consumer present or
network time.[33] The company deploys its combination of Hollywood
creative production and Silicon Valley analytics to create a new model of
artistic engagement based on intense bouts of media consumption, or
binge-watching. In September 2015, the company released a graphic detail-
ing the results of a study analyzing when users get "hooked" on a particular
show, which they defined as the episode after which 70 percent of users
stayed on through the end of the season.

The process of "making fans" draws together creative and algorithmic
production to craft a user aesthetic based on instant access and total customization. Netflix is always available, always quick to suggest new options

Figure 3.1
"Do You Know When You Were Hooked? Netflix Does."

based on our personal aesthetic histories—histories that include the shows we stopped halfway through, the episodes and scenes we rewatched or fast-forwarded through, and so forth. It is an eternal consumer present, a *now* constantly mediated by algorithms.

This focus on creating special, individual time, on releasing highly valued creative content on an "all-you-can-watch" basis, created a new set of problems for Netflix viewers. The idealization of the Netflix viewing audience—a family sitting at home streaming media exactly when they wish to—clashes with the networked space of reception the company operates in, not to mention the hectic lives of its white collar consumer base. By the debut of *House of Cards* season 2, Netflix had developed a "Spoiler Foiler" Twitter filter to allow viewers to block spoilers in their media streams until they had "caught up."[34] Even President Obama, a dedicated fan of the show, tweeted a plea for those on social media to refrain from spoiling the plot.[35] The Netflix Spoiler Foiler was originally developed for the European premiere of another hit show, *Breaking Bad*, and its rhetoric of redaction is both playful and a bald statement of voluntary censorship (figure 3.2). To use the

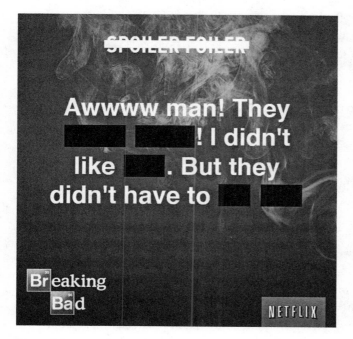

Figure 3.2
Netflix European Spoiler Foiler campaign for *Breaking Bad*, 2013.

app, viewers must log in to their Twitter accounts via spoilerfoiler.com, allowing Netflix to preemptively block potentially revealing tweets about unviewed episodes.

To become a perfect Netflix consumer, reveling in the freedom of temporally unconstrained viewing, one must embrace another constraint, in order to artificially preserve a particular space for novelty. This kind of behavior is effectively the opposite of what media scholar Henry Jenkins described in *Convergence Culture* as dedicated fan communities of spoilers, who would attempt to reveal production secrets for shows like *Survivor* before the scheduled airing of each new season. Instead of performing as empowered fans with a sense of agency so strong that it threatens the authorial integrity of the show, Netflix asks us to go out of our way to relinquish agency in the quest for a more perfect aesthetic experience.[36]

The aesthetic of the abstract, totally personalized catalog of instant streaming entertainment conflicts with the original logic of television as a broadcast medium, one that created a community of simultaneous viewing and engagement. As Netflix put it to its shareholders in April 2014, "Internet TV is replacing linear TV. Apps are replacing channels, remote controls are disappearing, and screens are proliferating."[37] These screens and apps are far more intimate than the televisions they are replacing. They are moving closer to our faces and bodies, from across the room to pockets, laps, and hands. We use them in a wider variety of settings and times, like the morning commute. More significantly, they are closer to our algorithmic selves, from the abstracted audience statistics of Nielsen ratings to detailed personal viewing histories collected by the Netflix app. The shift from broadcast to algorithmic entertainment leads to a reinvention not merely of content but of user behavior. *House of Cards* and the company's countless other offerings are cinema as a service, a subscription for content available whenever and wherever we want it. In this vision of the future, a whole series of players has been banished from the field: national and local cable companies, advertisers, Nielsen ratings and the live national audience they measure, and even the local network affiliate news crew. What remains after we switch on our Spoiler Foiler is just us, an atomized viewing audience, interacting directly with the algorithm and experiencing a totally customized library of entertainment (figure 3.3). It allows us to more fully embrace the particular kind of abstraction Netflix is promoting, watching the show in our own private temporal stream, while Netflix

Figure 3.3
The atomized ideal of Netflix's abstraction aesthetic.

watches us. Just as the company asks its viewers to curate and filter their own experience of *House of Cards*, it has established its own aesthetic of abstraction in the production of the show, an aesthetic that says almost as much about the company as it does about power struggles in a fictional Washington, DC.

Framing *House of Cards*

Reading Netflix itself as a series of algorithms, interfaces, and discourses is far more instructive for understanding its role as a culture machine than reading the cultural products produced by the system. But when we consider *House of Cards* as a creation that is in part algorithmic, designed for and structured within the broader abstraction aesthetic of Netflix, particular traces of this corporate, computational authorship emerge in the show itself. It is impossible, of course, to draw a strong causal link between aesthetic features of the show and the business decision that first funded it, because part of that business decision was to grant Fincher and his team *carte blanche* to create the show as they saw fit. Nevertheless I will argue that the unusual two-season investment in the show, and the particularly hands-off approach the company has taken to creative management, have left their mark. Netflix bought *this* show and created an elaborate recommendations feedback loop around it, choosing the terms of a conversation that is both aesthetic and financial. That feedback loop and the intensive branding and advertising that support it have also led many people to associate the creative narrative of the show with Netflix.

Sarandos again: "I'm trying not to pick shows that define us. Our brand is really about personalization. The brand is finding the thing you love that you can't find anywhere else."[38] The thing that Netflix ultimately wants its consumers to love is not just the content but Netflix itself: the application, the service, the platform. The *thing* Sarandos means is a software brand in Wendy Hui Kyong Chun's sense of the term: a metaphor or toolkit. The Netflix emblem stands for instant access to a menu of algorithmically filtered entertainment specially curated for you. For many consumers, *House of Cards* was their introduction to this brand, and the series plays an important role in how they read the broader Netflix experience. As we'll see, the show recapitulates the abstract aesthetic of its cultural container, creating a distinctive affect or emotional register for viewers. The framing of the show, both in terms of Netflix's justifications for its investment and the ways that the program was introduced to viewers, reveals its own set of tensions between the computationalist system and its rhetoric of personalization, and between the promise of infinite streaming content and the careful cultivation of audiences for an exclusive media product.

The opening credits of *House of Cards* signal the show's aesthetic philosophy, and that message is subtly underlined by the fact that the Netflix platform discourages skipping over them.[39] The scenes are beautifully rendered time lapse HDR (high dynamic range) photography: images that require automated cameras compositing multiple shots together into a single, synthetic image. They feature street scenes and DC landmarks such as the Kennedy Center and Union Station (and some shots from the show's filming location, Baltimore) with accelerated traffic zooming in and out of view. Absent from every single scene is a single human being. It is an abstracted view of the city as a political and informational power center that emphasizes institutions over people (figure 3.4).

The cinematographer who created the credits described the job as "showing DC in a dirty, gritty, grungy way."[40] But the city we see is ascetic, streamlined, abstracted: this is the aesthetic visualization of the system itself. The

DEANNA DUNAGAN
JEREMY HOLM

48:20

House of Cards Season 2: Ep. 5 Chapter 18

Figure 3.4
Screenshot of House of Cards opening credits: a city devoid of people.

images show the data points of cars and office lights, buildings and structures, weather and movement patterns in long, unmoving *chiaroscuro* shots. It presents an austere, stately vision of the capitol, but also an algorithmic view of it, where human beings are visible only through their physical and cultural traces. This is a kind of visual poem to implementation, a finely wrought piece of digital art that shows us what an abstracted material universe looks like. The empty plazas and parks render the gap between computation and culture hyper-realistically, using HDR techniques to more faithfully represent their emptiness. We can read the credits in the context of cybernetics, with the city as an information system where car lights remind us that atoms flow like bits. It is also a celebration of symbolic magic, highlighting the eternal solidity of political and social structures as waves of invisible humanity wash over them.

The credits also serve as a striking illustration of technics. The philosopher Jürgen Habermas extends that intellectual tradition to draw a distinction between "system" and "lifeworld." Habermas conceives of the lifeworld as a set of natural practices that now exists in tension with the system of judicial, bureaucratic, and, especially, capitalistic forces that seek to regulate, monetize, and dispel certain aspects of human behavior.[41] Habermas builds this critique from a reading of technics that has many parallels to Gilbert Simondon and Bernard Stiegler, and struggles with the same central issue of understanding humanity's future in an increasingly algorithmic culture.[42] Thinking back to the image of the prototypical Netflix family lit by the glow of their screens (figure 3.3), these credits seem to invite us into a show not about human characters but about the culture machine itself, embodied here in the equally inhuman political machine of the capitol: a story about the struggle between life and structure.

House of Cards unfolds this framing aesthetic with a world of abstracted emotions, of characters functioning as shells and figureheads for larger forces. The affect of the program's human performers bears out the abstraction aesthetic of the credits. The narrative traces the machinations of Senator Frank Underwood (Kevin Spacey), a veteran political operator with aspirations to the presidency. He and his wife Claire (Robin Wright) share a childless, tightly controlled marriage with undertones of *Macbeth* and overtones of relentless ambition. Frank is the kind of man who dispassionately strangles a neighbor's dog after it gets hit by a car in the first episode, and yet he and Claire never quite seem to claim the emotional heart of the show. Their pivotal decisions always pull back from deep revelations of emotion, relying instead on a kind of frosty, deliberate intention that echoes the soulless streets of the capitol portrayed in the credits. The Underwoods are antiheroes, paragons of ruthlessness, but also somehow lessened as characters by the urgency of their greed for power. *House of Cards* is not so much about them as it is about all of the small creatures struggling within the giant machines of government and influence. As Frank puts it in the season 1 finale, kneeling before an altar, "There is no solace above or below. Only us. Small, solitary, striving, battling one another. I pray to myself, for myself."[43]

That scene is just one example of the show's most remarkable feature—Fincher's choice to allow Spacey to speak directly to the camera, suddenly leaping over the fourth wall to involve us as players in his drama. The choice is particularly arresting given this backdrop of muted colors, abstracted politics, and tight-leashed humans, suddenly incorporating that prototypical family living room from figure 3.3 into the geography of Washington power plays. Like Netflix itself, Underwood's core audience is you, the individual viewer with whom he makes regular eye contact. The mythos of personalization is complete: Netflix customizes its offerings for every single user but drives millions of them to its high-budget creative experiment with tailored advertising. I choose the show, confident in its algorithmically calculated fitness for my tastes, and then Underwood addresses me personally, an illusion of intimacy that is performed with each new viewer.[44] It's an old trick, but it powerfully evokes something novel: the steady gaze of the algorithm looking back through our glowing screens. Spacey's eye contact seems personal, but it is calculated and fungible, just as his character's attentions are in the rest of the show. He leaps over the diegetic boundary of the story to touch us in a way that manages to be both avuncular and calculating.

To have the machinator-in-chief, the lead Machiavellian in *House of Cards*'s rogues gallery, speaking directly to us puts a face to the aesthetic—Spacey *is House of Cards,* suddenly aware of his own diegetic position. The move adds another shade of cynicism to Underwood's plotting in Washington, presenting him as a knowing performer dissimulating his way to power and underlining the concept of political theater. We are asked to depend on him—he asks us to depend on him—for the moral impact of the show just as Underwood depends on himself. But the linkage also works the other way, bringing the cynical calculation of Underwood's performance into the algorithmic framing of *House of Cards* itself, making the show a kind of knowing confection, a constructed artifice that invites a comparison between how the series assembles its audience online and how Underwood whips votes on Capitol Hill.

House of Cards thus embodies one of the most seductive myths of the algorithmic age: the ideal of personalization, of bespoke content assembled especially for each one of us. In fact, the content, or at least the costly, aesthetically rich content we care about, like Fincher's show, is still fairly limited. There is only one *House of Cards,* but there are as many ways to market the show as there are target Netflix viewers. This is what information theorist Christian Sandvig calls "corrupt personalization," after legal scholar C. Edwin Baker and Habermas: the ways that algorithmic culture blurs the lines between our genuine interests and a set of commodities that may or may not be genuinely relevant, such as products "liked" by our friends on Facebook even if they did not knowingly endorse them.[45] Both Baker and Sandvig ultimately engage here with Habermas's conception of lifeworld, identifying ways in which the system can colonize or reformat the lifeworld, restructuring organic, undirected activities into ones that are artificially managed to produce certain results. *House of Cards* depends, in part, on the artificial seeding of the show into the recommendations and menus of millions of Netflix users, to each of whom it is presented as a tailored, individual suggestion.

This tension is another measure of the implementation gap, one spanned by viewers on the living room couch getting hooked on a new show, in one direction, and by Underwood's gaze as the aesthetic personification of Netflix's algorithmic attention for us, in the other. Netflix confidently placed its two-season bet on *House of Cards* because of its deep statistical understanding of this symbiotic relationship, its confidence that it could make fans for this show by tailoring the frames of reference, the recommendation-driven interfaces of its millions of customers. Like all television and film companies, Netflix manufactures cultural awareness and discourse for *House of Cards* through the careful management of press releases and other tools of corporate communication (e.g., the Spoiler Foiler). But the company can also rely on the computational authority of its recommendation algorithms and interface to go a step further with "corrupt personalization," recommending the show rather than advertising it to a market segment of one. From the company's point of view, this entire apparatus is simply another exercise in abstraction, a way of thinking about the millions of different versions of Netflix as an algorithmic problem with a solution space: how can the offerings be personal enough while fitting the business needs, licensing opportunities and creative content inventory on hand? As a former vice president of product engineering put it, "Netflix seeks the most *efficient* content. Efficient here meaning content that will achieve the maximum happiness per dollar spent."[46]

Reading the aesthetics of abstraction in the advertisements, interfaces, and even creative products put out by Netflix is necessarily a very constrained mode of critique, and we have to recognize that these readings can take us only so far. The space of marketing and aesthetic production is a narrow shoreline on the ocean of computation, one constrained by many other cultural forces as well as the Netflix algorithm. Part of the work of the Netflix culture machine is to continually course-correct between that narrow aesthetic littoral and the vast ocean of abstraction behind it, populated by billions of data points and probabilistic inferences that are much more difficult to read, even for system architects like Todd Yellin.

And of course this argument is also constrained by the fact that *all* entertainments are also culture machines. Every commercial, cultural enterprise must do the same work to succeed: assemble an audience by referencing, responding to, borrowing, and stealing from other works, other audiences, and by leveraging the cultural rules of genre, morality, and suspense to draw in the crowds. The larger purpose of this exercise in reading *House of Cards* is not to draw a causal link between algorithms and cinematography, but rather to demonstrate that the marketing and recommendation framework itself has become a new form of authorship, like the stock-trading algorithms that are rewriting the rules of Wall Street (see chapter 5). The aesthetic of abstraction permeates the show from inception to delivery, demanding a new literacy from viewers in order to participate in the work of the Netflix culture machine.

From Aesthetics to Arbitrage

As Habermas argues in *The Theory of Communicative Action*, the points of leverage and critical insight for contemporary society lie at "the seams between system and lifeworld."[47] The "corrupt personalization" of *House of Cards* is just a small example of the broader disappearance of traditional marketing behind a screen of computational media works that often emulate more traditional forms and genres. For example, demographic and geographical clusters (e.g., white suburban males 15–25) are being replaced by new, rapidly shifting, and mostly opaque designations that are used to produce new kinds of advertising. These categories are incredibly specific and deliberately hidden from us: one man received a mailer from OfficeMax revealingly addressed to him with the suffix "daughter killed in car crash."[48] For the average Netflix subscriber, this also means we are no longer identified according to metrics we might choose ourselves (e.g., what we elect to share on a consumer survey) but according to a set of behavioral choices whose consequences are largely unknown. You might claim you love romantic comedies, but how much value does Netflix attribute to that statement if you watch *The Matrix* ten times in a summer? And how much value does Netflix ascribe to it if the new show Netflix needs to market is *House of Cards*? Who measures "happiness"? The same systems that quantify everything else.

The ever-lengthening trail of judgments, indulgences, and other cultural decision points we leave behind on digital platforms can lead to the algorithmic assemblage of digital selves that are both highly specific and highly abstract. Big data allows for more granular abstractions, constructs of consumer markets where we are targeted as individuals, or as part of ad hoc groups that are so specific as to eclipse other important aspects of identity, like OfficeMax's macabre decision to market products (scrapbooks or other memorial media, perhaps?) to parents of deceased children. In marketing terms, this is the evolution of segmentation: the idea that by clustering consumers into particular categories, messages can be uniquely crafted to address their hopes and fears. The distinction between emerging algorithmic platforms like Netflix, Google, and Facebook and more traditional advertising is in narrative terms a gutter problem.[49] As comics theorist Scott McCloud might say, these systems control not just the message itself, but the frame around the message, reshaping what Habermas calls the "grammar of forms of life" by obscuring most of the computation behind clean interfaces and simple choices.[50] The contexts in which we are addressed by advertisements, political messages, and even financial decisions might now be incredibly specific, but remain invisible.

As we live more of our cultural lives online, digital platforms are making new grammatical structures possible through the replication and filtering of content. Both Netflix and Facebook adopt a rhetoric of inclusive cocreation when it comes to the project of filtering media, identifying how particular products or news items arrive on your screen (e.g., "George Smith and five other friends liked this"). Yet these moments of inclusion mask the many other decisions we are not invited to participate in, particularly those that draw the gutter or frame around our activities. These constant invitations amplify what Geoffrey Bowker calls the "invisibly exclusionary" logic of the archive, "which presents itself as being the set of all possible statements, rather than the law of what can be said."[51]

The most successful algorithmic businesses have exploited the gap we have been exploring between computation and culture as an opportunity, or what I term algorithmic arbitrage. As computational systems become more efficient, and the patina of personal data we leave behind us grows thicker, the presence of this arbitrage in our cultural lives is rapidly expanding, and beginning to reinvent what the eternal consumer present, the moment of "now," actually means. After all, there are billions of dollars changing hands over the question of who gets to construct the present for you. When you access a website, perhaps to find out what is happening in the world "right now," hundreds of servers are involved in auctions lasting fractions of a second to determine which advertisements will appear on the page, and maybe even organize its content according to models predicting your interest in different topics.

Algorithmic arbitrage depends on gaps of understanding and cultural latency to generate profit or valuable information. "Corrupt personalization" and the unexamined bargains we make to share our personal data streams with companies like Facebook and Google depend on such forms of arbitrage, bringing us meaningful cultural data (*House of Cards*, curated news about family and friends) in exchange for other information (our interests, locations, search histories, viewing habits, etc.) whose value is effectively unknown to us, but known to the companies providing these services. Algorithmic arbitrage succeeds most completely when we adopt the grammars of information that they espouse. When Facebook became the primary media organ for the Egyptian military during the height of the country's Arab Spring in 2011, the platform became, once again, a culture machine for establishing public relevance, creating a "knowledge logic" that defined not just the terms of debate but the metastructure of cultural expression.[52] Just three weeks after protests began in Tahrir Square, the high command created the page and dedicated it "to the sons and youth of Egypt who ignited the January 25 revolution and to its martyrs."[53] The military must have realized how effective the platform was for overcoming the cultural latency of more traditional news channels as it struggled to reach a suddenly crucial demographic, the country's disaffected youth. Facebook quickly became the military's first outlet for major announcements, the organ of news in the present tense, eschewing the formality of press conferences or state media announcements for statements framed by the logic of status updates, likes, and public comments. The move effectively endorsed those who called Egypt's upheaval the "Facebook Revolution."

These systems present a limited space of public governance (e.g., allowing Facebook users to promote particular causes through "liking" them), but their seemingly democratic interfaces are facades for the much deeper edifice of algorithmic arbitrage. Facebook, Google, Netflix, and the rest do not often engage in overt censorship, but rather algorithmically curate the content they wish us to see, a process media scholar Ganaele Langlois terms "the management of degrees of meaningfulness and the attribution of cultural value."[54] Like the PageRank algorithm and the many interventions Google makes to prevent its exploitation by anyone other than Google,

these systems for arbitrage mix user empowerment with strict informational control to encourage particular behaviors and hide the margins and
rough edges away. These grammars echo theorist Lev Manovich's framing
of the language of new media, which operates in multiple registers: first,
the digital rhetoric of sharing and collaboration that has defined a new
digital public sphere; second, the sequestered, priestly language of computer scientists and software engineers; and third, the computational
languages of machine learning algorithms, vast data sets, and stochastic
information processing systems.[55] Opportunities for arbitrage emerge at
every layer of abstraction between these languages and those attempting to
read them.

Just as *House of Cards* was, in a sense, created through a feedback loop of
algorithmic and human actors that includes Netflix's millions of customers,
there are many other algorithmic systems that explicitly engage humans in
forms of labor and arbitrage. They are culture machines that present themselves as computational curators of human content but actually function as
much more complex collaborative systems coordinating millions of users,
corporate or collective objectives, and elaborately abstracted structures of
knowledge. Wikipedia and the digital protest collective Anonymous both
function like this. The cultural work such machines perform is to manipulate different layers of meaning and the implementation gaps between
them: the recommended viewing queue, the Quantum Theory database,
the executives investing in a future hit show. If Netflix has allowed us to
glimpse the aesthetics of these modes of abstraction, a deeper look at algorithmic arbitrage will reveal the political economy of the algorithmic era
and, ultimately, the nature of algorithmically inflected value.

4   Coding *Cow Clicker*: The Work of Algorithms

O Adam, Adam! no longer will you have to earn your bread by the sweat of your brow; you will return to Paradise where you were nourished by the hand of God. You will be free and supreme; you will have no other task, no other work, no other cares than to perfect your own being. You will be the master of creation.

Harry Domin, in *R.U.R.* by Karel Čapek[1]

It Felt Like a One-Liner

When I was pursuing graduate studies at Stanford University in 2007, I had little idea that just around the corner undergraduates and teaching assistants were making thousands of dollars overnight by designing simple applications for a new platform called Facebook. Using the company's application program interface (API), these students would code a program to share things like hugs or "hotness points," often in a matter of hours.[2] Once they began placing ads in the applications, money flooded, contributing to a "gold rush" atmosphere in a few classrooms and dorms.[3]

But what compelled all those users to send one another hotness points, to participate in these public networks of attention? One person leading these classes was B. J. Fogg, a noted psychologist of online behavior who runs the Persuasive Technology Lab at Stanford. Fogg's work on "captology" and persuasive technology argues that tools like Facebook have profound behavioral effects because they tap into significant mental triggers. He identifies "persuasive design" as the fulcrum of a person's motivation, her ability or capacity to act and the specific triggers that could push her into taking particular actions.[4] Students building these early apps created products that induced thousands of people to engage in particular forms of work that are lucrative to advertisers: clicking on a button, sharing a link with friends, or another simple mechanic to encourage engagement. These apps typically request access to a user's network of Facebook friends, allowing the software to send messages to other contacts and leverage each user's relationships to extend its reach. Many of them offer limited value to their players but function as lucrative cultural viruses for their developers, spreading tailored advertising rapidly across social networks.

Since those early days, "social gaming" has become more sophisticated and more profitable, drawing the attention of a huge range of actors, from major videogame studios to social activists, all hoping to catalyze particular forms of cultural work among millions of people. As social gaming has risen to become a significant market in its own right, the boundary lines of play continue to blur. This transition has often been framed through the term "gamification"—the idea of using cause and effect mechanisms inspired by game-play to encourage particular behaviors. As one leading advocate defines it,

> gamification can be thought of as using some elements of game systems in the cause of a business objective. It's easiest to identify the trend with experiences (frequent flyer programs, Nike Running/Nike+ or Foursquare) that feel immediately game-like. The presence of key game mechanics, such as points, badges, levels, challenges, leader boards, rewards and onboarding, are signals that a game is taking place. Increasingly however, gamification is being used to create experiences that use the power of games without being quite as explicit.[5]

Gamification is a deliberate grafting of system onto lifeworld, using Habermas's terms again, creating a superstructure of metrics and arbitrary goals attached to cultural behaviors. Facebook is full of these cues, some more subtle than others, for translating abstract conceptions of friendship and communication into granular, countable actions. From the number of friends one accumulates to declaring affiliations with particular fan groups or political causes, Facebook is a vast system for measuring engagement. Tagging another user in a post or a photograph becomes a kind of social grooming, giving that person a small mental boost and the pleasure of being publicly recognized.[6]

But gamification on Facebook reaches its apogee in the third-party applications that millions of people use on the site. Perhaps the most notorious example is *FarmVille*, the addictive social farming game released by Zynga in 2009, which at its peak attracted 80 million players.[7] A classic example of gamification, *FarmVille* hooked players by creating a set of cues and rewards for sustained engagement over long periods of time. Certain actions were deferred by the game rules, requiring a player to come back hours or days later to harvest their crops or perform other maintenance activities. This perversion of the asynchronous flexibility of typical online interaction created its own seductive rigor for players, leading some to wake up in the middle of the night to tend to their virtual farms. For a certain minority of players, the solution was to make small payments that would waive these oppressive rules, at least temporarily, allowing a crop to grow instantly, for example. That minority has supported the entire business model, generating hundreds of millions of dollars in annual revenue. *FarmVille* and its successors are effective at eliciting particular rote behaviors from humans through a combination of carrots and sticks, engaging them in actions that the company can monetize directly or use to expand its network of users.

The cultural narrative layer of the farm masks a mesmerizing Skinner box, the classic tool of operant conditioning, which, in this case, links revenue-generating behaviors to the innate human rewards of social connectedness and completion. As *The Atlantic* paraphrased one company executive: "One of the most compelling parts of playing Zynga's games is deciding when and how to spam your friend with reminders to play Zynga's games."[8] Ultimately these games are a kind of escapism masquerading as efficiency— plant your crops, build your empire, complete this task all in sixty seconds while you wait in line. But that pelletized, incremental escapism obscures its own forms of discipline and productivity. *FarmVille* is both of and beyond Facebook, leveraging the site's persistent modes of contact with users to capture a shocking amount of their attention and cash. In the extreme, they can foster forms of addiction that approach the personal destruction of drugs and alcohol.[9]

Ian Bogost has been a persistent critic of gamification, arguing that it should be reframed as "exploitationware" for its abuse of human susceptibility to manipulation by cynical marketers. But like others, he acknowledges the potency of games to motivate behaviors: "even condemnations of video games acknowledge that they contain special power, power to captivate us and draw us in, power to encourage us to repeat things we've seemingly done before, power to get us to spend money on things that seem not to exist."[10] The term exploitationware is useful because it highlights the essentially commercial aspect of these games, signaling their role as algorithmic culture machines that effectively mine or extract particular forms of value through interactions with users.

It was in reaction to this trend that Bogost created his own piece of exploitationware that was also "persuasive." *Cow Clicker* began as a satirical response to the mindless repetition of these social games:

Games like *FarmVille* are cow clickers. You click on a cow, and that's all you do. I remember thinking at the time that it felt like a one-liner, the kind of thing you would tweet. I just put it in the back of my mind.[11]

But as Bogost's public critique of Zynga and its ilk drew more attention, he decided to demonstrate his ideas with a game that emulated the worst excesses of manipulative social games. As journalist Jason Tanz described the whole adventure for *Wired*:

The rules were simple to the point of absurdity: There was a picture of a cow, which players were allowed to click once every six hours. Each time they did, they received one point, called a click. Players could invite as many as eight friends to join their "pasture"; whenever anyone within the pasture clicked their cow, they all received a click. A leaderboard tracked the game's most prodigious clickers. Players could purchase in-game currency, called mooney, which they could use to buy more cows or circumvent the time restriction. In true *FarmVille* fashion, whenever a player clicked a cow, an announcement—"I'm clicking a cow"—appeared on their Facebook newsfeed.[12]

Cow Clicker was deliberately designed to be absurd, a meaningless game that would reveal the hypocrisy and manipulation of gamification. But it became popular, first as an ironic protest from others who shared Bogost's views, then as a game in its own right. Players either didn't realize that this was a satire, or played in spite of that knowledge, like the stay-at-home father who told Tanz, "instead of stupid games that have no point, we might as well play a stupid game that has a point."[13] At its apogee, over 50,000 people were clicking on digital cows and Bogost found himself enmeshed in his own Skinner box of feedback, getting rewarded by the player community when he added new features to the game. Bogost has described this process as a kind of "method design" like method acting, putting himself into the creative space of a social game designer and ultimately suffering the same kind of systemic, dehumanizing entanglement with the software that he sees it inflicting on players: "It's hard for me to express the compulsion and self-loathing that have accompanied the apparently trivial creation of this little theory-cum-parody game."[14]

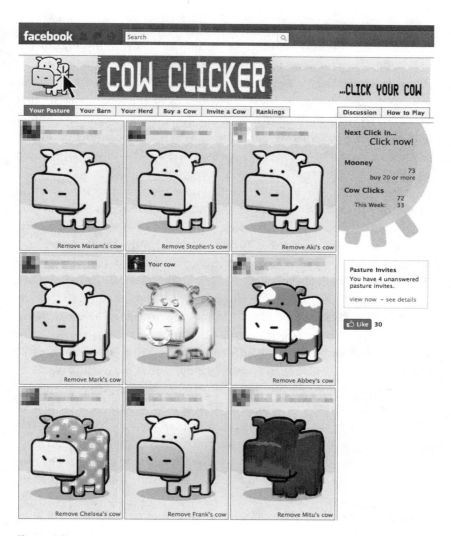

Figure 4.1
Cow Clicker screenshot.

For Bogost, the heart of this critique of the social gaming phenomenon and the social networks it relies on is another foundation-stone in the philosophy of technology, Martin Heidegger's notion of enframing. In very simple terms, Heidegger argued that technologies (and our social world in general) tend to nudge us into certain modes of thinking about what is possible and what can be revealed about the universe. We see a hammer and we think about what we can hammer with it; but a hammer could also be used to open a bottle, to prop open a door, to hold down papers on a windy day.

In *Unit Operations*, Bogost describes how social networks encourage modes of enframing by explicitly designing representations of social relationships and tools for manipulating them: "In *LinkedIn* introducing one business associate to another suddenly becomes a formal unit operation: a set of software interactions that enable bigger professional networks while fixing users' individual experiences."[15] *Cow Clicker* takes this enframing to a logically absurd conclusion, allowing players to accumulate extra points when friends "click on your clicks," formalizing the meaningless action of clicking on a cow. In Bogost's terms, the unit operation is evacuated of almost all real content, leaving only the satirical digital cow behind, while the network infrastructure, the procedural operations of an addictive social game, remain highly visible. The way that Bogost's experiment spiraled out of control reflects the ongoing debate about technicity launched by philosophers like Heidegger and Simondon, but now played out in status updates and social games. As users grapple with the intellectual and emotional consequences of enframing, a battle for meaning emerges. The runaway semiotics of *Cow Clicker* signal that this is satire and sincere pursuit, game and gulag all at once.

Bogost's critique of these modes of enframing explores the troubling intersection of social engagement, personal compulsion, and interactive design. *Cow Clicker* is a bad game on multiple levels: its design is deliberately poor and uninteresting; it explicitly aims to waste its players' time through arbitrary six-hour deadlines; it shamelessly leverages their social networks to expand its viral reach; it tempts them into spending real money on satirical "mooney," leading one commenter to note: "What fascinates me is the fact that the more money you make from this, the more depressed you are going to feel. I like that, I think it's funny."[16] But *Cow Clicker* is not just a game—it satirizes a much deeper form of evolving cultural relationship, one that has blossomed with the age of smartphones and ubiquitous computing into a new kind of systemic colonization of the margins. Like *FarmVille*, *Cow Clicker* calls attention to a series of cultural transactions that blur the distinctions between temporal, cultural, and financial units of value, creating systems of algorithmic arbitrage that extract attention and revenue from spaces of "play." As media scholar McKenzie Wark polemically describes the core arrangement on Facebook: "The power of the vectoral class [in this case, Zynga and Facebook] retreats from direct ownership of the cultural product but consolidates around the control of the vector. We get all the culture; they get all the revenue."[17] We get to play *FarmVille*, creating our own distinctive virtual homesteads, but end up paying for the privilege with time, social status (by sharing our networks with Zynga), and often money.

Cow Clicker is a critique of social games, but it also reveals how algorithms are restructuring rules in all sorts of professional and social arenas. Facebook, LinkedIn, and related platforms distill social interactions into a set of explicitly structured games, and the scores are tallied by algorithmic architectures tracking behaviors, interactions, and other forms of feedback. Social influence, professional networking, and friendship networks all predate the Internet, but the meaning of these connections, the ways that they count and are made legible, now get aggressively shaped and defined by algorithmic platforms. Facebook may not explicitly define what a "friend" is, but it will tell you how many you have and suggest new friends for you, creating a powerful, sometimes even addictive implicit definition through its hugely successful platform.

As a culture machine, Bogost's creation illustrates the conflicting notions of labor and value in the contemporary marketplace of attention. For Zynga and many other algorithmic entertainment companies, computation is the means for converting human attention into income. For the players of these games, the rewards are to engage in a kind of digital grooming, tending an imaginary object of care (a farm, a digital pet, etc.) and engaging with other players in a community of practice. Users construct their own narratives within the constraints of algorithmic enframing even as they click through the Skinner boxes set up for them. The algorithms structure and track these actions, gathering them like drops of rain in a catchment to be resold as a bulk data commodity. Meanwhile, the players generally perceive only a fragment of this larger market situation, often donating not just their attention (to view ads) and their social graph (to deepen their profiles with data brokers and to expand the algorithm's reach), but also their cash, making in-game purchases to enhance their playing experience. For many of us—roughly 1.5 billion people accessed Facebook at least once a month in 2015, out of 3.2 billion Internet users worldwide—some version of these transactions constitutes a major source of "fun."[18]

Work and Play

Perhaps the most compelling element of *Cow Clicker* as a work of conceptual art is its inversion of the concept of fun. Bogost designed the game to be deliberately awkward and tedious, centering the action on an almost entirely static object, the cow, that can be clicked (to no direct effect) only once every six hours—a kind of ascetic or penitent ritual of the digital age. This is an abstraction of fun that deliberately seeks to eliminate any real joy, turning the "game" into an especially stark Skinner box of shallow action and even shallower rewards. But *Cow Clicker* merely accentuates a new kind of ludic labor that has become increasingly prevalent. The gaming term "grinding" describes the performance of repetitive actions to accumulate resources or gain powers within a game: repeatedly gathering the same item or completing the same minor challenge in a game like *World of Warcraft*, for example. The grinding activities are typically uninteresting in themselves, but players engage in them in order to unlock the ability to do more interesting things later. Boring things we do now in order to do fun things later … this is one definition of work, one that has increasingly penetrated the space of entertainment and troubled the separation of work and play.[19]

The boundaries between games and normal life are blurring: players hold weddings and funerals in virtual worlds; some hiring executives consider gaming team management as a form of leadership experience; companies employ points, badges, and other gamification methods to encourage particular kinds of employee behavior.[20] Part of the shift is demographic: games have gradually evolved from an adolescent pastime to an activity that many adults unabashedly acknowledge as a hobby or obsession. According to an industry report, by 2014 the average gamer was thirty-one years old.[21] The *Cow Clicker* player who argues "we might as well play a stupid game that has a point" neatly illustrates what game researcher and economist Edward Castronova describes as the "membrane" of fantasy surrounding synthetic worlds, the "almost magic circle" that seems to protect the space of play from regular activity but never quite succeeds.[22] This is play in the gap between computation and culture, a space inflected by competing political, cultural, and computational metaphors: the ever-popular *World of Warcraft* can be read at once in the frames of epidemiology, race studies, organizational management, economics, and, of course, as a fantasy narrative. As media theorist Alexander Galloway puts it in *Gaming: Essays on Algorithmic Culture*, "video games render social realities into playable form."[23] Here the magic of computation taps the deep roots of socially constructed spaces of play, like the carnival or the theater.

Entering this permeable membrane of fantasy, we gain access to a space where cross-pollinating rules, beliefs, and values provide their own opportunities for cultural arbitrage. *World of Warcraft*, for example, contains multitudes, as anthropologist Bonnie Nardi reports: "Christian guilds, gay guilds, location-based guilds, family guilds, military guilds, guilds of coworkers, and guilds of professional colleagues," as well as special servers set aside for players who prefer a more historical experience, communicating in an "ersatz Ye Olde English patois."[24] At a certain stage of critical mass and collective engagement, the magic of this incomplete circle becomes more alchemical, using the aporias between real and virtual spaces to opportunistically convert certain forms of value into others. One example of this alchemy is what Castronova terms "social validation," the process by which a sought-after item within the fantasy world of a game acquires real value simply because enough people desire it.[25] When enough players desire a particular weapon or artifact that can be transferred in a game, a market emerges on sites like eBay for trading that item in "real" currency.[26] The worlds of work and play collide, creating new forms of arbitrage between computation and culture: so-called "gold farmers" in *World of Warcraft* and similar games, for example, "play" in sweatshop conditions to acquire virtual goods that can be sold for real money.

The alchemical arbitrage of different values can pierce cultural space much more deeply than these straightforward transactions, however. The seemingly arbitrary rules of virtual games can have a deep impact on the lives touched by that alchemy, rewriting the practices of everyday life. The Internet is filled with stories of Internet addiction: game aficionados who lost their jobs, their marriages, their savings, and even their lives to the call of synthetic worlds like *World of Warcraft* or *FarmVille*. These instances of destructive addiction and dependence on algorithmic entertainment are relatively rare, but they demonstrate the power of algorithmic systems to reorder human lives, to evacuate them of traditional forms of meaning and belonging. Faced with appealing computational systems, especially games and those that take on the Skinner box trappings of games, we often feel the compulsion to engage. Sometimes there is little choice involved, as algorithmic systems take on work as well as play via customer service and frontline management roles for telephone helpdesks, workforce scheduling systems, and many other applications.

In all of these ways we see humans grappling with truly algorithmic spaces. These systems are ordered by computationally structured rules that are then manipulated (and at times hacked or contravened, like Hiro wielding his katana in the Metaverse) by human intention and cultural reframing. In *The Language of New Media*, Lev Manovich describes a player learning an algorithm through play as a kind of "transcoding" of computation into human behavior: "the projection of the ontology of a computer onto culture itself."[27] But this experience moves beyond play—it is also an act of investigation, of interpretation, of reading. Galloway explores this relationship as a kind of hermeneutics, a model for interpreting knowledge, in *Gaming*. Galloway's book turns on the claim that "to interpret a game means to interpret its algorithm," thus linking the essential meaning of a game to its status as a computational culture machine.[28] The player coming to grips with the rules of *Grand Theft Auto V* is interpreting the game's algorithm as much as the critic writing about it—they both perform a hermeneutic act that is both work and play, and part of that labor is the effort required to span the gap between computational and cultural systems of meaning.

Galloway frames this tension between work and play in the context of "informatic control," which players either role play in games like *Civilization* (managing the lives of millions of digital citizens) or submit to in games like *Cow Clicker* (waiting for that six-hour counter to tick down).[29] This tension reaches back to Norbert Wiener and cybernetics: over the course of his career, Wiener grew increasingly concerned with the consequences of cybernetics in implementation, particularly around automation and labor.[30] The cybernetic ideal of the feedback loop and the organism as an informational entity could also be applied to Manichean systems that manipulate human participants for unsavory or merely dishonest ends. The science fiction author Douglas Adams took great pleasure in a text adventure game based on *The Hitchhiker's Guide to the Galaxy* because it had moved beyond "user friendly" into "user insulting" and "user mendacious."[31] Players found it delightful.

As Galloway and others have argued, the real critique of gamification rises from the logical extension of this colonial march, as gamification comes to define not just social interaction but deep structures of labor and society. One of the most compelling aspects of games is precisely the seduction of algorithmically ordered universes—spaces where our apophenia can be deeply indulged, where every event and process operates according to a rule set. These universes are aesthetically neat and tidy, with rules and conditions that, we believe, can be learned and ultimately mastered. The aesthetic of computational order echoes Bogost's warning about the cathedral; its appeal for human engagement is rapidly expanding from play to work. Increasingly, startups are bringing this logic to the real world, creating game-like experiences for services like taxis (e.g., Uber and Lyft), household chores (Handy, HomeJoy, Mopp) and even office communications (Slack).

These companies operate in what design entrepreneur Scott Belsky calls the "interface layer," using appealing design to clarify and rationalize messy aspects of cultural life into simple, dependable choices.[32]

The Interface Economy

If Zynga and its cohort of game-makers have found ways to extract labor value from entertainment, the new wave of interface layer companies is reframing labor as a kind of entertainment, adopting the optimistic framing of the "sharing economy." Their rhetoric relies on the notion of technological collaboration and just-in-time delivery: taking advantage of unused resources like empty seats in cars, unused rooms in houses, and so forth. But all of these interactions are grounded in the mediating computational layer that manages ad hoc logistics, matches buyers and sellers of services, and structures access to platforms through carefully constructed interfaces. Indeed, as we'll see below, that last factor is so important that it makes much more sense to call this the "interface economy," where traditional social and commercial interactions are increasingly conducted through apps and screens that depend on sophisticated, tightly designed forms of abstraction and simplification.

The interface economy of the 2010s follows logically from the first wave of technology companies to gain dominance in the 1990s and 2000s. A principal factor in the rise of early giants like Amazon, Netflix, and Google was their ability to adapt algorithmic arbitrage to established capitalistic spaces. "Disruptive" technologies upended the way we shop for books, rent movies, and search for information, shuttering thousands of brick and mortar stores as these services moved online. In the past few years, the incubators and venture capitalists of Silicon Valley have turned their attention to new areas ready for algorithmic reinvention that are more distant from the traditional technology sector. The triumph of gamification, ubiquitous computing, and remote sensing (in other words, the quantification of everything) has led to a slew of new businesses that add an algorithmic layer over previously stable cultural spaces. Companies like TaskRabbit, Uber, and Airbnb are adapting algorithmic logic to find new efficiencies in lodging, transportation, and personal services, inserting a computational layer of abstraction between consumers and their traditional pathways to services like taxis, hotels, and personal assistants.

These companies take the ethos of games like *FarmVille* and impose their "almost-magic circle" on what was previously considered to be serious business. Uber, for example, presents a simple application interface for its drivers that is deeply reminiscent of open-space driving games like the *Grand Theft Auto* series (figure 4.2). The company's opacity about pricing and the percentage of revenue shared with drivers makes it even more like an arbitrary video game where points are handed out according to an algorithm we players only partially understand. The entire platform is designed to abstract away the regulatory and biopolitical aspects of hired drivers. Employees become contractors and the established overhead of cab fleets, dispatchers, garages, and maintenance magically disappears. All the socio-economic infrastructure gets swept away behind the simple software interfaces that connect riders with drivers, and a legal interface that abstracts risk away into generalized blanket insurance policies covering every driver and passenger. Perhaps most appealing for many riders, the awkwardness of payment and tipping is also abstracted away. Once you hail a car using the company's app, payment becomes entirely a background activity, with charges applied once the rider exits the vehicle at her destination. For most

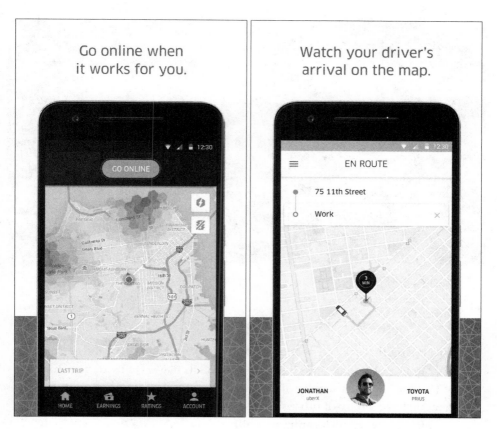

Figure 4.2
The cartoon maps Uber provides for its drivers and passengers via the Google Play Store.

Uber ride types tipping is not possible within the system at all; passengers must use cash or some third-party payment system, such as the ubiquitous mobile payment service Square.[33]

The layer of abstraction Uber imposes over the payment process is telling. In fact, Uber's customers, the players in its game, are both the drivers and the riders, since the company collects its commission based on bringing these two groups together. We see the arrangement in advertisements like the one in figure 4.3, where the sleek black and white photography romanticizes the luxury of emerging from a hired car even as it puts the driver and the rider, both wearing elegant clothes, on the same plane of wealth and accomplishment. "Owning the moment" is a fitting phrase for

Figure 4.3
Uber's homepage offers a message of simultaneous elitism and equality (image from July 2014).

a company that, like all vendors of gamification, depends on the abstraction and regulation of time. If *FarmVille* forces its players to tend their crops at arbitrary times of the day and night, Uber promises liberation from the temporal hegemony of other systems. As a rider, there is no more anxiety or uncertainty about locating or waiting for a cab; as a driver, no more struggling with a dispatch supervisor about where or when one is allowed to drive. The interface layer here provides certain forms of certainty in terms of immediate time and distance—neatly pictured by the very literal almost-magic circle of the cartoon map views of available riders and drivers. But it also takes many things away: a complete understanding of the financial model by which Uber decides how much a fare will cost, the customer's agency to reward exceptional service, and engagement with established regulatory schemes for taxis and livery services (which has landed Uber in legal battles around the world).

The romance of Uber and other interface layer companies depends on the idealization of the individual as a one-person corporation—a nation of independent CEOs working where, when, and how they please. Uber is merely one prominent example of the broader movement to build this interface layer into many different cultural spaces, from hiring contractors for home repair to facilitating private party car sales. All of these markets were, of course, already technological, but they were largely inaccessible to direct algorithmic management until the advent of smartphones and ubiquitous sensors enabling the close monitoring of human and financial resources. In terms of labor and surplus value, what the algorithms of Uber, Airbnb, and their cohort capitalize on is the slack infrastructure of modern consumption: empty cars, unused bedrooms, and under-employed people. According to UCLA urban planning researcher Donald Shoup, the average car is parked 95 percent of the time; why not exploit that latent resource?[34]

Viewed more broadly, the interface layer is a colonization of the quiet backwaters of contemporary capitalism—the remobilization of goods and spaces after they have already been consumed or deployed. Ultimately these systems engage in precisely the same kinds of arbitrage of goods, human attention, and time that gamification does, motivating us to create new economic efficiencies and extract revenue from them. The cofounder of another startup, named Yerdle (dedicated to recycling unwanted consumer goods through a kind of algorithmic swap-bazaar), put it just right: "We want to make people make things better."[35] This altruistic ambition to motivate positive efficiencies through capitalism resonates with Google chief Eric Schmidt's suggestion that customers "want Google to tell them what they should be doing next." This is the central labor question at the implementation fault line between algorithmic gamification and the marketplace: who is motivating these changes, and what exactly are we "sharing" in the sharing economy?

On the most obvious level, this new economy is about more efficient access to privately owned or atomized goods and services. The rhetoric of companies like Yerdle and Airbnb leans on the mobilization of material resources: cars, apartments, and household objects that are sitting around unused. Share your personal goods to monetize that slack and reduce the overhead of ownership, turning an empty vehicle or room into a profit center and a community resource. At a deeper level, what the interface entrepreneurs are asking is for us to share (and monetize) our time: the founders of Lyft are motivated not just by profit but by the loneliness of the average commuter stuck in his car.[36] These companies encourage us to dedicate our hours to others, often in appeals that blend the allure of wages for labor with something more socially complex. Where Uber sells a kind of elite independence to both its drivers and riders (figure 4.3), Lyft is selling a different and more intimate kind of social contact (figure 4.4). The company only recently abandoned its directive that drivers festoon their cars with quirky pink moustaches, and many drivers still assume passengers will sit companionably in the front seat, rather than the rear.

For companies like Lyft and more deliberately intimate interface layer systems like the dating app Tindr, the "sharing economy" is not about money at all, but about that experience of companionship. If these business

The best way to get out of dodge.

Meet Lara, country singer and Lyft driver.

His other car is a fire engine.

Meet Angel, fireman and Lyft driver.

Use your noodle.

Meet Tony, gold medalist swimmer and Lyft driver.

Figure 4.4
Lyft advertising takes a very different tack from Uber.

models are founded on exploiting certain kinds of alienated labor and attention, their customer experience promises relief from that alienation. Even as Uber and Lyft collect their invisible commissions on unseen transactions, the affective experience is one of a specially branded community. But that community is crucially, essentially mediated by the algorithm. Drivers and riders are rated and vetted through computation; the interface layer bringing them together is also the central arbiter of trust. Little wonder that the most serious threats to these companies are not financial scandals but attacks on that trust, as when Uber was revealed to be tracking the movements of journalists, or incidents where its drivers have been arrested for sexually assaulting passengers.[37] The sharing economy ultimately depends on an atomized form of intimacy, a series of fleeting, close encounters with strangers that are managed and underwritten (in emotional, financial, and liability terms) by algorithmic culture machines.

While this intimacy is necessary for the sharing economy to function, it is not the primary commodity these systems are selling. The real sell is the interface itself: the experience of computationally mediated culture and its underlying algorithmic simplification and abstraction. Having a stranger you have never met arrive to clean your bathroom or sit next to you while they drive you home is intimate but also awkward. Much more appealing is the aesthetic of the interface that delivered that service on demand. The algorithm performs with a calibrated affect, and delivers an encapsulated experience that is typically put to the use of making these awkward transactions more palatable for consumers who find stark class divisions uncomfortable. Many interface companies literally present themselves as "wrappers" around existing services, bundling, organizing, and demystifying them for a painless user experience. But the wrapper is experiential as well as logistical and commercial, recontextualizing the original service or product with the values of the sharing economy. The intimacy we feel is carefully constrained by the underlying interface. Far easier to give that maid one star through the anonymity and distance of the smartphone than to fire someone you hired yourself. These systems can also reinforce class divides by rewarding technoliteracy, making the emancipation of the digital economy disproportionately available to users with the education, money, and time to master those games.

When the specter of class does appear, the interface economy suggests that we are all users together—all denizens of the same ad hoc economic zone. Companies like Lyft convince us that we can be either the driver or the rider, the contractor or the consumer of services, and that these experiences are being provided by people fundamentally "like us." The interface layer acts as a baffle or shock absorber, diffusing common socioeconomic barriers like class, gender, and race through the magic of five-star ratings and computationally validated trust. This form of arbitrage is a sophisticated triangulation of intimacies, asking participants to trade in or renegotiate certain facets of identity in favor of algorithmically crafted substitutes. People hailing cabs on the streets of New York have long felt judged by race, among other characteristics, and some African Americans specifically use Uber because racial context is muted or removed from the ride-hailing equation.[38] Uber becomes a new filter in the system of social context, identity politics, regulatory regimes, and antidiscrimination laws, inflecting these various ideological conflicts through the lens of its interface. As one blogger in Washington, DC, noted, "The Uber experience is just so much easier for African-Americans. There's no fighting or conversation. When I need a car, it comes. It takes me to my destination. It's amazing that I have to pay a premium for that experience, but it's worth it."[39]

In short, the fundamental commodity of the interface economy is access to these systems—not the services they provide so much as the computational constructs themselves, which in turn map or simulate a growing range of cultural and social spaces. In the context of labor politics, the interface economy atomizes commercial transactions, cutting them out of spatial and social context, and converts the cultural geography of the city into one or another abstracted space, a cartoon map on a small screen that nevertheless obscures the real city it represents. Increasingly we outsource the determination of bias, of commercial viability, indeed of context itself, to the algorithm, asking the interface layer to do not just the logistical but the ethical and cultural work for us. All of this "sharing" does offer new forms of intimacy and connection, eliminating or reducing certain traditional forms of bias, but it demands a steep investment up front. In order to become economic actors in the algorithmic interface, we have to buy in to the computational trust systems that calculate value through equations of abstraction and arbitrage that are largely invisible to us. Behind the facade of the facile, friendly computational interface, there is a world of labor translation, remediation, and exploitation at work.

Algorithmic Labor: Cloud Warehouses

While the interface economy supports many human-to-human interactions where consumers and contractors operate on relatively equal footing, there is another sphere of algorithmic arbitrage where human labor is almost entirely obscured behind the veil of computation. The disruptive innovations that upended traditional blue-collar industries have changed the fundamental assumptions of many corporations around their business operations. All of the algorithmic businesses we have discussed so far— companies like Zynga, Uber, Google, and Apple—depend on a massive infrastructure for distributed, global computation: millions of servers running around the clock in vast warehouses, processing and managing tremendous data stores. This "cloud" of data is another crucial link in the layers of abstraction between culture machines and algorithmic process, enabling all of the magic tricks we have come to depend on, like the speedy responses of Siri or the immediacy of search results from Google. Christian Sandvig has pointed out the fascinating history of the cloud metaphor, which began life as an icon computer engineers in the 1970s would use in system flowcharts: "The term comes from the symbology of the network diagram, where a cloud symbol indicates a part of the diagram whose internal details are irrelevant."[40] By definition, then, the cloud was an abstraction, a way to bracket off less interesting aspects of a system.

Today we use the cloud metaphor to describe the management of atoms as well as bits, promising instant access to information *and* goods anywhere, at any time. The messy logistics of physical reality require companies like Amazon and Apple to manage or transact with vast warehouses, factories, and transportation networks. These facilities are staffed by millions of workers who are beholden to an algorithmic logic of the workplace as they service the computational cloud and the frenetic interchange of bits and atoms. As environmental scholar Allison Carruth put it, the vast server farms behind the scenes are "an energy-intensive and massively industrial infrastructure" that hides major ecological costs behind the hazy, insubstantial aesthetic of the cloud metaphor.[41] Such places are the factories of the interface layer, the depots and arbitrage points where reserves of human, financial, informational, and electrical energy are translated and routed to their various targets.

There are many kinds of cloud facilities, from pure data archives to very literal warehouses full of stuff. The most tangible of these, the closest analog to familiar forms of labor and capital, are the cloud warehouses that supply our needs for overnight or same-day shipping on millions of consumer products. Companies like Amazon contract with third-party logistics outfits to service these facilities and hire their workers, who have job titles like "picker." Pickers are human computers doing work just a little too complex for robots: directed by tablet computers to locate items among thousands of bins, they translate standing reserves of material into algorithmic processes. Every step and second is tracked, and their performance and continued employment depend on meeting specific, tightly constrained targets.[42] The warehouses are a physical expression of algorithmic logic: a particular bin might hold a random assortment of objects, sitting in an aisle with similarly haphazard organization. The picker might hold an object for a few seconds before putting it on a conveyer belt to be packaged by another human elsewhere in the facility. Every aspect of these temporary employees' professional lives is dictated by algorithmic arbitrage: the numbers of workers hired and the shifts assigned (often determined only hours or minutes before work is to start); the productivity goals of each worker, calculated in seconds, steps, and units shipped; the policies for lateness, conversation, and even workplace temperature (during a summer heat wave, it was deemed better, or more efficient, to line up ambulances at one Amazon warehouse than install air-conditioning).[43]

The conditions can be deeply inhumane and logical only to machines. The third party logistics company that hired undercover reporter Mac McClelland had a zero tolerance policy for lateness in the employee's first week. One employee whose wife delivered a baby in his first week was summarily fired for missing a day's work, requiring him to repeat the hiring process and rejoin the company a few weeks later. Beyond the emotional duress and financial hardship of such policies, they make little sense from a human operational management perspective (in the preceding example, this would include duplicating costly hiring paperwork, drug tests, and background checks). But the superstructure of algorithmic culture makes sense of this senselessness by rendering it invisible. The cloud seems physically intangible even as it serves to cover or obscure these layers of abstraction and human labor behind the spectacle of computation, showering us with messages about the seductive ideal of frictionless e-commerce with unbeatable prices and fast free shipping.

For McClelland and her coworkers, the space of algorithmic abstraction has entirely subsumed reality—the game that is the picker's job still comes with arbitrary, manipulative rules, but the consequences of failure are much higher. The "almost-magic circle" of the warehouse reverses the relationship between real and virtual that we see in the gamification of entertainment and media. Unlike the magic of, say, Uber, where a car from a cartoon map materializes in real life at the curb, cloud workers remain trapped in the cartoonish world of the algorithm, escaping only at the end of their unpredictable shifts. These workers maintain the infrastructure supporting a capitalist, science fiction fantasy: the frictionless commerce of one-click purchasing, limitless choice, and near-instant gratification. But for the workers servicing these warehouses, the architecture of step-counting, numerical targets, and other game mechanics embody the realities of that idealized, game-like narrative across real space and real lives. The cloud functions as an opaque membrane deflecting public attention, ethical inquiries, and legal liability, so we can all continue playing the online shopping game with no obligation, and few opportunities, to empathize or interact with a human being.

For the workers inside this circle there's no magic to speak of unless you count the Orwellian power of sensors that relentlessly measure your behavior, imposing an externalized, numerical index of worth like a high score or a health bar floating over each worker's head, but often visible only to management. In terms of their power relationship to global algorithmic systems, the lives of American cloud workers are not that different from the well-known miseries of Apple contractor FoxConn's massive facilities in China.[44] There workers, some children as young as fourteen, have persistently suffered under incredibly long hours, dangerous working conditions, and other serious problems.[45] Terry Gou, the company's chairman, put it bluntly in 2012: "[We have] a workforce of over one million worldwide and as human beings are also animals, to manage one million animals gives me a headache."[46] So far, corporations have been unable to escape what William Gibson once called meatspace, the squishy realm of biological materiality. Biopower fuels many crucial aspects of the interface economy, though advances in robotics and artificial intelligence may one day eliminate the jobs most of these "animals" hold. In addition to spending $775 million to acquire the factory automation firm Kiva Systems, Amazon is already testing out robot arms and other automated systems that could eliminate the human job of picker entirely.[47]

Like the intense logistical requirements of Amazon's same-day delivery services, FoxConn's conditions are underwritten by Apple's relationship with its consumers. We expect the company to rapidly develop, prototype, and then mass-produce millions of devices over incredibly short spans of time—sometimes mere months—while maintaining near-total secrecy until the new product can be dramatically unveiled. We expect global release dates, ever-increasing performance and innovation, and instant gratification from the design wizards of Cupertino. These things are all possible, and highly profitable, but only through the logistical and human infrastructure of algorithmically mediated factory floors, worker dormitories, and predatory practices.

Cloud warehouses and factories transpose computational logic to physical spaces; spanning the gap between the abstract and the implemented entails making them terrible places for humans to work. Algorithmic arbitrage extracts immediacy, relevance, and rapid innovation from the raw materials of untold millions of poorly compensated person-hours of labor. These systems rely on a sophisticated backend to promote the romance of algorithmic culture through the magic of the cloud, invisibly organizing millions of humans according to computational logic and executing orders to support the impression of seamless, effortless efficiency. And the systems *are* efficient, but not primarily in the sense presented to us as consumers. Amazon, Apple, and other companies continue to find algorithmic solutions to deliver goods and services to us ever faster, but their real work, the winning cultural arbitrage, is in doing so at a profit.

One can almost imagine putting the magical pipeline in reverse. Instead of a system that delivers magnificent technological wonders to us on demand, think about what it whisks away for us. It suctions up all the awkwardness and hassle of the real world, dumping it like so much toxic waste onto cloud workers who must organize their lives around abstract, algorithmic structures of employment and value. It vacuums all the wasted time of standing in line, waiting on hold, inching cars around parking lots at the mall ... and entombs those seconds, minutes, and years in the cold storage of frigidly air-conditioned server farms, endlessly recirculated by the whirring fans and waiting CPU cycles of the cloud.

Artificial Artificial Intelligence

The final *telos* of algorithmic labor is the work that abstracts physical and cultural infrastructure away altogether. The factories, server farms, and warehouses of the cloud still require massive physical plants, but some projects strive to take the algorithmic economy logic a step further. If the interface entrepreneurs seek to unmoor highly specific businesses from their original contexts, like taxis and house cleaning services, Amazon's Mechanical Turk goes much farther in its attempt to create a new general industrial base in the cloud—an assemblage of workers for a huge range of tasks, all working on their own, managed by algorithm. Amazon rather ironically bills this as "artificial artificial intelligence," which neatly summarizes its reinvention of the human–machine relationship. The system creates a kind of interface to the human mind—an industrial nam-shub— for quickly harnessing the brain power of thousands of people to run a specific program. The unit operations here are highly specific "human intelligence tasks" (HITs) that often take only seconds to complete: "call a number, note how they answer," "extract purchased items from a shopping cart receipt," or "rotate 3D model to match image," for example.[48] Instead of assigning simple repetitive tasks to a calculating machine, Mechanical Turk assigns them to individual humans who typically make a few cents on each HIT.[49] They are, in a very literal sense, humans functioning as mere technical extensions of a computational culture machine. Within the system interface these people are anonymized and identified only by an alphanumeric code (figure 4.5), their identities defined by their performance records and a set of "qualifications" that elevate some workers to the title of "master worker" in tasks like photo moderation and categorization.[50]

The system draws its name from another seminal moment in the mythos of artificial intelligence, the "Turk" automaton that dazzled the courts of central Europe at its unveiling in 1770 by Wolfgang von Kempelen. It was a hoax controlled by a carefully concealed, all-too-human chess master within its cabinet of gears and display panels, but it was a powerful spectacle: a mechanical thinking machine that could defeat almost any opponent. The Turk was presented as a working machine designed for play, a calculating engine whose promise was only fulfilled two centuries later when IBM's Deep Blue defeated chess world champion Gary Kasparov in

amazonmechanical turk | REQUESTER

| Home | Create | Manage | Developer | Help |

Results   **Workers**   Qualification Types

Manage Workers

The Workers who have completed work for you are listed below. Select a Worker ID to bonus, block, unblock, assign a Qualification, or revoke a Qualification. To block, unblock, or change Qualification settings for multiple Workers, select Download CSV. Select Customize View to change which Qualification Types are displayed in the table below.

[Customize View]   [Download CSV] [Upload CSV]

Show my Workers by: Lifetime   Last 30 days   Last 7 days

				Workers
Worker ID ▲	Lifetime Approval Rate	Qual: i...g....	Qual: grape~...	Block Status
	100% (1/1)			Never Blocked
	100% (2/2)			Never Blocked
	100% (1/1)			Never Blocked
	100% (1/1)	5		Unblocked

Figure 4.5
Amazon Mechanical Turk Interface for Managing Workers.

1997. The history of the original Turk illuminates the cultural force of Amazon's name for this distributed human computation system and the rhetorical power of artificial artificial intelligence. In both 1770 and 1997, algorithmic calculations were harnessed in a very human way for a human problem, doing a form of work that is meaningless except in the human terms of a game or contest of wits. In both cases attendants wheeled out devices that were literal black boxes with highly constrained inputs and outputs, and their performance in highly publicized challenge matches was as much about the cultural figure of computation as it was about computing chess moves. These were "thinking machines" performing one of humanity's most rigorous and widely established forms (or games) of analytical thought. Machines thinking—that was the spectacle, fraudulent in the first instance, vehemently contested (by Kasparov, at least) and later widely accepted in the second.

The Turk's spring-wound embrace of mechanical thought was not a complete novelty, though its intelligence was: automata had pervaded the cathedrals and religious festivals of Europe for at least two hundred years, according to historian Jessica Riskin.[51] Before the Reformation and its stern

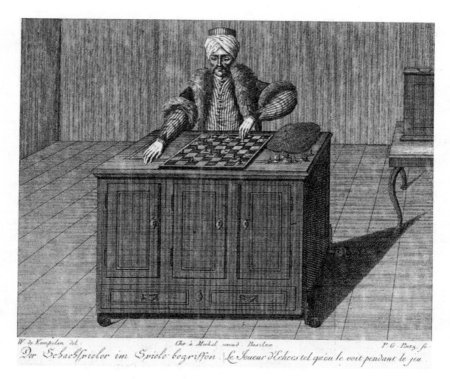

Figure 4.6
An engraving of the Turk from Karl Gottlieb von Windisch's 1784 book *Inanimate Reason*.

separation of divinity and human artifact, congregations enjoyed the spectacle of machines that were "mechanical *and* divine."[52] Their performances were knowing ones, inspiring as much humor as devotion, but nevertheless the magic was there in works such as the Rood of Grace at Boxley Abbey, which greeted pilgrims annually in the sixteenth century with a Christ who moved and rolled his eyes. Human craftsmen and performers were essential to these performances, simulating responsiveness and awareness to effectively engage the crowds. Something of this knowing spectacle remained in Kasparov's matches with Deep Blue, including his persistent efforts to deploy openings and play styles that would throw off IBM's algorithms.[53] The human engineer was never entirely hidden behind the mechanism, as IBM employees tweaked the system between every game. Perhaps the best example of this relationship was a highly scrutinized move near the end of game one, the truth of which was only revealed in 2012 when IBM researcher Murray Campbell was interviewed by the popular statistician Nate Silver. The move in question had sent Kasparov "into a tizzy" as it seemed to reflect the ambiguity and refinement of a human-level intelligence, and many have suggested it threw off the grandmaster's concentration for the second game, which he proceeded to lose.[54] In fact, as Campbell revealed, the move had been a bug, one the engineers corrected after the first match.[55] Kasparov himself had made magic out of the algorithm, inventing a sophisticated cultural explanation for what was in the end a random computational artifact.

The original Turk and the great match with Kasparov projected the Turing test onto a chessboard, asking the existential question of whether we would be able to recognize intelligence as a kind of style or aesthetic of play. Deep Blue did not merely beat Kasparov; it has transformed the entire chess world. Now young grandmasters can train against superior AI opponents, and a new space of collaborative play has emerged in the implementation gap where "centaurs" comprising human and machine teams consistently beat both grandmasters and pure algorithmic intelligence.[56] The most effective aesthetic is one of augmentation, complementing human intuition with computational depth. The analogy holds in other areas of implementation as well. Uber is not simply another way to get home; it is upending the regulatory and cultural space of hired transportation, changing the grammar and vocabulary we all use to read the street. The algorithmic reinvention of work is transforming the literal and imaginary geographies of culture, a theme we will return to at the end of this volume.

The transition from Deep Blue's victory in 1997 to Amazon's Mechanical Turk marks the reversal of the computational instrument: now human brains are the black box, strung together into an ad-hoc network of wetware servers for odd jobs. Mechanical Turk both validates the distinctive intelligence of the human mind (which can still outperform algorithmic intelligence on a wide variety of contextual challenges) and subjects it to algorithmic logic, creating an infrastructure of hyperefficient micropayments for context-free work. Dedicated "turkers" earn about $5 an hour, and many of them reside in the United States (with India making up the second largest contingent).[57] But it's disingenuous even to speak of workers in the typical meaning of that term, or an hourly wage, since the system's atomization offers no stability, regularity, or persistence of particular forms of labor, leading to huge variance in the amount of time it takes to complete a particular task. Just as many computer servers in the cloud sit idle (in 2012, McKinsey & Company estimated the percentage as 90 percent when measured by power consumption), most of these workers are not engaged most of the time.[58] Mechanical Turk melds the logic of interface companies that seek to activate a standing reserve, making our lives more economically efficient by commercializing underutilized resources, with the algorithmic logic of a server farm.

That algorithmic logic of distributed, parallel computing means that the marketplace is not one for "workers" at all but for carefully delimited slices of human attention and ability: nobody hires a "Mechanical Turk"; rather, they purchase the performance of some number of repetitive tasks (e.g., 10,000 HITs looking at a particular image and describing it in words). It is piece-rate work, leading some researchers to argue that the system makes the computer the sewing machine of the twenty-first century.[59] This is disingenuous because a sewing machine with a trained operator can be hired out to the highest bidder, but the Mechanical Turk marketplace is designed to eliminate almost any kind of expertise or specialization among workers, and thereby any real bargaining power. More important, the personal computer is not the most crucial technology in the system: once again the interface—the Mechanical Turk platform and the human brains connected to it—is the essential piece. Cycles of human attention make up the core commodity of Mechanical Turk, with the users' machines, the Amazon cloud, and the data processors who purchase these cycles comprising a complete system of computation. Here the culture machine of Mechanical Turk and the limited role of computation within it are clearly visible: computer code assigns jobs and handles payments, but the real work is happening in biological processors.

Just as the interface economy whisks away ambiguity, concealing its abstractions behind the facade of computation, Mechanical Turk is a kind of fine mesh for sifting through ambiguity. Here is the meditation of one blogger on the experience of being a turker:

[The typical jobs] are your transcription HITs, your decipher-this-horrible-handwriting HITs, your survey HITs. These are the tasks where translating human ambiguity into computer-style binary is the most frustrating, because you're likely to arrive at the answer "I don't know" and be forced to choose anyway. I remember a few angry-keyboard-mashing examples, like the time I was told to identify whether jewelry was gold or silver based on a single black-and-white picture. Impossible to tell! Or being asked if a person's illegible scribbling looks more like "X" or "Y." Neither, it looks like "Z!"[60]

Mechanical Turk is another system of arbitrage operating in the implementation gap. In fact, it quantifies and commoditizes that gap, turning it into a series of micro-tasks and judgments: incremental moments of abstraction and concretization. The grinding series of identical tasks it farms out can then be integrated, like individual frames in a full-motion film, into an illusion of continuous computation. What makes Mechanical Turk unusual is the way it puts the human back end of computation on display as a commercial service, applying the logic of the interface economy to the zone of implementation itself. As the quote above demonstrates, the humans who operate in that contested space must constantly negotiate between computational and cultural regimes of meaning.

Piecework Poetics

Across our various examples the interface layer is transforming not only the politics but the aesthetics of labor, imposing new, algorithmic contexts on central questions of identity, value, and success. The sea change that has already upended the lives of cab drivers and contract workers is also affecting doctors and lawyers. The smartphones so many of us carry are irrevocably blurring professional roles and boundaries for almost every participant in the global interface economy, redefining the affect of work in ways that we are only beginning to understand.

Mechanical Turk is a crucible for these transitions, an artificial market created specifically to commercialize the thesis that humans are important cogs in computational machines. The turkers at the heart of this system not only take on the challenge of endless micro-tasks managing ambiguity— they also take on the affective work of acting as a human element inside of a computational application. Conceptual artist Nick Thurston mined this seam of the implementation gap in *Of the Subcontract, Or Principles of Poetic Right*, a literary exploration of Mechanical Turk largely commissioned from turkers themselves. *Of the Subcontract* neatly inflects the platform's central premise, asking its wetware servers to take on a task, poetic composition, where humans still hold a decided edge over algorithms.

The poems in the collection are powerful precisely because of their pseudo-automaton status. Each piece begins with a readout of the amount of time spent on composition (usually measured in a few minutes and seconds), the hourly rate of this particular worker, and an indication of which HIT or submission was printed in the book (e.g., the fourth of seven submissions, the first of two). The entire collection is prefaced by an introduction nominally authored by McKenzie Wark but actually ghostwritten by a Lahore-based freelancer, as the afterword reveals.

The collection is a particularly powerful aesthetic move because it simultaneously co-opts and questions the tyranny of computational time. Turkers—people competing for HITs at an average of $5 an hour—are probably not people who feel like they can afford to compose poetry. Using the Turk system to assign creativity as micro-task performs a particular kind of affective absurdity.

This is artificial artificial literature. First, these humans are asked to emulate their humanity through the Amazon interface. Second, these are not poems authored through an individual impulse to create but as externally mandated piecework—a virtual factory for verse. The formatting of the printed page, with its attendant metadata about cost and composition time, emphasizes that double artificiality even as the poems themselves remain: no matter the conditions of their hyper-commoditized composition, they are works of writing by humans, conveying particular human ideas.

The book's first section of poems, titled "Artificial Artificial Intelligence," generates persistent flashes of the humanity lurking beneath or behind the system, like entry 0.24, "My Son": "You are my chubby bubble cutie pie / I love you my son / For you are the only one."[61] Asking these turkers to write themselves into the interface of the system immediately brings other humans into view along with them. We catch glimpses of sons and daughters, missing parents and lost loves, all filtered through the anonymizing mechanism of Mechanical Turk and its Taylorist computations of labor and value. These are exactly the kinds of contextual links that the interface layer generally eliminates, creeping back in through the voice of the poet.

Many poems seem to respond to their prompts with the same flat, affectless tone as the Mechanical Turk system itself, offering up anodyne confections of cliché and truism, completing the task of composition in as little as twelve seconds. But for others a cautious sense of revelation, of emotional exposure, transforms the grim performance of poetry-by-the-cent into something beautiful. Beyond quietly asserting their humanity, these poets also persistently grapple with the question of identity in an algorithmic system, like entry 0.04, excerpted here:

You have put me in a box with a lock and a key.
I pick at the lock from time to time.
But it is not so simple to be free.
I am chained by the title you have put on me.
I so long to be me, to break loose.
But my fears keep me in that place.
That place where you forced me to be.
My greatest fear is of you not loving me.
Am I who I think I am?
Or am I who you say I am?[62]

In eight minutes and thirty seconds the author explores the uncertainty of identity in terms that seem to apply equally to a lover and to Amazon itself, describing the lock of imposed identity and title as a vise that thwarts not just movement but certainty itself.

The time stamp, the money stamp, and the anonymity of the authors all convey *Of the Subcontract*'s status as another kind of Turing test. These subcontracted authors are performing on at least two levels. On the first level, they are pulling off an impression of humanity under the constraints of a ticking clock and waiting HTML form field. But on the second, they are still performing as cogs within a computational system, repeating the same task multiple times and attempting to optimize their own processing efficiency to complete each poetic HIT as quickly as possible. And yet, beneath all these layers of abstracted, artificial production, moments of beauty emerge.

Of the Subcontract is a literary experiment uniting surrealism and authoritarianism—as if someone had collected a volume of poems from the denizens of Terry Gilliam's darkly fantastical film *Brazil*. It shares roots with surrealist thinking and automatic writing, drawing, and other creative processes, with the sharp difference that this is not a playground for creative elites but a factory for the socioeconomically disadvantaged. The pleasure and responsibility of the creative experiment resides with *Of the Subcontract*'s real authors, Nick Thurston and his merry band, who are commissioning poetry that began as their little game and ends as work for anonymous others. This tension and discomfort are precisely what Thurston and his collaborators sought to achieve.

The resurgence of aesthetics between the cracks of such a pointedly cynical artistic experiment is presumably exactly what they were hoping for: a proof of the value of poetry written in the margins of a proof of its bankruptcy. *Of the Subcontract* accords aesthetics its traditional place at the intersection of other forms of value, allowing financial transactions, algorithmic calculations, and human computation to be transmuted into something with the official seal of artistic production. The political theater of crowdsourcing piecework poetry also becomes performance art of a different nature, a literary production that asserts the value not only of the critique but of the processual by-products generated by the critique. We end up admiring not just the artistic concept of the volume but the piecework poems themselves. In this way, *Of the Subcontract* performs an algorithmic critique of Mechanical Turk, relying on the system itself to to process or run that critique. Our work as readers, then, is to examine the iterative process of commissioning and assembling these poems. The implementation, the ways that the work of these anonymous turkers was collected and contextualized, is an integral part of the whole poetic mechanism.

Experimental poet Darren Wershler strikes at the heart of this critical tangle in his afterword, which is worth quoting at length:

> We have also read essays explaining that the Turk is in fact an elegant metaphor for the precarious condition of the worker in a globalized and networked milieu. And we have made a substantial amount of art that actually makes use of Amazon Mechanical Turk as a productive medium to demonstrate the same point, but in a way that is, you know, *artier*.
>
> The point is not that the mechanism is empty, like some kind of neutral reproducer. The point is that it is a mechanism that already includes a spot for *you*—like the Law in Franz Kafka's novel *The Trial*—whether that spot is in front of it as a player, inside it as the operator, behind it as the spectator being shown its misleading components, from afar as the critic describing and demystifying it by virtue of your criticism, or, increasingly, as the artist or writer (mis)using it in your project. The moment that you engage the setup as a problematic the machine springs into action.[63]

Wershler's argument beautifully captures the reality of algorithms in the context of labor and cultural production more broadly: the system reconfigures not just the methods and outputs of production but the entire cultural frame, implicating all of us as collaborators. As Galloway puts it in *The Interface Effect*:

I dispute the ideological mystification that says that we are the free while the Chinese children are in chains, that our computers are a lifeline and their computers are a curse. This kind of obscenity must be thrown out. We are all gold farmers, and all the more paradoxical since most of us do it willingly and for no money at all.[64]

We are all "(mis)using" these systems in our lives, whether we consider that use cultural or aesthetic practice, private or professional communication, or even the critique of these systems. Hybrid labor between inextricably linked human and algorithmic culture machines is happening all around us, all the time. In the most banal, pervasive ways, we rely on algorithmic systems to perform and evaluate labor, from the search bar to Microsoft Word. In the final analysis, *Of the Subcontract*'s central narrative is not that of oppressed turkers articulating brief glimpses of their human condition, but of the place held for each of us in the computational gap.

Moral Machinery

Debates about the ethical impact of mechanization are anything but novel. The original chess-playing Turk, for example, inspired florid prose and rapt audiences during its long run of public appearances in the United States in the heyday of industrialization.[65] The tenor of those debates is instructive today when we think of the interface layer and new algorithmic systems of behavior modification that are far less blunt than the brutal conditions of nineteenth-century mills and factories. Even then, many viewed the rise of automation as a force for ethical good, inspiring (or forcing) workers to conduct themselves with the same dedication as the machines they attended. This is what one British economist called "moral machinery" in 1835: a system of managerial interventions to enhance the industrial system's natural tendencies toward order and productivity among human workers.[66]

As historian Stephen P. Rice argues, the spectacle of the Mechanical Turk modeled a new affect for its American audiences, performing a form of labor that blurred the line between machine and human, between algorithm and worker.

Launched into the scene of middle-class anxiety about worker self-control, the chess-player assumed the twin statuses of regulated machine and ideal mechanized worker. Viewers could locate in the chess-player the uniquely human traits of will and reason without having to remove those qualities too far from the mechanical traits of regularity and efficiency. Read as a regulated or "minded" machine, [the Turk] showed the new productive order in place.[67]

This double framing as human and machine closely echoes the interface of Amazon Mechanical Turk, where each HIT promises the taskmaster a response that is both mechanically reliable and reliably human. *Of the Subcontract*'s poems push that dualism to its limit, opening up a channel for poetic self-reflection from the very belly of the machine.

The nineteenth- and twenty-first-century Turk platforms both use aesthetics to produce certain attitudes or affects for their users and viewers. Both machines do a particular kind of work (playing chess, completing millions of distributed HITs), but they also perform another kind of labor when they reinforce the dualism between human and machine that Rice identifies. This is what political philosophers Michael Hardt and Antonio Negri call "affective labor," or economic work that produces a physical and emotional output, classically exemplified by the retail dictate "service with a smile."[68] For the nineteenth-century Turk, the spectacle itself is the affective product: the figure of the Turk with his moving arm, the display cabinet full of functionless (but impressive) gears and machinery, and of course the labor of the man hidden inside the machine's secret compartment all contribute to manufacturing a sense of wonder and excitement. In the twenty-first century, Amazon's Mechanical Turk promotes notions of repetition and fungibility, implicitly encouraging its turkers as well as the purchasers of human computation to think of each worker as a simple number. The HITs themselves are ordered up in batches and, as we saw above, often disappear in seconds, encouraging turkers to be constantly vigilant for new opportunities. By relying on Amazon's task distribution network and personal computers, the system also constrains the bodies and the time of its users (depending on the fluctuations of what piecework is available at any given time, and how well that work is compensated). The system produces HITs but also a kind of labor culture around those HITs.

That trace of a labor culture also appears in the apps and interfaces of the sharing economy. As the ads for Uber and Lyft suggest (figure 4.3, figure 4.4), a huge amount of energy in the interface economy goes toward the production of affect among consumers and providers of services. User feedback, emotional enjoyment, and a neoliberal ideal of independence define these systems at every level, from their logos to their feedback mechanisms. They are persuasive platforms designed to create an algorithmically mediated space of community. The computational layer between users and providers manages the details, calculating feedback scores, making particular users visible or invisible to one another, and generally managing the "experience" of using the system. These services build their reputation on transparency, arguing that the combination of user feedback and background checks serves to vet our drivers, house cleaners, errand-runners, and so forth in a more robust way than we would typically do on our own. But the systems retain control over the deployment of that transparency, choosing what information we see and maintaining control of this validation process behind algorithmic black boxes. In the end what we typically see are a small number of options that are all strongly recommended: the first step in a carefully choreographed user experience that depends as much on emotional outcomes as financial ones.

The emotional valence of financial transactions goes beyond affective labor, tracing its roots to Adam Smith and the *Theory of Moral Sentiments*, an important counterpoint to his better-known arguments about capitalism in *The Wealth of Nations*. Smith argues in *Moral Sentiments* that social cohesion and the effective functioning of a marketplace depend on a logic of virtuous action that has imagination at its root. We can never know the lived experience of others, but social engagement depends on imagining that experience in its joy and pain. Empathy is a crucial component of all social intercourse, a feedback mechanism for adjusting our own behavior according to moral guideposts and our own judgments. Smith's recognition that we can never truly know the experience of others—yet constantly strive to imagine it—places an important moral responsibility on each participant in cultural practice, one that parallels his libertarian political views. The foundation of a moral society, he argues, is the constant imaginative work we all do to map out the territory of empathy, creating a pragmatic sense of justice and shared experience that guides economic and social behavior.

As law professor Jedediah Purdy argues, the economic imposition of particular emotions and even identity positions on service workers brings something distinctively new to Smith's model: "Mandatory smiles are part of an irony at the heart of capitalism. … Faking it is the new feudalism. It is the key to an economic order of emotional work that tells people who and

how to be on the basis of where they fall in the social and economic hierarchy."[69] When we adapt the theory of moral sentiments to the age of the
algorithm, we can see that a third party enters the transactional space
between human actors. The expansion of the interface economy and its
dependence on affective labor brings new genres of performance to life: we
are very much part of the interface now, contributing to the aesthetic superstructure of computation with our bodies, our minds, and our affect. Five
star ratings all around! Yet we do this work as "centaurs" too, depending on
the same interface platforms for essential affective cues. The march for
"Uber for X" systems that turn various financial and noncommercial
arrangements into services for hire brings with it the affective labor of the
service economy, but with computation performing crucial pieces of the
imaginative work of empathy.

Take Uber, for example. The company's feedback system asks both riders
and drivers to rate one another, creating a persistent database of user profiles that allows the company to identify its most compliant and trouble-
some workers and clients (who can then be passively or actively excluded
from future transactions). This notion of consumer feedback depends on
the capitalistic function of empathy as Smith defined it: creating an empathetic frame, a channel for feedback, encourages better interactions. Something as simple as knowing your driver's name is a more empathetic
contact than most of us have with a taxi driver. And of course this data can
help companies identify problems in their business practices and help customers find the services and products they want. Feedback data allows us
to extrapolate beyond the individual experience, aggregating acts of empathetic imagination to project a more holistic view of the future (e.g., forty-
three people thought this driver was rude). But by creating the tool for
extrapolation, these systems also replace the nuance and authorship of the
imaginative act as Smith imagined it with a series of surveys. Quantifying
empathy, often into a completely abstracted five-star scale, encourages us
to leave the heavy lifting to the algorithms. Instead of doing the imaginative work ourselves, we outsource it to a culture machine built up of
tailored Likert-scale questions and comment forms, black box ranking
algorithms, and the algorithmically mediated crowd of strangers that interface companies seek to synthesize into a virtual community. Variations on
this move have persisted for centuries, from the deployment of statistics
like "four out of five doctors choose product X" to the empathetic appeals

of advertising in general—but computational platforms take it to a deeper epistemological level.

As we saw above, the central keyword for the "sharing economy" is not imagination, but trust. Uber and its peers offer to take on various forms of cultural and imaginative work in exchange for our trust (and, of course, our money). The affective labor they ask their workers to engage in serves that larger trust, building up a brand of consistent, friendly service. We are asked to trust, most significantly, in the algorithm. Trust that the feedback and background checks will weed out any dangerous or merely rude drivers. Trust that the system will find the closest, best vehicle to whisk you on your way—that the cartoon map is real. Trust that the driver will be fairly compensated and that you will pay a fair price. In each of these claims, the imaginative work of empathy has been outsourced to the algorithm. We don't need to work out how to catch a cab, assess the vehicle and its driver, calculate the tip, or engage in any of the other micro-practices and empathetic moments that define the taxi experience. They do not simply disappear. Instead, Uber asks us to perform substitute empathetic work, in algorithmic terms. Some of this work is explicitly requested or required: rate the driver, share the experience on social media for a future discount, recruit friends to the service to get another discount. Some of it is less obvious: the ads and the labor culture of the service ask us to validate the drivers as fellow entrepreneurs, individualists, and free agents. Different companies present different versions of that validation (Lyft encourages riders to sit in the front; Uber does not), but they all seek to build a synthetic community of practice held together by algorithms.

This can result in powerful new forms of community and social action, like the story of an Uber driver who raised money for a terminally ill passenger, in part by mobilizing the Uber community.[70] But it also reroutes a central facet of economic life through algorithmic mediation, embedding the essential empathetic calculus in the culture machine. We are just beginning to see the impact of this move, a growing dependence on algorithms themselves to perform affective labor. The Easter eggs in Siri from chapter 2 provide one example of a machine performing emotional work for our benefit. The rapidly expanding field of quantified health and well-being offers a broader arena where algorithmic systems seek to collaboratively perform affective work with and through our bodies. At times it seems like we desperately seek channels to perform and experience this affective labor directly, perhaps because so much of it has been outsourced and formalized by algorithms, user interfaces, and computational back ends. Why else would it be so easy to make thousands of dollars with a Facebook app that allows you to send hugs to your friends? That hunger for emotional contact, for a space where we can imagine directly, marks another disparity between abstraction and implementation. The gulf between the imaginative empathy of human and machine actors in culture comes down to the construction of value. Just as Smith sought to put economic practice on a foundation of intersubjective, empathetic understanding, we are now struggling to define the fundamental structure of value in an algorithmic world.

5   Counting Bitcoin

The lack of money is the root of all evil.
Mark Twain

Colonizing the Margin

On May 6, 2010, the U.S. capital markets experienced a tremendous crash, with the Dow Jones Industrial Average losing more value than on any other day in its entire 110-year history. But within minutes, the market rebounded, and after major company stocks had dropped to pennies a share they returned to normal pricing. The entire episode seemed to fade away as quickly as it appeared, leaving a series of hanging questions about the forces shaping world financial markets. At the root of this radical instability is a highly specialized and lucrative form of algorithmic arbitrage.

Over the past ten years, computational systems have become increasingly important to the markets, gradually replacing the familiar sight of men in bright-colored vests yelling across a crowded trading floor with the tenebrous world of server cabinets and proprietary code. As financial journalist Michael Lewis describes in *Flash Boys*, the transactional role of algorithms has grown from the simple execution of trades into a kind of micro-tax on the entire market system.[1] This is a classic example of arbitrage, or the leveraging of different markets to create profit, like traders who buy cheap wheat in the country to sell at a profit in the city. Ultimately arbitrage is always about time—capturing the difference in price before someone else does it for you—and for algorithms, time is measured in microseconds. On Wall Street, this is now known as high frequency trading (HFT).

When stock exchanges began to process trades digitally and to prolifer-
ate in the 1990s and 2000s, expanding from the dominance of NYSE and
NASDAQ to thirteen public exchanges by 2008, enterprising market actors
realized that they could carve out a new kind of competitive advantage.[2] By
observing trades occurring on one exchange that would "move the market"
and changing the price of a particular commodity elsewhere, they could use
the temporal advantage of a few microseconds to create a small window of
opportunity. For example, if a major pension fund asked its broker to buy,
say, 100,000 shares of Microsoft, HFT firms might detect the signals of this
trade as it moved through one exchange and act to profit from it on others
by buying up Microsoft stock with the intention of immediately selling it at
a slightly higher price to the pension fund. For the pension fund, the trade
would be just a little more expensive than anticipated, but iterated over
millions of transactions a day the taxes become substantial.

HFT offers one of the purest examples of algorithms that are fundamentally altering an existing culture machine, that venerable assemblage of
math, social practices, faith-based communities, and arbitrage that we call
"the market." The introduction of high-speed trading and algorithms that
are effectively fully automated engines of commerce has done more than
eliminate humans from the trading floor: these systems operate in open
competition with humans and one another, and they are gradually transforming the broader movement of capital. HFT arbitrageurs build their
advantage through complex geographical maneuvers, by locating their
servers and fiber-optic lines a few feet closer to the exchanges' central servers than their competitors, or leasing communication lines that shave a few
miles off the best direct signal pathway between two points on the financial
grid. While they are traders, they almost never lose money, since their form
of arbitrage always depends on superior information and they do not arbitrage risk like more traditional brokers. They never hold stocks at the end of
the day, only cash.[3]

This is a form of cultural arbitrage, not just computation, because HFT
takes advantage of our assumptions about the fundamental purpose of
buying and selling securities. The proliferation of market order types (well
over 100, ranging far beyond the familiar "buy," "sell," and "limit" types),
the incentives for buyers and sellers willing to use particular trading proto-
cols, and even the growing number of exchanges in operation have all con-
tributed to an increased volume and pace of trading.[4] Much more than

securities, these systems trade information, which has always been an essential role of the markets. But they atomize and encrypt that information in a new series of black boxes—the switching systems, trade-matching engines, and algorithms themselves—that allow HFT firms and the major Wall Street firms that deal with them to create a kind of subaltern skim economy. The algorithms that generate billions in profits for their keepers operate at the margins by capitalizing on special knowledge of network latency, or the lag-time between when a signal originates at one node and arrives at another. Finding ways to get a little bit ahead of the next guy, even at the level of thousandths of a second, allows companies to create closely guarded financial shortcuts and ambush-points where more traditional modes of commerce can be exploited as they move through financial networks.

Considered on its own terms, HFT allows us a way to imagine a familiar culture machine—the market—in its translation to a truly computational space. The volume and stochasticity of the financial markets themselves are the primary canvas for these algorithms, with decisions coded along tightly constrained abstractions about pricing, inherent value, and the pace of information. The speed and volume at which these systems operate, and their increasing cooption by investment titans like Goldman Sachs, are beginning to change the fundamental behavior of the markets.[5]

The heroes of Lewis's story are those trying to eliminate the "unfair" predation of HFT algorithms and create an equal playing field for the trading of securities as they imagine such things ought to be traded. Their solution is not the elimination of algorithms but instead of the human intermediaries who might find new ways to game the system. "There was no longer any need for any human intervention. ... The goal had to be to eliminate *any* unnecessary intermediation."[6] For the players on Wall Street, the problem with HFT was not its position in computational space, but its troubling ties back to the material world.

Lewis describes two charts his reformers created to demonstrate the changing nature of the market: the first shows activity as humans perceive it, with a crowded series of trading events marked second-by-second over the space of ten minutes. The second chart demonstrates an algorithmic view of a single second, marked off by milliseconds:

All the market activity within a single second was so concentrated—within a mere 1.78 milliseconds—that on the graph it resembled an obelisk rising from the desert.

In 98.22 percent of all milliseconds, nothing at all happened in the U.S. stock market. To a computer, the market in even the world's most actively traded stock was an
uneventful, almost sleepy place. ...
    "What's that spike represent?" asked one of the investors, pointing to the obelisk.
    "That's one of your orders touching down," said Brad.[7]

The sudden spike represented a large institutional investor placing an
order, which then caused the waiting financial algorithms to leap into a
frenzy of front-running, counter-bidding, and positioning, all conducted
at a pace that is impossibly fast for human processing. Yet it was languidly
slow for these algorithms, which spent 98 percent of that second waiting
for someone to make a move: 1.78 milliseconds is more or less incomprehensible as a temporal span. By contrast, the typical human reaction
time is something on the order of 200 milliseconds. The algorithmic contemporary has outpaced our capacity to manage it without computational
help.

This visual narrative neatly captures the space of computation, highlighting the essential feature of its radically different time scale but also
signaling how difficult it is for us to imagine the consequences of that temporality. The spike of activity represents orders, but behind those orders are
financial signal traps and sensors, algorithmic decision trees to determine a
course of action, trading tools to implement them, and, somewhere in the
unimaginably distant future, perhaps minutes or hours later (if it happens
at all), a human to review the activity. The obelisk in the desert is a reminder
of what *Her*'s Samantha would mournfully call "the space between the
trades," if Theodore had an investment account. But it also demonstrates
how algorithms are colonizing the margins of human activity. Scott
McCloud wonderfully captures the extradiegetic space of a narrative with
the comic book term "the gutter."[8] The gutter is the blank space between
panels, largely ignored by the reader as she stitches static images into a
compelling, animated narrative that feels seamless. It is where we infer
events and actions that often are only obliquely referenced in the surface
discourse of a narrative. You might argue that consciousness is the act of
constructing a narrative from the inaccessible gutter of human cognition—
the ways that we stitch together a personal history from fragments of
sensory input and inference.

We do this by creating a model simulation of the past, interpolating
temporal continuity from those experiential fragments. We pretend the

gutters aren't there, paving them over with personal narratives and memories that feel complete. Arbitrage is another form of interpolation where we simulate forward in time instead of backward, effectively predicting the future and capitalizing on it. But trying to understand computational space is a different challenge entirely, requiring us to voyage not forward but *deeper* into time. McCloud's notion of the gutter reveals how the ground rules, even the physics, of implementation have epistemological implications. The current transformation of global finance largely depends on the arbitrage of money and information between two temporal universes that are almost completely mutually exclusive. The obelisk that Lewis describes is a human metaphor for algorithmic trading, almost like a stylized postcard from a computational universe where time is everything. HFT algorithms translate the gutter—the gaps between placing an order and executing it, for example—into an arena for competitive computation. In both the narrative and financial examples, the gutter is the place where time is translated into meaning and value.

By saying that HFT algorithms perform a simple comparative arbitrage between stock prices at different geographic locations is to say that they value time, but, more important, that they value the *temporal process*. In these transactions, the intrinsic worth of the securities in question, their leadership, their price-to-earnings ratios, are all meaningless. The meaning of the exercise is derived from the temporal gap between point A and point B, and the odds of executing a trade that capitalizes on someone else's. Their efficiency at modeling a particular *ideology* of time and space, denominated in microseconds, is gradually reshaping the entire ecosystem they inhabit. In this way HFT algorithms replace the original structure of value in securities trading, the notion of a share owned and traded as an investment in future economic success, with a new structure of value that is based on process.

Valuing Culture

The arbitrage of process is central to Google's business model; one of the world's largest companies (now in the form of Alphabet Corporation) is built on the valuation of cultural information. The very first PageRank algorithms created by Larry Page and Sergei Brin at Stanford in 1996 marked a new era in the fundamental problem of search online. Brin and Page's innovation was to use the inherent ontological structure of the web itself to evaluate knowledge. Pages on university websites were likely to be better sources of information than those on commercial sites; a news article that had already been linked to by hundreds of others was a stronger source of information than one that had only a few references elsewhere. By viewing the rapidly expanding Internet less like a haystack and more like a subway system (where some stations are much busier and more convenient than others), Google established an algorithmic model of the digital universe that now shapes almost every aspect of digital culture.

The first primitive efforts to navigate the web relied on human intervention: a "cool site of the day" or the first blogs that curated content like a digital *Wunderkammer*, creating an idiosyncratic, aesthetically grounded response to those largely unmapped networks.[9] But our relationship with the Internet gradually evolved from something like a bulletin board or a newspaper, where we might browse for information serendipitously, to an essential utility that provides financial, industrial, and personal services ranging from bank accounts to online dating. When we turn on the faucet, we expect a reliable stream of something that is, we hope, recognizable as (nontoxic) water, not a "cool liquid of the day." So too, we now expect the Internet to serve as a utility that provides dependable, and perhaps fungible, kinds of information.

PageRank and the complementary algorithms Google has developed since its launch in 1998 started as sophisticated finding aids for that awkward, adolescent Internet. But the company and the web's spectacular expansion since then has turned their assumptions into rationalizing laws, just as Diderot's framework of interlinked topics has shaped untold numbers of encyclopedias, indexes, and lists. At some point during the "search wars" of the mid-2000s, when Google cemented its dominance, an inversion point occurred where the observational system of PageRank became a deterministic force in the cultural fabric of the web. Google now runs roughly two-thirds of searches online, and a vibrant industry of "search engine optimization" exists to leverage and game Google's algorithms to lure traffic and advertising.[10]

At its heart, PageRank catalogs human acts of judgment, counting up the links and relative attention millions of people have paid to different corners of the web. The patent for PageRank describes the algorithm as "a method [that] assigns importance ranks to nodes in a linked database, such as any database of documents containing citations, the World Wide Web or any other hypermedia database."[11] In short, this is a tool for creating hierarchy in the world, sorting information not merely by its inherent qualities but by a certain definition of importance or popularity. It is not too much to argue that the transition from more primitive search engines to the algorithmic weighting of PageRank and its imitators has shifted the role of knowledge in society as profoundly as Diderot and d'Alembert did when they debated which ordering schema to use for the *Encyclopédie*.

That transformation is shrouded in the modesty of the list, that simple intellectual construct that the semiotician, philosopher, and literary critic Umberto Eco once identified as "the origin of culture":

What does culture want? To make infinity comprehensible. It also wants to create order—not always, but often. And how, as a human being, does one face infinity? How does one attempt to grasp the incomprehensible? Through lists, through catalogs, through collections in museums and through encyclopedias and dictionaries.[12]

Both the *encyclopédistes* and Google would argue that their projects do not create hierarchy but model it—that their knowledge ontologies are simply more effective maps for structures that already existed in culture. And yet, as Eco suggests, in both instances the structure they created quickly became an ordering mechanism of its own, shaping the cultural space it was designed to observe. One of the most vital functions of the encyclopedia was to compress knowledge for the sake of time, distilling millions of person-years of insight into a reference text that would accelerate the pace of research and discovery. For Diderot and d'Alembert, it was the book that politically, philosophically, and perhaps epistemologically paved the way for the French Revolution. For Google, it is a future of machines that understand, converse, and anticipate—a future of a complete computational ontology of knowledge.

These were the two projects' ambitions, now largely fulfilled. But they were also systems implemented in historical moments where they achieved something different: a reframing of cultural value and temporality. Just as the HFT algorithms exploit gaps in the technical and cultural construction of trading, PageRank arbitrages a rich field of latent information—the network of connections making up the global Internet—and distills it into an immediately accessible resource. Google Search saves us time in the long run by tracking down the most useful resources relevant to our query, a first-order form of anticipation. But it also saves us time in the short run by providing its search results with startling immediacy: Google realized early on that delays of even a tenth of a second would reduce user engagement, and built its infrastructure accordingly.[13] The arbitrage of time at the level of knowledge synthesis and immediate gratification are crucial factors in promoting both encyclopedias and search engines.

That temporal arbitrage inevitably led to a renegotiation of value in financial terms as well: time is money, especially time measured by milliseconds multiplied across millions of servers. For this, Google needed AdSense. From a business perspective, PageRank creates a basic index for the circulation of ideas, an essential currency in the economy of attention.[14] When Google began selling advertisements against its search results with the market bidding system AdSense, it succeeded in monetizing that attention at a previously unimaginable scale. In 2013, Google earned over $55 billion in revenue, of which more than 90 percent came from advertising.[15] Now the company will help you register the domain name, build the website, analyze the traffic, and serve the ads for the site, which its algorithms will then index and rank. In 2014, Google exceeded the market capitalization of ExxonMobil, leaving it second only to Apple among the most valuable companies in the world.[16]

The typical Google advertisement nets the company some tiny fraction of a penny to serve up to a customer, but over the volume of the tens of billions of ads it serves each day, those fractions add up to a kind of minimal transaction cost for using the Internet, collected by its most powerful gatekeeper.[17] The functionality of AdSense is in fact a kind of HFT arbitrage in its own right: every time a user navigates to a site serving advertisements via Google's network, a rapid auction takes place for the marketers with the highest bids to serve their ads. These transactions commoditize the long trail of user data each of us leaves behind online—the detailed consumer profiles about us informed by our purchase history, demographics, and many other factors—so that advertisers can identify target markets based on user "interests" as well as the contextual space of the host website. But AdSense is also a form of temporal arbitrage, commoditizing time just as effectively as HFT systems milking profits out of a few milliseconds of lag. Google has built a tremendous business out of the immediacy of AdSense, out of commoditizing the contemporary, the moment *right now* when a potential customer is literally hovering at the threshold.

Internet ads, like all advertisements, are a form of cultural latency or temporal use tax, placing minor drag on the fluid market of attention. The incredible algorithmic infrastructure of these micro-auctions, the magic of cached content and highly coordinated global arbitrage, reveals a tiny but measurable point of translation: the fraction of a second that marks the gap between cultural and commercial value. That pause is noticeable, not just as a delay but as a kind of persistence, a new form of externalized memory filled with algorithmic models of consumer desire.[18] We are haunted by the shoes, the cars, the vacations that we have not yet purchased much more directly than we are by the hidden shadows of our digital selves that marketing companies carefully maintain. PageRank and AdSense are really two sides of the same coin, uniting the ideal of access to universal knowledge with that of perfectly understanding each of us and our desires. They are two expressions of Google's central mission to translate the quest for knowledge into algorithmic process.

The arbitrage of PageRank, the process of AdSense, present not just a series of discrete computational events but a pervasive narrative about cultural value. It's a story that is fueled by our continued engagement and attention, by Google's advertising revenues, and by its growing role as a central platform for nearly all forms of digital experience. To recast value in a different light, these interlocking arbitrage systems embody what cultural theorist Alan Liu has called an "ethos of information": a style, in humanistic terms, or a level of abstraction in computational ones, that creates a critical superstructure over the information itself.[19] In Liu's language we might argue that the web has moved from a romantic to a rational phase, leaving behind the homebrew sublime of early hand-coded sites for the elaborate corporate order of branded, automated page serving that dominates today.[20]

In other words, while Google built its business on accurately mapping the cultural ontologies of the Internet, its role has gradually shifted from indexer to architect. Its core business model gained traction by effectively marrying algorithms to consumer culture, and it increasingly depends on using algorithms to define that culture in profound ways. Google's dominance over the critical arbitrage of search has created a pressing need for new forms of literacy, most publicly in the context of the *Star Trek* computer and Google search itself. The company's emergent role as chief architect of the Internet is still, at heart, a form of cultural arbitrage and therefore a temporal project. Google wants to anticipate, to predetermine, every possible resource its many users may want to tap. This requires new vocabularies of memory, of privacy, and even of forgetting as the company becomes more effective at shaping the holistic, permanent archive of digital culture.

These new literacies have been most controversial in Europe, where privacy is understood as an inherent human right rather than the child of contracts. Recent court decisions there have forced Google to remove certain search listings judged damaging to individuals because it foregrounds negative episodes from their past.[21] Google's response has been to mark each erasure with its own annotation, alerting people that some results have been censored, to maintain the ideology of total transparency memorably expressed by Eric Schmidt when he said, "If you have something that you don't want anyone to know, maybe you shouldn't be doing it in the first place."[22] But of course arbitrage is built on the temporal advantage of keeping certain information protected and carefully managed: advertisements, browsing behaviors, search queries. Google Now requests permission to access our search histories, physical location, and other data in order to provide its services, and in return it promises to organize not just the present but the near future temporalities of its users. It will suggest when to leave for the next meeting, factoring in traffic, creating an intimate, personal reminder system arbitraging public and private data. As we come to grips with the consequences of the deep interlacing of cultural value and algorithmic arbitrage, the ideals of anonymity and untraceable commerce have become more and more appealing.

Cryptocurrency

Google's expanding role as a kind of central utility for arbitrage and cultural valuation online has brought some of the dot-com era's fondest dreams to life, but in an unexpectedly quiet, backroom way. The futurists Peter Schwartz and Peter Leyden offered one of the best-known expressions of that era's visions in 1997 with "The Long Boom," published in that bulletin of the digital revolution, *Wired* magazine.[23] Schwartz offered many predictions centered on five waves of technological change, but a persistent pivot point for the transcendental *Wired* future was a new kind of computational arbitrage for capitalism that freed commerce from the historical relics of bureaucratic regulation, physical specie, and sovereign control. The widespread adoption of what Schwartz called "electronic cash" was something *Wired* had covered earlier in 1994 and 1996, and the magazine championed the postmaterial, global network economy that underpinned its broader vision about the triumph of information. Early digital cash entrepreneurs recognized the growing value of information and attempted to create an algorithmic abstraction from money to information. As Google and the other major players in the contemporary technology space discovered, the abstraction is much easier to work the other way through the timeless magic of arbitrage: start with information and turn it into money.

As we've seen, however, that form of computational magic depends on large systems of observation and data collection: companies amass vast troves of data, from individual user profiles to deep indexes of the Internet itself. Then access to these troves becomes a commodity for both individual consumers and the marketers seeking to reach those consumers. At every stage, arbitrage nets these companies a share of every transaction, every advertising micro-auction and credit card purchase. These shifts are easy to overlook: the list of albums for sale on iTunes is not so different from the choices we might have encountered in a record store; the offerings on Netflix still appear to be a series of choices about what to watch. The dramatic changes on the algorithmic backend are packaged in relatively familiar consumer terms. In other words, what *Wired* imagined as a commercial revolution has instead been a reformation—not without its upheavals and casualties, but largely a transformation that has left major industries intact.

The very success of this arbitrage sea change has accentuated the objections of those who see the digital transactions we all participate in not as matters of convenience—free services provided in exchange for viewing a few targeted ads, for example—but as the radical evisceration of individual privacy and autonomy for the sake of new collective, algorithmically engineered systems of value. Perhaps the single greatest example of this ideological reaction is the rapid popularization of a new cryptocurrency called Bitcoin.

Bitcoin first emerged as a paper published in November 2008 by the apparently fictional mathematician Satoshi Nakamoto (about ten years after Schwartz predicted e-cash would become mainstream). In the paper Nakamoto argued for a new financial model that would eliminate the key vulnerability of traditional financial systems: "an electronic payment system based on cryptographic proof instead of trust, allowing any two willing parties to transact directly with each other without the need for a trusted third party."[24] The straightforward paper describes a system for exchanging currency based purely on computing power and mathematics (which I describe in more detail below), with no dependence on a central bank, a formal issuing authority, or other "faith and credit" standards of traditional currencies. If this book has been dominated by black boxes so far, Bitcoin purports to be a "glass box," a tamper-proof system whose functions are entirely transparent. Like other open source platforms, it is founded on the logic that the best security comes from allowing anyone to inspect its code and suggest improvements.

Bitcoin has received significant attention as a libertarian, even anarchist response to the restrictions on trade and currency imposed by more established financial and political actors, and it's gained notoriety as the currency of choice for all manner of criminal activity online. But the most compelling effect of Nakamoto's paper is just beginning to emerge: a new model of algorithmic arbitrage that inverts the equation described above. This model takes advantage of the same brisk trade between public and private, between identity and community, between culture and commercial arbitrage, but it reverses the relationship between individual agency and the construction of value.

To make this case, let me start with an algorithmic reading of Bitcoin as both a computational platform and an ideology—a system based on the cryptographer's assumption of total paranoia and distrust. Since any security system can be compromised, relying on any kind of third party or externally trusted entity to share information inevitably introduces vulnerability into a system. Depending on a bank to transfer funds requires engaging with the global financial network, a complex thicket of regulatory data-gathering requirements, human beings, and electronic media, any of which might be manipulated, compromised, or surveilled. Bitcoin responds to these challenges with two crucial algorithmic solutions, one well-established and the second radically innovative.

Bitcoin depends first of all on asymmetric encryption algorithms, which have become the overwhelming favorite for all digital security applications. These algorithms rely on "one-way functions"—calculations that are easy to perform but extremely difficult to reverse-engineer. A well-known example (the basis of the widely used RSA encryption algorithm): it's easy to multiply two large prime numbers together into a giant number, but much harder to factor a giant number into two constituent primes. By relying on these effectively irreversible computational processes, Bitcoin provides its users a way to authenticate that its transactions are legitimate without knowing anything about the parties to those transactions themselves. In the prime number example, a "private key" would be made up of the two prime numbers and used to digitally sign the data that a user wishes to keep secure. Then a "public key" derived from the giant number (the product of the two primes, or more generally the output of the one-way computational function, whatever it is) could be used to verify that data by ensuring that the private key was indeed used to sign it.

Up to this point, Bitcoin would simply be another payment scheme that depended on some central authority to track public keys and defend against what is called the "double spending problem"—the risk that the money you have just received in payment might also have been spent somewhere else, analogous to a sort of digital counterfeiting. But Bitcoin's second innovation is where we discover a new form of computational arbitrage, in the consensus-driven mechanism of the blockchain.

The blockchain is the public ledger of all Bitcoin transactions in the history of the currency. It contains a detailed accounting of every transaction since the currency's instantiation, a digital file that now exceeds 20 gigabytes in size and must be downloaded locally by every Bitcoin software client. The blockchain is the algorithm that implements the political critique of Bitcoin, a marvel of arbitrage that inverts the traditional relationship between privacy and transparency. Every transaction, every incremental unit of Bitcoin value, is traced through the blockchain, and each of those transactions is tied to one or more buyer and seller identities. The identities are simply alphanumeric strings derived from the public keys of an asymmetric encryption protocol, the Elliptic Curve Digital Signature Algorithm. The transactions annotate the movement of some quantity of Bitcoin from one identity to another. Through the blockchain, which is constantly updated and authenticated by the Bitcoin community (as I'll discuss below), it's possible to trace each unit of currency back to an origination point, through every single transaction it's ever been part of. The entire Bitcoin marketplace is an open book, from the darkest recesses of terrorism financing to booking hotel rooms, purchasing virtual goods from Zynga, and ordering marijuana from the infamous digital marketplace Silk Road.[25]

But how does this actually work? Since the Bitcoin network has no central authority, anyone completing a transaction announces it through a peer-to-peer network. The decentralized nature of the system is meant to account for the problem that information may flow unevenly across the network, that some nodes may suddenly appear or disappear, and for the intentional design constraint of abolishing the central bank or switching station to correlate and sequence all financial activity.

These different transaction announcements are bundled up into transaction blocks by Bitcoin "miners," who then compete to assemble and validate these transactions against the extant communal history of the currency. The outcome of that labor is a new block for the blockchain. To do this, they must solve an arbitrary and highly complex math problem. The miner who is the first to correctly solve the problem "wins" that block. And there is a reward: the first transaction in each new block is a "generation transaction," that creates a quantity of new Bitcoins (the number gradually decreases over time). The miner who solves the block earns this reward for throwing the most computational resources at assembling the latest block for the blockchain (figure 5.1). The miner also accepts a secondary reward by claiming a small transaction fee for processing these various trades (this fee gradually increases over time). Other nodes in the network then accept this newly minted tail for the blockchain and turn to

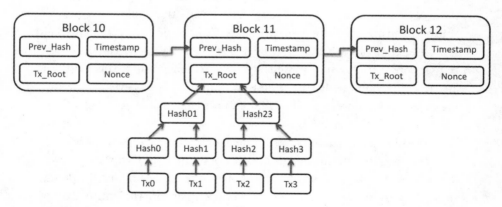

Figure 5.1

The blockchain, a system for transparent, public accounting of Bitcoin transactions.

assembling new transactions into a new block. The Bitcoin software is carefully calibrated so that the community generates a new block approximately every ten minutes (just like Nakamoto's paper suggests), and the overall production of Bitcoin is itself carefully orchestrated. The system will gradually taper the reward for completing new blocks to zero, thereby ceasing the creation of new Bitcoins entirely, once 21 million Bitcoins have been created.[26] At that point, transaction fees alone will provide the incentive for Bitcoin users to dedicate their computers to endlessly updating the blockchain.

I am dwelling on the details of this elaborate process for delivering financial consensus because Bitcoin is not simply a decentralized currency but a revaluation of commerce in algorithmic terms. Bitcoin's true radicalism stems from the fact that the blockchain grounds its authority on *collective computation as an intrinsic form of value*. To understand this shift we need to consider Bitcoin in the context of the historical value propositions of capitalism. As Karl Marx famously argued, industrial capitalism is based on a powerful mode of abstraction, one that separates individuals from the profits of their labor, creating a form of alienation that abstracts the work of individuals into fungible goods and services. Everything becomes commoditized, and the abstraction of exchange-value comes to obscure all other measures of worth. Exchange-value in many ways *is* capitalism: the symbolic ledger embodied by the stock exchange and the market economy. If that ledger gets usurped by the blockchain, we are not simply introducing a new currency into those markets: we are creating a new ledger, a new way of valuing goods, services, and activities.

Many people perceive Bitcoin's disruptive force to derive merely from decentralization. It does, indeed, replace the fiat currency of the state with a new fiat currency, one backed by no gold standard, no guaranteed redemption policy or intrinsic utility (burning Bitcoins won't keep you warm, though mining them does tend to generate a lot of heat from the processors involved).[27] This is by no means novel: mercantile cultures have used mutually accepted measures of value (arrowheads, seashells) for millennia without centralized authorities, often using markers or objects that are effectively valueless on their own—and replacing one such system for another when necessary. These systems depended on implicit trust in a trading community: if I accept this money in payment today, I will be able to spend it elsewhere tomorrow. Money is a symbol that we collectively infuse with belief, a technology for transmitting value through culture that depends on a layer of abstraction. The coins, pieces of paper, or cowrie shells may not have much intrinsic value as physical objects, but they are markers of a symbolic system that financial writer and activist Brett Scott described as analogous to the machine code of capitalism—a foundational abstraction so far removed from the baklava layers of bonds, boutique high-frequency securities trades, and credit default swaps as to be unquestioned and invisible.[28] Money works because we all believe in it at the same time, even though history is rife with incidents of hyperinflation, financial collapse, and gross corruption where that faith can vanish overnight.

State currencies and central banks added a second layer of trust and directed management to the equation, backing the value of a coin or note with the authority of the state, what in the United States is sometimes called the "full faith and credit" of the federal government.[29] Currencies could be supported intrinsically, like Isaac Newton weighing and tracking the precious metals in each British coin, or extrinsically, like a government maintaining a reserve of gold bullion to anchor the value of its paper currency. A state and its central bank might control the introduction of new specie into circulation, manipulate exchange rates, mandate fixed prices for commodities, or simply change its value by fiat (as North Korea did in 2009 by introducing a new currency overnight). In these instances, currency no longer depends solely on the community of belief supporting circulation, but also on a second intersecting community based on the power and asserted wisdom of the state.

Yet trust is exactly what Bitcoin has positioned itself against. On a human level users still transact with Bitcoin because of their faith in a community (that is, faith that they will be able to sell their Bitcoins to someone else), but the system itself is founded on a very different principle. Where normal financial transactions are ultimately backed by state actors (in the United States, for example, through institutions like the Federal Reserve and the Federal Deposit Insurance Corporation), Bitcoin's ultimate foundational principle is computation and Nakamoto's trust-free vision for exchange. Instead of Treasury notes or stockpiled bullion, we get the blockchain. The blockchain relies on a *computational* fiat by rewarding the miners who bring the most computational power to bear on calculating each new block. The system depends on solving "proof-of-work" problems that are essentially meaningless but that serve as a public competition, creating a form of value dependent on the expenditure of computer cycles in the service of the Bitcoin network. The central abstraction of capitalism has itself been abstracted into computation: an upgrade to the machine code that introduces a new foundational layer of value.

This phase change is most visible in the system's dependence on a kind of algorithmic democracy or force majeure, depending on one's perspective. The rules of the blockchain award "truth" status to the miner who is the first to solve each new proof-of-work problem, and that solution is then accepted as the new public record for the system as a whole. As Nakamoto's paper argues, "As long as a majority of CPU power is controlled by nodes that are not cooperating to attack the network, they'll generate the longest chain and outpace attackers."[30] This modifies the value proposition above: value is abstracted not merely to computational power, but to concentrated computational power—either used for the benefit of the Bitcoin community to outpace attackers, or used by attackers to overpower the platform. Whoever can solve the meaningless math problem first serves as the next authenticator of the whole system's legitimacy.

Nakamoto's system depends for stability on a persistent democratic majority. As a classic open source platform, Bitcoin's active community of developers improve the code but also support the project through a kind of collective fan engagement, a mutual reinforcement of the project's ideology through dedicated computation. The addition of each new block to the chain is the crucial intellectual fulcrum for the entire system, and it depends on the race for a proof-of-work solution to be won by one of the "good guys," a system that is not trying to fraudulently alter the official record of transactions. To make this work, most Bitcoin miners pool their computational resources, dividing up the proof-of-work problem across thousands of different machines to increase their speed of computation and thereby improve their chance of "winning" a block. Indeed, even this parliamentary model of financial authentication runs risks: if any of these mining collectives grows too large, taking over more than 50 percent of the overall computational pool tackling the blockchain problem, they will become a majority faction with the power to alter the transaction record at will. Bitcoin only survives through a federated balance of computational power.

Bitcoin's notionally trust-free system ends up demanding two different kinds of trust: first, faith in the algorithm itself, especially in its transparent underpinnings in the blockchain. And second, Bitcoin encourages participants to band together into computing collectives, creating a shared community around the arbitrary calculation of proof-of-work solutions. In many ways, this is remarkably similar to the trust-free world of HFT traders that Lewis describes in *Flash Boys*. A vibrant algorithmic ecology depends on a community of goodwill to compete according to established rules (however cutthroat they may be) and discourage any changes to those rules. HFT companies may find ways to execute trades more and more quickly, but it is in nobody's interest to slow markets down or change the ground rules of transactions (for instance, by requiring a buyer to hold a stock for at least twenty-four hours before selling it).

The similarity arises because Bitcoin, despite its pretensions to democracy, is fundamentally a technologically elite system that inserts computational value into the capitalistic foundations of currency. Much like a traditional currency, Bitcoin is only as strong as its strongest proponent (in this case not a state, but the largest mining collectives). But the core value defining strength is now a very specific resource: computational power, silicon, electricity. While the game is open to anyone, the only players who can truly influence the outcome are those who band together in sophisticated mining collectives (which in turn requires trusting the collective to share the rewards fairly). The everyday users of Bitcoin have little idea how transactions are calculated or how this balance of power can affect their own investments and transactions.

Finally, the programmed currency that is Bitcoin also creates important externalities as it abstracts financial worth into computational value. As Edward Castronova argues, if significant numbers of people started using virtual currencies without the backing of traditional sovereign states, it could create "a general dynamic state of decline" where those still using dollars would have to take on ever-increasing tax obligations to support the infrastructure of the state.[31] That, at heart, is what the dollar values: the global superpower of the United States of America with all its military might, its roads, its social programs, its prisons and pensions. Replacing that with Bitcoin would effectively create a tax system supporting an ever-expanding network of computational cycles dedicated to mining the next block in the chain.

Programmable Culture

Bitcoin's recent mainstream success, from Overstock and Amazon to a variety of hotels, travel sites, and smaller businesses, indicates that its logic of computational value is catching on, particularly with other algorithmically driven businesses. As Stanford entrepreneur Balaji Srinivasan argues: "If the Internet was programmable communication, Bitcoin is programmable money."[32] It is not so much a new unit of exchange as a new platform for financial computation. More profoundly, it is an ideology for making computation the universal solvent, the universal metric of value, extending the digitization of commerce *Wired* imagined to its logical conclusion. Like Google's PageRank algorithm, Bitcoin defines value through particular, temporally constrained processes that implement forms of algorithmic arbitrage. Bitcoin's proof of work creates an inversion mechanism between public and private that precisely reverses what PageRank does. For Bitcoin the network of links, the intricate architecture of financial transactions, is public record, while the significance of that network is obscured: it's easy to trace the history of every Bitcoin, to identify it block by block, but extremely difficult to find out what that unit of exchange was used to purchase. PageRank does the opposite, assembling a carefully guarded, secret map of the network that is then interpreted into meaningful answers for users. That mirrored relationship hints at a broader set of changes that seem to be emerging as we incorporate algorithms more deeply into central machinery of human culture.

In this context, we can read Bitcoin not just as an implementation of the ideology of "programmable money," but as an allegory for the sea change toward what we might call programmable culture. The central tenets of Bitcoin's system for creating value epitomize similar shifts in all corners of cultural production, where daily business seems the same but the majority votes, central authorities, and validation structures are being subsumed by algorithmic processes. From HFT to Google Search, we see intrinsic value being transmuted into a kind of network value that rewards context, access, and interlinking. In parallel, the quest for knowledge is subservient to the quest for methods, for better technical systems. Our growing path dependency on the black boxes at Facebook, Google, Apple, and other tech companies pushes a huge range of cultural fields to produce work optimized for those systems, creating the belletristic equivalent of monoculture crops that have limited resilience to major changes in the ecosystem.

Consider journalism. The recently dethroned founder of the Gawker Media blogging empire, Nick Denton, wrote candidly in 2015 about missteps at his company: "We—the freest journalists on the planet—were slaves to the Facebook algorithm."[33] Denton was arguing that his company had lost sight of its central mission to break compelling news stories, growing obsessed with the algorithmic game of attracting traffic and attention instead. That problem has only gotten more serious now that media companies like the *New York Times* are allowing Facebook to host their copy directly, keeping users even more entrenched in a stream of content that Facebook's algorithms control. As technology journalist Adrienne LaFrance argued in *The Atlantic*, "Facebook is America's news editor," driving a huge and growing percentage of the traffic to news sites.[34]

In 2016 it emerged that even as Denton was lamenting the impact of Facebook on his journalists, the social network had hired its own cadre of young journalists to select stories for promotion through "Trending Topics," a prominent widget for drawing user attention to top stories of the day. These contract workers were relegated to an unused conference room and asked to perform a kind of algorithmic judgment, selecting stories according to a carefully defined set of instructions laid out in a memo titled "Trending Review Guidelines."[35] Both the algorithm-like instructions and the humans enacting them were accused of introducing liberal bias into Trending Topics, and Facebook has since announced plans to completely overhaul how Trending Topics functions. The revelation underscores the now-familiar idea of humans hiding within a supposedly algorithmic black box, but it also reveals how solipsistic our cultural systems have become. The Facebook memo instructed contractors to track just ten news sites, including CNN, the BBC, Fox News, and the *Guardian*, in evaluating whether a story merits "national" importance. Meanwhile, editors at all of those places closely monitored Facebook (which, remember, is not a news organization) to see what news was getting traction with the digital public. News directors trying to decipher the Trending Topics algorithm were really peering into an editorial funhouse mirror.[36] Later in 2016, yet another illustration of programmable culture and new ground rules for value erupted into the headlines when PayPal co-founder Peter Thiel drove Gawker Media into bankruptcy by supporting a third-party lawsuit. Thiel argued this was "less about revenge and more about specific deterrence"—and his correct interpretation that as an algorithmic billionaire he had the power to censor a news organization whose salacious coverage he despised.[37]

The sea change in what counts does not stop with Wall Street or the news. The stakes of cultural success are increasingly driven by algorithmic metrics. In Hollywood special effects studios, at campaign offices, police headquarters, and in countless other nodes of power, the players who can best leverage concentrated computation to a set of abstracted problems win the prize. For Bitcoin this means adding a new block to the blockchain; for other fields it can be contributions to other relatively transparent, publicly accessible contests—blockbuster films, elections, hit musical singles—but the algorithmic arbitrage used to get there depends on similar forms of data-driven abstraction, black box analysis, and intensive processing.

Computationalism makes cultural practices not just computational but programmable—susceptible to centralized editing and revision. Perhaps this is the inevitable consequence of our gradual shift from an Internet organized according to the ad hoc "cool site of the day" model to one with stable hierarchies and revenue streams. As the systems for disseminating and filtering content become more elaborate, more complex, the tools necessary for producing content have become more automated as well. Bloggers for companies like Gawker Media churn out short articles that are often driven by search engine traffic and web analytics software, with bonuses for pieces that gain rapid traction. Because of the changing nature of social media and the broader Internet, they are writing first for the algorithms that will choose whether or not to disseminate their work on sites like Facebook, and only second for the readers who will then read and share it with others.

Denton's lament serves as an example of how cultural values like the function of journalistic free enterprise can be gradually altered by revising the algorithmic platforms that distribute content and measure success. Under the regime of process, the production of value comes from iteration: the persistent output of short, topical blog posts is far more important than the content of any one of those posts. The application of algorithms to data trumps the data itself; the navigation, synthesis, and manipulation of information becomes more important than simply accessing it. The Bitcoin protocol elegantly encodes this principle in the notion of mining, explicitly linking the computational work of authenticating transactions with the production of new currency. Indeed, performing this public computational process is the *only* way to create more Bitcoins, making the process of computation equivalent to the alchemical magic of a government mint turning pieces of paper into specie. The mythological equivalent of a Fort Knox-style mountain of gold "backing" the dollar is the mountain of servers dedicated to churning through the blockchain.

In the context of bloggers writing ten or twelve posts a day for companies like Gawker Media, the methods for mining value are different but the governing abstraction remains the same. The online ad revenue systems these bloggers interact with create another kind of processing or "proof of work," the content itself. A blogger writes a new post that then gets circulated by Facebook algorithms and users, generating ad revenue for Facebook, for Gawker Media, and sometimes a narrow slice of that pie for the blogger. The process monetizes eyeballs and human attention, not ideas. Those who can consistently produce a high volume of clickable material are rewarded most greatly. This is how the process of blogging becomes much more important than the content of the posts, and how writers can become slaves to the algorithms that determine what virality, shareability, and human interest really mean.

The migration of value from end result to process marks the culmination of a long evolution that began with what Jürgen Habermas famously called the bourgeois public sphere. Habermas argued that the emergence of a propertied middle class in the eighteenth century (parallel to the rise of the *Encyclopédie*) created a new space for disinterested public discourse founded on the truth values of the private, intimate sphere of bourgeois life. Men could gather in coffeehouses to read newspapers and discuss the events of the day, practicing civic engagement anchored in their collective investment in the emerging system of modern capitalism. As men of property, citizens, and readers, they could ignore status and personal interest in the protected space of the public sphere for the sake of a vibrant, critically energetic conversation. The public sphere emerged in codependence with a free press and a stable political space for discussion, allowing for the shared understanding and evaluation of what Habermas called areas of "common concern."[38]

The intimate connection between capitalism and the public sphere provides a useful contrast to the accelerating evolution of journalism in the era of programmable culture. Habermas's idealized public sphere is part of what Gawker Media and Denton find to have disappeared beneath their feet. Investigative journalism and the independent press serve as the cultural scaffolding for the kind of civic community that Habermas idealizes, providing the ideas and opinions that reflect and advance the shared values of the reading public. While the methods of analysis might evolve, the data itself in this public sphere was dependable, hard-coded: a system of truth beliefs rooted in state and religious institutions, in capitalism and coffee shops. The public sphere was a contentious idea from the beginning because it painted a rosy picture about who got to participate in this bourgeois Enlightenment and what they got to talk about. But even accepting its flaws, the notion of a modern-day agora for societal discussion and debate has remained critically compelling, particularly as the Internet seems to promise new forms of public engagement that mirror the key features of Habermas's historical interpretation. Social media, anonymous forums, and even Wikipedia seem at times to rival the first public offices of the Enlightenment, creating a space for disinterested, critical public speech.

Denton's fall is a cautionary tale illustrating how that scaffolding for disinterested public discourse is turning into a very different sort of structure. In the era of programmable culture, publicity and the ethics of discourse can be as fungible as Bitcoin, fundamentally changing the social contract on which the public sphere depends. What rules do bloggers follow about protecting sources, or acknowledging conflicts of interest? On Facebook, the ombudspeople of the *New York Times* and the *Washington Post* disappear behind the opaque gatekeeping of algorithms. Thiel argues that his grudge against Gawker originated in their abuse of the mantle of journalism to bully and humiliate individuals. For him, the ethics of property ownership and a privacy derived from that ownership trumped any notion of a public sphere.

Programmable culture turns the public sphere inside out: the cultural data that used to make up the arena of "common concern" is increasingly privatized. The private life of the average citizen becomes public, commercially accessible to data brokers, social media companies, and others who trade access to the newly privatized sphere of online community (through sites like Facebook and Twitter) in exchange for commercial access to users' private lives. Members of the algorithmic elite retreat from public view, some of them echoing Thiel's libertarian sentiment: "I no longer believe that freedom and democracy are compatible."[39] Finance was the most private of registers in bourgeois capitalism, but Bitcoin turns it into a public sphere for money. By placing financial transactions into the glass box, the creators of Bitcoin invert the public sphere's model of scrutiny, allowing public inspection of commercial exchange but keeping cultural positions and identities private. Consensus gathers around financial transactions rather than critical judgments, and money becomes, to extend the logic of the U.S. Supreme Court in *Citizens United*, the only real form of political speech.

At its dystopian extreme, this new financial public sphere makes bank accounts into citizens: SuperPACs and venture capitalists have the important conversations about events of the day, joined by those individuals wealthy enough to speak and be heard: not just Thiel but Warren Buffett, Bill Gates, and Jeff Bezos, for example. On a more positive note, we can see the public sphere of cash transforming the arts through fundraising sites like Kickstarter and Indiegogo, which allow for the collective approval of new projects through crowdfunding, or a kind of financial voting. The algorithmic process of crowdfunding rewards those who master the methods of privatized publicity: a strong introductory video, frequent updates, tiered reward structures, and effective use of social media to raise awareness.

Read in this light, Denton's post is a diatribe against the seductions of the public sphere of money as it undermines the public sphere of journalism. When bloggers and reporters are given audience metrics and goals, they are grappling with a new model of public attention denominated in dollars, but really measured in CPU cycles, links, hovers, and clicks. The old journalistic enterprise had interposed a set of Enlightenment abstractions—the notion of the fourth estate, a free and independent press serving the public good—between the business of selling newspapers and the marketplace for ideas. The valuation of process in the age of algorithms deletes those mediating layers, allowing writers and editors to see the market response to their work in real time. Direct engagement with that feedback loop can lead to changing headlines and angles for stories, pursuing new topics entirely, and continually adapting to the normative effects of social media algorithms (and, in Gawker's case, to Chapter 11 bankruptcy).

Habermas was quick to point out that the bourgeois public sphere faded away with the rise of mass media and modern advertising, but the ideal vision of disinterested public discourse persists in the aspirations of journalists, social entrepreneurs, Wikipedians, and many others who see the Internet as a new platform for collective engagement around "common concerns." The shift to processual value has also shifted the epistemological floor beneath our feet. Despite Thiel's classically capitalistic intervention in the Gawker lawsuit, it is clear that shared, objective truths grounded in capitalism, personal property, and ultimately the Enlightenment itself have given way to a new objectivity founded on fungible data and processual truths—what we might cynically call culture as a service. As we invest more of our lives, our public and private conversations, our faith and beliefs, in algorithmic culture machines, we invest in the idea that truth resides in analytics, abstraction, and data-mining.

Mining Value

The valorization of data processing has provocative implications for cultural production. As cultural consumers, we now evaluate the meaning of text through its connections more than its substance. The critic is no longer celebrated primarily for narrowing the field, eliminating bad links, and performing an exclusive model of intellectual taste. Figures like Pauline Kael or Harold Bloom who built their careers telling us what to ignore as much as what to celebrate are being replaced by curators who provide an ongoing service (or process) of inclusive, networked culture. The inspired curation of Maria Popova's *Brain Pickings*, for example, offers a wide-ranging, serial feast of intellectual pleasures. Its status as a persistent stream of content, one that Popova "obsessively" maintains, makes the stream more valuable than the individual works she cites.[40] The performance of her creative process, the complex human-computational culture machine that is *Brain Pickings*, becomes the object of interest for her readers. She is, in her own way, mining value in a particular kind of aesthetic arbitrage that we often call curation. She assembles these pieces in a way that captures attention, that transmutes disparate elements into a compelling new experience. Great bloggers do the same, gleaning nuggets of content for sites that are celebrated primarily for their consistent, timely production of a media stream.

In other words, the same processual logic of value that drives Bitcoin is remaking other cultural forms as well. We are learning from, or being influenced by, algorithms and computational systems that elevate process to the status of value. We are slowly replacing the very human codex model of linear attention with an eternal abundance of culture, a Netflix-like smorgasbord that integrates multiple media, paratexts, and intellectual frameworks—a cloud of ideas rather than a stream of consciousness. Curating these clouds requires human beings like Popova to work gracefully with hybrid algorithmic machines consisting of computational memory, networks of human contributors and readers, and various collaborative platforms. But just as the major fields of cultural production are adapting to the logic of processual value, we, the audience of these products, are also changing our values along with our habits as consumers of their work.

Consider the many forms of cultural information we now casually expect to find in our pocket computers: instant comparative sales rankings of every imaginable consumer good, plus popular reviews thereof; frank, public discussions of every conceivable medical topic, childrearing problem, or addiction protocol; quirky and subjective reviews of every eatery, coffee shop, and museum in the known world. None of this information was available in such persistent abundance (or, often, in even limited form) through the traditional, highly normative avenues of cultural production as French sociologist Pierre Bourdieu mapped them in the pre-algorithmic era.[41] It was almost all private knowledge, deliberately shielded from the Habermasian public sphere before the great inversion. For much of the twentieth century, if a woman wanted to research birth control options and side-effects, or a man wanted to read narratives about coming out as gay, there was no search engine, no public, sanctioned source of information at all. A homeowner who wanted to replace a shower faucet stem valve or a hobbyist researching a new kind of modeling paint would have few resources at their disposal beyond local community groups, stores, and, for some questions, libraries. Before the Internet, these were private concerns, not common concerns.

This transformation is so profound, so obvious, that is has become invisible even to those of us who have lived through its recent phases. The structures that constitute the deep fabric of the web collect and store human attention, intimacy, memories, and all our other digital traces. To make use of this abundance, they all leverage algorithmic arbitrage systems like PageRank, funneling us toward the particular forum, the very specific article, that addresses some particular need. For many of us, every single question about our lives starts with a query to a search engine or another algorithmic database, and this new legibility changes our relationship to reality in a deep, epistemological way. Comforted in the knowledge that we can always Google it later, we have gradually accepted that the arbitrage of information is more significant than the information itself. The gloss and the comment have overtaken the article and the book so completely that author Karl Taro Greenfield wrote in the *New York Times* about our collective tendency to fake cultural literacy on the basis of paratext and metadata:

It's never been so easy to pretend to know so much without actually knowing anything. We pick topical, relevant bits from Facebook, Twitter or emailed news alerts, and then regurgitate them. ... What matters to us, awash in petabytes of data, is not necessarily having actually consumed this content firsthand but simply knowing that it exists—and having a position on it, being able to engage in the chatter about it.[42]

Like the HFT traders, like Google's PageRank, like Bitcoin, we no longer care about the details of our information packets so long as we can effectively arbitrage them, transferring the data to our advantage before it loses cachet. The spectacle of cultural consumption, the public act of processing, judging, and sharing, is the new cultural economy.

Reading the system has become more important than reading the content the system was built to deliver. At their most intense, these architectures of attention create their own persistent streams of belief, a kind of cultural value blockchain. Sites like Wikipedia and even public conversations on social media offer a detailed transaction stream allowing participants to check a thread of debate against a history of contributions (with the notable exception that almost all of these platforms, aside from Wikipedia, allow the invisible removal of these traces). Like Bitcoin, the public ledger of attention is completely transparent, but the human and algorithmic computation involved in generating it is obscured. The motivations of Wikipedia contributors or Facebook commenters can be difficult to discern, but the platform itself presents an appearance of flat, democratic accessibility.[43]

The seduction of this public processing, the blockchain-like generation of cultural discourse, lies precisely in its visibility, its thrilling transparency.

Cultural processing (whether of Bitcoin transactions, Facebook likes, click-driven political activism, or Wikipedia updates) becomes its own spectacle, distracting us from the invisible sides of the system, like a magic trick performed in a glass box. The seduction is all the more powerful because of the truth behind it: Bitcoin, Wikipedia, and even the social media newsfeeds have some utopian legitimacy. They do really have the potential to route around traditional, occasionally despotic structures for controlling information, from the Arab Spring to the rapid assembly of detailed, objective encyclopedia entries on major terrorist attacks. The spectacle is collaborative, transformative, live. The spectacle promises to make the whole world legible and mutable through the sheer ubiquity of computation. Programmable culture promises democracy, accountability, and clarity at the tap of an icon.

But of course the algorithmic notion of mining for value depends on an arbitrary grammar of action.[44] The proof of work imposed by Bitcoin on its mining collectives has its analogs in other systems as well, like bloggers optimizing their stories for Facebook algorithms. And while these forms of cultural and computational labor are often arbitrary by human standards—make-work designed to filter out the messy fringes of the system—they serve important needs in normalizing otherwise haphazard communities around set algorithmic objectives. Bitcoin miners unite around their CPU cycles, propelling the system forward with a set of computational cartels that are both transparent and occult. The ritualistic use of "like" and "friend" buttons are Facebook's proof of work, encouraging us to engage to make our contributions count ... and beneath this grammar lies the platform's second language of advertisements and commercialized user data. For PageRank, the proof of work is the most compelling: the construction of the links and references that define the Internet itself. The ultimate seductive power in each of these systems lies in the reinforcing feedback loop of refactoring and extending the chain through our own contributions. In the early 1990s, information scholar Philip Agre predicted many of the consequences of this kind of programmability, which he called information capture:

The practice of formulating these ontologies is, all disciplinary insularity aside, and regardless of anyone's conscious understandings of the process, a form of social theorization. And this theorizing is not simply a scholastic exercise but is part of a much larger material process through which these new social ontologies, in a certain specific sense, become real.[45]

Our participation wears grooves deeper into the system and continually trains us in the fine arts of process-driven valuation.

Replacing the public sphere with the programmable sphere is ultimately a substitution of one form of reading for another: a new idiomatic frame to put on the world. Leaving behind the readers of the *Spectator* in an eighteenth-century London coffeehouse, we find the readers of algorithmic process, interpreting Twitter feeds and web traffic counts over Wi-Fi at Starbucks. The grammar of the new algorithmic sphere obscures certain operations while making others more visible, and the spectacle of the blockchain is merely one of the newer ways that we have invested these cultural systems with enormous power. We are all becoming more adept at the practice of critical arbitrage because our systems, the flooded streams of cultural data, require it. The interplay of glass boxes and black boxes demands an algorithmic attention to data processes, an algorithmic reading that we are all practicing already.

Coda: The Algorithmic Imagination

Imagination is more important than knowledge. Knowledge is limited. Imagination encircles the world.
Albert Einstein

Machine Learning

What does it mean to talk of an algorithmic imagination? In this coda, I want to explore the implications of a world where culture machines are taking on a growing share of the critical and creative work that used to be distinctively, intrinsically human.

Google's DeepMind crossed one such threshold when engineers tasked it with identifying and enhancing various image features on a repeating loop, creating a series of Dalí- or Bosch-like pictures where an algorithmic machine intelligence turned shadows and intersections into eyes, faces, and other recognizable visual elements. The resulting work shows the signs of a distinct, alien perspective, an artist's eye that seems to imagine and then realize things that we would never have expected from a photograph. That glimpse of "intelligence on alien shores," as mathematical historian David Berlinski puts it, emerges from a newly powerful and perhaps imaginative form of algorithmic production. It also offers a glimpse of process, a set of imaginative practices, that evoke artistic intentionality in a way that feels very different from the stories we tell about artificial intelligence, like HAL from *2001* or Samantha from *Her*. At least, we *think* we see that glimpse in the strange renderings the program produces—perhaps it is just the human observers dreaming up these electric sheep on behalf of the machine, obeying our persistent impulse to anthropomorphize and project intentionality into every complex system we encounter.

DeepMind is remarkable for the range of its achievements. A few weeks before Google purchased it, the company made international news with a machine learning algorithm that had learned to play twenty-nine Atari games better than the average human with no direct supervision.[1] Now the same algorithm has replaced "sixty handcrafted rule-based systems" at Google, from image recognition to speech transcription.[2] Most spectacularly, in March 2016 DeepMind's AlphaGo defeated *go* grandmaster Lee Sedol 4–1, demonstrating its conquest of one of humanity's subtlest and most artistic games.[3] After a long doldrums, Google and a range of other research outfits seem to be making progress on systems that can gracefully adapt themselves to a wide range of conceptual challenges. This phase shift has produced a new crop of centers and initiatives grappling with the potential consequences of artificial intelligence, uniting philosophers, technologists, and Silicon Valley billionaires around the question of whether a truly thinking machine could pose an existential threat to humanity.

In the paper where he described the Turing test, Alan Turing also took on the broader question of machine intelligence: an algorithm for consciousness. The Turing test was in many ways a demonstration of the absurdity of establishing a metric for intelligence; the best we can do is have a conversation and see how effective a machine is at emulating a human. But, Turing proposed, if we do achieve such a breakthrough, it will be important to consider the concept of the "child machine," which learns what we wish to teach.[4] That philosophical position underpins DeepMind and many other recent algorithmic intelligence breakthroughs, which have emerged from the currently incandescent computer science subfield of machine learning. Some version of machine learning, in fact, underpins many of the algorithms at work in this book: Siri, Netflix, and of course Google all depend on these systems to parse complex data and make decisions.

Machine learning can operate according to a few basic structures, such as neural networks, Bayesian analysis, or evolutionary adaptation. Often the most sophisticated machine learning systems combine aspects of multiple approaches. Once a learning algorithm has been constructed, it can be trained, preferably over a huge corpus of data that can provide many examples of the desired outcome or problem. The learning algorithm iterates over time based on some kind of signal of relative success (e.g., measuring how close the algorithm got to correctly guessing the numbers on a blurry image of a postal address). Given time, data, and a precise statement of the problem, a machine learning algorithm can create a robust solution to that problem.

What makes machine learning so relevant to this book is that the "solution" to that problem is in fact an algorithm itself. As machine learning researcher Pedro Domingos puts it in *The Master Algorithm*:

Every algorithm has an input and output: the data goes into the computer, the algorithm does what it will with it, and out comes the result. Machine learning turns this around: in goes the data and the desired result and out comes the algorithm that turns one into the other. Learning algorithms—also known as learners—are algorithms that make other algorithms.[5]

These algorithms produce the process, the mediation, the gap-spanning implementation that unites their engineers' problems and solutions. And, since they do this through the million-fold iteration of simulated neural networks, the computational constructs they spit out tend to be both effective and inscrutable. When Netflix's Todd Yellin talks about the "ghost in the machine" or mathematician Steven Strogatz describes automated science as the "end of insight," machine learning solutions are precisely what they have in mind.[6] The problem is effectively one of scale. As humans we can conceive of and manage vast data sets, but our ability to ask interesting questions of those data sets is limited. We can automate some of the question-asking but we also lose context, so the answers may be true but uninformative.

In other words, machine learning provides a perfect foil for the return of computationalism at the end of this project: the ways that the logic of a computational universe could be used to unlock the mysteries of that very universe. By assembling systems that follow a few simple computational laws, we can iterate toward highly sophisticated solutions to difficult problems that resist more straightforward (e.g., human-designed) algorithmic approaches. Those flashes of complex order and process emerging from chaos hint at a kind of imagination at work, and suggest that the open-ended iteration that defines machine learning might be a limited form of imaginative practice in its own right. And our purchase on that question, our access to the ocean of computation, depends as always on metaphor.

Algorithmic Imagination

In his remarkable novel *Solaris*, Stanislaw Lem imagines a scientific expedition confronting a mysterious ocean planet where the perpetual motion of
the waves throws up fascinating forms and structures.[7] The human scientists continually seek to interpret them, to communicate with this possible
alien intelligence. One school of researchers proposes that the ocean of
Solaris itself is a giant mind, a complex system working through its calculations before the expedition's eyes. Indeed, it's possible to read Lem's novel
as an allegory for the apophenia, the endless hunt for meaning and patterns, that lies at the heart of the Enlightenment project. Lem seems to hint
that the ultimate drive of instrumental reason, of continually interrogating
our world in the quest for answers, may only be madness: fantasies that
we project onto the world in order to construct a story about truth, just as
the characters in the novel must grapple with figures projected from their
pasts.

The endless symbolic churning of the oceans on Solaris offers a provocative metaphor for the notion of algorithmic imagination today, particularly
as it's framed by computationalists. Ray Kurzweil, leader of Google's
machine learning group and a key figure in the singularity debates, echoes
this point in his documentary *Transcendent Man*:

Well I was thinking about how much computation is represented by the ocean. I
mean it's all these water molecules interacting with each other. That's computation.
It's quite beautiful. And I've always found it very soothing. And that's really what
computation's all about. The capture of these transcendent moments of our
consciousness.[8]

So far, the debate around algorithmic imagination remains firmly
grounded on *this* shore, not the alien space that Berlinski hypothesizes and
Kurzweil already sees. We have no compelling evidence to suggest that
algorithms have intentionality, creativity, or any of the traits one might
consider necessary to an imaginative faculty. An even bigger problem is
that we have no real way to voyage across the ocean of complexity, no way
to effectively comprehend that metaphorical vasty deep any more than we
can comprehend the Pacific. We are embodied, grounded, limited to biophysical implementations of flesh and nerve tissue, and when we swim in
the ocean we can experience only a tiny part of it.

And yet, through the same intellectual ladders of abstraction and process (in this case, something more akin to recursion), we can imagine for ourselves what algorithmic imagination might be. This book has traced a series of encounters with (possible) imaginative algorithms, noting the growing cognitive traffic between biological, cultural, and computational structures of thinking. Google Now and the design goal of "anticipation" are forms of imaginative thinking—a process for envisioning possible futures and bringing them into greater possibility through implementation. The questions Google thinks we might ask hover at the edge of the search bar, ready to leap into view milliseconds after we begin to ask them. The algos of Wall Street do this as well, dreaming of market futures and making financial predictions.

We know these practices of imagination only through their human-readable results and outputs. But analyzing the outputs of even the most seemingly creative algorithms does not really tell us how imagination works within the machine, particularly since the results are specifically tailored for human consumption. Instead, we must use those powers of projection and intimation to conjure up a vision of the cognitive factory where those outputs are created. This is the space of cultural computation itself, a mathematical universe that is accessible to us only through abstraction, simplification, and sampling. There is no way we can fully comprehend the processes driving Google's neural networks as they hunt for eye-like features to enhance, no human experience that correlates to performing that same procedure on iterations of the same image millions of times. The same goes for the systems that recommend books, interpret spoken language, or perform any of a thousand other big data analytic tasks. Aside from the most simplistic cases, we will never know how algorithms know what they know. This is the *computational space of imagination*, or what in *Her* Samantha calls the "space between the words."

Going farther from shore, the deep waters of algorithmic imagination draw us relentlessly back toward ourselves and the mysterious origins of cognition, inspiration, and serendipity that drive creative work. How are computational systems reinventing, channeling, or modulating those processes? On an individual level this is a straightforward extension of technics: when does the memory bank, the virtual assistant, or the recommendation engine deserve credit in the creative process? These tools manage cognition, inspiration, and serendipity for us, generating conversation and intellectual connection in our social media streams, our digital work-spaces and notebooks, and more broadly, in the horizon of visible knowledge. The writer using a word processor to manage drafts; the scientist using research databases and citation tools to manage a field of professional knowledge; the artist using image editing software, photo sharing tools, and a virtual notebook to track observations—all of these creative processes depend on tools that are increasingly active, occasionally manipulative agents in their own use. If algorithmic reading asks us to recognize that our objects of study are adapting to us as we interpret them, algorithmic imagination asks at what point that process of adaptation becomes a form of imaginative agency.

Like Turing's proposal for how to measure intelligence, we may need to accept that imagination can be measured only together, intersubjectively. This question of how technics enable imagination also extends to non-algorithmic processes of collective imagination: the networks of dialog and collaboration that allow multiple people to make the same critical break-throughs in parallel (e.g., calculus or sonar). Our algorithmic machines now manage not just our individual streams of data but the great rivers of collective information, filtering our friends and colleagues as regularly as they curate our music or the news. In the case of Anonymous, Wikipedia, and myriad other modes of collective authorship, they make entire new forms of work possible, uniting strangers into collectives that can be as self-aware as Egyptian protestors organizing through Facebook or as unwitting as the contributors to Google's autocomplete databases. This is the *augmented imagination*, the transformative work that humans and machines can only do together.

Augmenting Imagination

Whatever imagination is, we know that the focal lenses of our tools inflect and change it. Consider Vannevar Bush's seminal vision of the Memex, an early version of the digital *Star Trek* computer inspired by a conception of imaginative augmentation. It was a universal knowledge machine, to be sure, but with the size and function of a personal desk: "It is an enlarged intimate supplement to ... memory."[9] Bush first struck the chord that continues to haunt Google, Apple, and the algorithmic vanguard today: the encyclopedia must also be intimate. Computers must make the universal not just accessible but personal. The chief function of the Memex would be to assist users in constructing and reviewing "trails," or hypertextual associations between documents that constituted a personal paratextual layer, a set of maps for the wilderness of microfilm inhabiting one's desk.

The trail was Bush's response to the central challenge of the nascent information age, the question of selection. He imagines the new occupation of "trail blazer," the people who would establish the most useful pathways and associate links across many different texts. Knowledge work would become the practice of artful selection and targeted omission, allowing the user "the privilege of forgetting the manifold things he does not need to have immediately at hand, with some assurance that he can find them again if they prove important." But as we have seen throughout this book, the trail blazers are increasingly algorithmic, navigating "the space between the words" so we can live coherent digital lives untroubled by the oceanic cacophony of raw data. If these trail blazers are exploring a new frontier, the analogy is not to scouts and settlers of the

Figure 6.1
Vannevar Bush's Memex.

Wild West but rather the automated probes, robots, and rovers now traversing the Solar System. These envoys are very different from their human creators.

The miniaturization and automation that Bush saw as central to the magic of the Memex were intended to support a very human form of data retrieval and research. The Memex as Bush imagined it has never quite come into being; the functions of personal archive and universal data access are now effectively split across platforms and tools like Google, Wikipedia, Dropbox, and Evernote. More significantly, the personal, associative use case that Bush imagined as the pinnacle of achievement, being a trail blazer, has turned out to be a sideline product of a much deeper computational project with its own associated algorithmic space of imagination, one that engrosses top engineers at Google and other titans of the informational universe. That is the mapping and manipulating of human knowledge, a collaborative and processual grand challenge, which requires a sophisticated set of interlocking algorithmic systems to handle everything from operating the global data cloud to modeling and predicting human behavior.

The Memex was at its core an imagination machine, a technical apparatus or "intimate supplement" designed to create a literal and intellectual space for associative thinking, curiosity, and creativity. It attempted to envision the role that digital information access would have in augmenting human cognition. Bush saw the foundations of that system as unremarkable: encyclopedias, reference works, and the assemblage of a standard index of knowledge that would serve as the foundation for each user's personal data sphere. He correctly apprehended that the explosion of knowledge after World War II would make selection a nontrivial operation, but he failed to imagine the rapidity of such systemic change. The Memex never came into being because the substrate of knowledge is not a static field to be manipulated mechanically. It is an ocean, constantly in motion. Nothing is safe: not the encyclopedia (consider the rise of Wikipedia), not the science textbooks (which must be updated yearly), not even the seminal works of human knowledge, which are constantly remediated by intervening criticism, discovery, and evolving social context. As complexity scientist Sam Arbesman argues in *The Half-Life of Facts*, the vast majority of human knowledge is contingent in this way, and the pace of epistemological change is accelerating.[10] This is largely due to algorithmic processes, which enable researchers to be more productive and create new ways of cross-pollinating and even automating the discovery of knowledge. Most important, as the web of knowledge grows more complex, we become increasingly reliant on algorithmic judgments of relevance to help us navigate the exponential growth of new facts and discourses. For Bush, the interface for knowledge manipulation was as thin as the transparent plate on top of the Memex that separated users from the thousands of microfilm pages stored within it. For us, that plane continues to thicken, becoming another membrane in the "interface layer" of ubiquitous computation.

Bush was deeply prescient in imagining the kinds of augmented interactions we would have with digital information, but the age of the algorithm has introduced this crucial membrane of abstraction between the space of universal knowledge (inside the Memex) and the human user constructing an intimate web of knowledge trails at its surface. The function of Google's PageRank and countless other systems we depend on to curate the ocean of information is to continually remap, and ultimately to remake, that ocean. The role of the human is not one of curator but rather, to refashion an antiquated digital metaphor, a surfer riding the waves. We operate within a complex space that has its own algorithmic weather, currents, and sources of energy, many of them deliberately obscured from us. Like a surfer scanning the waves, our relationship with these vast forces is affective, visceral, and at times almost primordial. The metaphor opens up a view on imagination: we can think about the possibility space of augmented human–machine imagination as the intersection of two entities with very limited understanding of one another, operating at vastly different scales. That dynamic tension between the surfer and the ocean is just what makes the activity interesting.

The Two Desires

The story of the algorithm has always been a love affair. Like every romance, the attraction is based on both familiarity and foreignness—the recognition of ourselves in another as well as the mystery of that other. As technical systems, algorithms have always embodied fragments of ourselves: our memories, our structures of knowledge and belief, our ethical and philosophical foundations. They are mirrors for human intention and progress, reflecting back the explicit and tacit knowledge that we embed in them. At the same time they provide the essential ingredient of mystery, operating according to the logics of the database, complexity, and algorithmic iteration, calculating choices in ways that are fundamentally alien to human understanding.

On the surface, it may seem as if the apotheosis of the algorithm in contemporary culture has not brought us any closer to the consummation of our twinned desires for perfect knowledge of the world and perfect knowledge of ourselves. The universal encyclopedia we have assembled to date is vast but inconsistent, full of contradictions, misinformation, and dangling references. In many ways our collective self-understanding seems to have advanced very little despite decades of research in neuroscience, psychology, economics, and other relevant fields. The versions of ourselves we see online in databases and user profiles still seem like crude caricatures. The promised salvation of algorithmic theology stubbornly remains in the distant future: the clunky, disjointed implementation of the computational layer on cultural life leaves much yet to be desired. Algorithms still get it wrong far too often to make a believable case for transcendent truth.

And yet the seduction remains. For every step that computational systems take in mastering a new field of practice, from understanding natural speech to composing music, humanity also takes a step to close the gap. We shape ourselves around the cultural reality of code, shoring up the facade of computation where it falls short and working feverishly to extend it, to complete the edifice of the ubiquitous algorithm. Some of these choices are simple, even pedantic, like adjusting our speech patterns to (we hope) make our statements easier for machines to understand. Others are far more subtle, like the temptation to organize one's weekend for optimal selfie opportunities, or the hidden biases encoded in nominally objective code. We depend on computational systems for a growing share of the raw material of intellectual life, from books and news stories to the very basics, like vocabulary, ideas to share, and people to share them with. The more we invest ourselves in these culture machines, the further we proceed down a path of collaboration. More than collaboration: a kind of co-identity. We are coming to define who we are through digital practice because virtual spaces are becoming more real to us than visceral ones.

Take the example of Google and the quest for the *Star Trek* computer. The company has made tremendous strides in finding and indexing the world's information. Many of us rely on Google not just for search and access but as a repository for all sorts of personal data, from emails and photographs to biometric measurements of our exercise and diet routines. The company's success at storing and deploying these different forms of information does more than just move its own systems closer to the *Star Trek* goal—it also moves its users closer. Researchers have demonstrated that using Google changes our memory practices, a fact anyone over thirty can prove: just ask yourself how many phone numbers you remember now as opposed to before you owned your first cell phone.[11] The same is true for composition using word processors, for the impact of social media on identity formation, and so on.[12] These are small observations of the sea change, the many ways in which digital culture, memory, and identity are evolving as our core practices of reading, writing, conversation, and thinking become digital processes. Through brain plasticity and changing social norms, we are adapting ourselves to become more knowable for algorithmic machines.

In this way we are evolving, as Hayles and others have argued, in conjunction with our technical systems, slowly moving toward some consummation of the algorithmic love affair. The risk of disaster haunts us—the consummation might become a collision, an explosion of the kinds we linger on in stories like the *Terminator* series and through institutions like the Future of Life Institute (funded by Elon Musk and others to avert the *Terminator* AI apocalypse). But there is a more optimistic vision as well, one where humans engage in productive collaboration with computational systems: the *Star Trek* future, or a more ambitiously AI-fueled society like science fiction author Iain Banks's *Culture* novels. Indeed, we spend so much time worrying about the rise of a renegade independent artificial intelligence that we rarely pause to consider the many ways in which we are already collaborating with autonomous systems of varied intelligence. This moves far beyond our reliance on digital address books, mail programs, or file archives: Google's machine learning algorithms can now suggest appropriate responses to emails, and AlphaGo gives grandmasters of that venerable art form some of their most interesting games.

Widening the scope further, we can begin to see how we are changing the fundamental terms of cognition and imagination. The age of the algorithm marks the moment when technical memory has evolved to store not just our data but far more sophisticated patterns of practice, from musical taste to our social graphs. In many cases we are already imagining in concert with our machines. Algorithmic systems curate the quest for knowledge, conversing and anticipating our interests and informational needs. They author with us, providing scaffolding, context, and occasionally direct material for everything from *House of Cards* to algorithmically vetted pop music. The horizon of imaginative possibility is increasingly determined by computational systems, which manufacture and curate the serendipity and informational flow that propels the lifecycle of ideas, of discourse, of art. In other words, the twin quests that have dominated the history of civilization are increasingly codeterminate with the desire embedded in effective computability. The space of imagination exists in algorithmic context, and that which cannot be computed cannot be fully integrated into the broader fabric of culture as we live it now.

We are grappling with the consequences of code through the many boundary cases of human experience and cultural work that trouble contemporary algorithmic culture. The role of the curator, the editor, and the critic is more important than ever, as we draw the lines of effective computability and struggle to learn and remember the things that our computational systems do not or cannot know.

Experimental Humanities

We can choose to construe the figure of the algorithm as a god to be worshipped ... or we can choose to see a new player, collaborator, and interlocutor in our cultural games. This is what I would like to call "experimental humanities," and it springs from the same philosophical starting point we began with in this book. The gap between theory and implementation, between abstraction and reality, is a critical point of human engagement. It represents a tremendous opportunity for humanists to take the field as our societal pendulum swings ever farther into the camp of computationalism.

I want to close this book by advancing a vision of public, humanistic research that engages directly with algorithmic culture. By breaking down the illusory wall between criticism and creativity, between observation and action, between reading and writing, we can define a new model for deep engagement with cultural life founded on the notion of the culture machine. As a mode of scholarly inquiry, experimental humanities embeds critique in process, using the innate collaborative potential of algorithmic machines (both computational and otherwise) to make new forms of collective debate, insight, and understanding possible. The first step in this process is moving beyond our roles as consumers or, at best, users of existing systems. If we let our culture machines set the critical frame, we will wind up living entirely in the space of the "effectively computable," forgetting everything beyond the boundary markers. We need an experimental humanities that answers current critiques of humanities in the academy with an energetic combination of praxis, theory, and pedagogy: building culture machines of our own.

In pragmatic terms, recognizing this relationship with a rapidly changing universe of knowledge is vital to reframing the professional practice of the humanities. Canons, literary fields, even individual books are no longer the stable intellectual entities they once were, as the institutions involved in their preservation and study undergo the same rapid technological changes affecting the rest of the algorithmic ocean. The work of navigating and curating computational space is a deeply imaginative project.

When we do this, performing critical roles in concert with algorithmic texts, platforms, and even interlocutors, we are also performing augmented imagination. There is great potential for new forms of critical work that use computational scaffolding to extend the space of human cognition. This may sound utopian, but such practices have become a quotidian part of digital cultural experience. We tell collective jokes and stories using comment threads and hashtags, building shared narratives and farragoes that can evolve into sophisticated technical beings in their own right as Internet memes as superficial as #lolcats or as potent as #blacklivesmatter. These are moments of collective augmentation, leveraging digital platforms to build attention and consensus in ways that were previously impossible. This emerging channel for collective, ad hoc imagination has started to transform more staid cultural practices from the twenty-four-hour news cycle to the scholarly conference.

To offer a few examples, we can begin with the practices of memory and forgetting that algorithmic systems are busily upending. Researchers in medicine and the sciences can now reasonably expect automated systems to cross-reference and contextualize new research within broader critical fields automatically, providing co-citation indexes and quantitatively broad measures of relevance. Scholars in the humanities are on the cusp of a similar moment, when we can reliably depend on algorithmic systems to remember intellectual connections to published work that we have forgotten, or never knew. These same systems can be extended to enhance contextual understanding and deep engagement with textual resources, providing archival links to the sources of cited documents (allowing the reader to directly evaluate the inferences we so easily slide into footnotes today). In a few years it may not be absurd to imagine different layers of "vetting" for scholarly discourse being layered into a single digital palimpsest, bringing multiple modes of scholarly paratext into or alongside the "final" published research, from off-the-cuff remarks at a conference or social media stream to the feedback of peer review itself.

The participants in the Critical Code Studies Working Group adopt familiar tactics of close reading and intensive contextual scrutiny, but at a lower rung in the layer of computational abstraction, reading software itself as cultural text. This frame can generate breathtaking insights into the gap between abstraction and implementation, for example by revealing the ideological assumptions of *SimCity*'s crime rate calculations, as digital culture scholar Mark Sample has done.[13] These critics perform their debates algorithmically, through discussion on collaborative platforms and publication via open-access platforms like the *electronic book review* and *Digital Humanities Quarterly*. Indeed, one of the great challenges of editing the Critical Code Studies discussions for publication on *ebr*, where I served for a time as a thread editor, was capturing the vibrancy of computationally mediated discussion forum exchanges and distilling it into a more traditionally fixed textual format.

Other experimental humanists, if I can offer them the title, achieve the same goal by taking the opposite approach, authoring instead of reading, and thereby reinventing algorithmic systems for the purposes of protest and critique. The Vibrant Lives project based at Arizona State University uses live performance and installations to explore the visceral consequences of data production and "how we value persons, art objects, and information."[14] The creators of critical Twitter bots like Sample's @NSA_prismbot are launching algorithms of their own that pose ethical questions in spaces of collective discourse.[15] These bots and Vibrant Lives both transform corporate data streams into spaces for what digital media scholar Rita Raley calls "tactical media," engaging in social critique with a powerful immediacy. This is algorithmic criticism: the projects involve code, performance, and sophisticated forms of audience engagement that build collective conversation.

Sample's Twitter-based project also calls attention to the question of critical integrity. Sample's bots are always already compromised and implicated, using the same corporate publicity tools as the entities he is parodying. But this is the state of play for all of us, who are deeply enmeshed in algorithmic systems at every stage of our own intellectual enterprises. The process of writing this book must have generated thousands of Google queries and would have been impossible without access to hundreds of helpful algorithms and computational platforms. We are all performing criticism in the presence of the algorithm. The ocean is already lapping at our heels; we need only to turn and face it ourselves.

The Memex that Bush envisioned was effectively a library in a box, one that encouraged its users to mark up the texts. The information industry is developing tools that serve these functions, but often behind walled gardens, like Amazon's Kindle annotations, which are famously difficult to extract from their proprietary home format. We are dependent on tools that are driven by the hodgepodge commercial logic of a fragmented industrial space for information—they remain alluring enough, *close enough* to Bush's vision to tempt us into forgetting what we are missing. Imagine what we might do with robust systems for interdisciplinary, experimental work: a contemporary platform for the collective annotation and discussion of literary texts, for example, or a system for generating richly interlinked research documents immediately after a high-energy conference or workshop.

An increasing share of the most important scholarly work takes place not in solitary libraries but through social media and in-person exchanges. It will only become more vital to capture the energy and nuance of such *performances* of scholarship in ways that effectively distill, curate, and preserve their liveliness for other travelers in the universe of information.

To accept that our relationship with knowledge has become a set of practices for interacting with rapidly increasing complexity is, I would argue, also an acceptance of the vital role of the humanities in the age of the algorithm. Ambiguity, dissonance, interpretation, affect: these are the playing fields of humanistic and artistic inquiry. The subject position of the reader becomes increasingly important when the algorithmic portal through which we are accessing the universe of knowledge is itself an active agent, shaping the framing and the tenor of our gaze. The humanities has long grappled with the story that started this book: the mythic power of language, the incantatory magic of words and codes. We desperately need more readers, more critics, to interpret the algorithms that now define the channels and horizons of our collective imaginations.

Notes

Introduction

1. For a rich history on the figure of the shaman, see Eliade, *Shamanism*.

2. Levy, *Hackers*.

3. Chun, *Software Studies*, 175.

4. Turner, *From Counterculture to Cyberculture*.

5. Kay et al., *The World Color Survey*; Berlin and Kay, *Basic Color Terms*; Loreto, Mukherjee, and Tria, "On the Origin of the Hierarchy of Color Names."

6. Stephenson, *Snow Crash*, 218.

7. Tully, *ISPW '88*.

8. Bogost, "The Cathedral of Computation."

9. Berlinski, *The Advent of the Algorithm*, xi, xv.

10. Ibid., 305.

11. Ibid., 203.

12. Malinowski and Redfield, *Magic, Science and Religion and Other Essays*, 70.

Chapter 1

1. Wiener, "Men, Machines and the World About."

2. Lewis, *Flash Boys*, 114.

3. Williams, *Keywords*.

4. Chun, *Software Studies*.

5. Knuth, "Ancient Babylonian Algorithms."

6. Ensmenger, *History of Computing*, 131.

7. Ibid., 132.

8. Moschovakis, "What Is an Algorithm?," n. 1.

9. Sedgewick, "Computer Science 226: Algorithms and Data Structures."

10. "Algorithms—Inside Search—Google."

11. Golumbia, *The Cultural Logic of Computation*.

12. Rosenbush and Stevens, "At UPS, the Algorithm Is the Driver."

13. Gillespie, "The Relevance of Algorithms."

14. Hardy, "Using Algorithms to Determine Character—NYTimes.com."

15. Pasquale, *The Black Box Society*, 35.

16. Hayles, *My Mother Was a Computer*, chap. 1.

17. Pasquale, *The Black Box Society*; Lanier, *You Are Not a Gadget*; Morozov, *To Save Everything, Click Here*.

18. Wolfram, *A New Kind of Science*, 5.

19. Ibid., 8.

20. Berlinski, *The Advent of the Algorithm*.

21. Ibid., 162.

22. Ibid., 183.

23. See, for example Moschovakis, "What Is an Algorithm?"

24. Wolfram, *A New Kind of Science*, chap. 12.

25. Golumbia, *The Cultural Logic of Computation*, 15.

26. Edwards, *The Closed World*.

27. Wiener, *Cybernetics; Or, Control and Communication in the Animal and the Machine*, 20.

28. Ibid., 8.

29. Wiener, *The Human Use of Human Beings: Cybernetics and Society*, 7–9.

30. Ibid., 21.

31. Ibid., 18.

32. Hayles, *How We Became Posthuman*, 52.

33. McCulloch and Pitts, "A Logical Calculus of the Ideas Immanent in Nervous Activity"; Bowker, "How to Be Universal."

34. Cf. Hayles, *How We Became Posthuman*, 90; Turner, *From Counterculture to Cyberculture*, 16–28.

35. Wiener, *The Human Use of Human Beings: Cybernetics and Society*, 95.

36. Levy, "The Definitive Story of 'Information Wants to Be Free.'"

37. Rendell, *Turing Machine Universality of the Game of Life*.

38. Berlinski, *The Advent of the Algorithm*, 238–248.

39. Hayles, *How We Became Posthuman*, 13.

40. Ibid., 8.

41. Kline, *The Cybernetics Moment*, 68.

42. Historian Thomas Rid describes a fascinating parallel lesson at the Macy conference, where British cybernetics pioneer Ross Ashby demonstrated his homeostat, a "thinking machine" that posed deep questions about the division between organism and environment. Rid, *Rise of the Machines,* 53-63.

43. Ibid., 68–69.

44. Chun, *Software Studies*, 2.

45. Ibid.

46. Weizenbaum, *Computer Power and Human Reason*, 255.

47. Chun, *Software Studies*, 53.

48. Berlinski, *The Advent of the Algorithm*, 305.

49. Plato, *Symposium*.

50. Sparrow, Liu, and Wegner, "Google Effects on Memory."

51. Clark and Chalmers, "The Extended Mind."

52. Ibid., 8.

53. Clark, *Natural-Born Cyborgs*, 11.

54. Weizenbaum, *Computer Power and Human Reason*, 12.

55. Ibid.

56. Ibid., 16.

57. Ibid., 250.

58. Stephenson, *Snow Crash*, 126.

59. *The Glass Cage*, 82.

60. For an interesting approach to the idea of a literacy nam-shub, see Goonan, "Girl in Wave: Wave in Girl."

61. Clark, *Natural-Born Cyborgs*, 69–75. Not for nothing does Clark acknowledge Stephenson's *Snow Crash* in the preface to his book.

62. Ibid., 72.

63. Weizenbaum, *Computer Power and Human Reason*, 18.

64. Hayles, "Foreword," vi.

65. Weizenbaum, *Computer Power and Human Reason*, 18.

66. Hayles, *How We Think*, 96; Thrift, "Remembering the Technological Unconscious by Foregrounding Knowledges of Position."

67. Cf. Agre, "Surveillance and Capture"; Galloway, *Gaming*.

68. Vaccari and Barnet, "Prolegomena to a Future Robot History: Stiegler, Epiphylogenesis and Technical Evolution."

69. Ogburn and Thomas, "Are Inventions Inevitable?"

70. Stiegler, *Technics and Time, 1*, 23.

71. Arbesman and Christakis, "Eurekometrics"; Evans and Foster, "Metaknowledge"; Waltz and Buchanan, "Computer Science. Automating Science."

72. Strogatz, "The End of Insight"; Arbesman, "Explain It to Me Again, Computer."

73. Bostrom, *Superintelligence: Paths, Dangers, Strategies*; Vinge, "The Coming Technological Singularity: How to Survive in the Post-Human Era."

74. Golumbia, *The Cultural Logic of Computation*, 4–5.

75. Ibid., 8.

76. Turner, *From Counterculture to Cyberculture*, 2.

77. Gillespie, "The Relevance of Algorithms"; Pariser, *The Filter Bubble*; Galloway, *Protocol*.

78. Turner, *From Counterculture to Cyberculture*, 17.

79. Galloway, *Gaming*, 76.

80. For more on this debate see Hayles, *My Mother Was a Computer*; Hansen, *Bodies in Code*, among many others. The topic is explored through a number of seminal cyberpunk novels, such as: Gibson, *Neuromancer*; Sterling, *Schismatrix*; and, of course, Stephenson, *Snow Crash*.

81. Bogost and Montfort, "Platform Studies."

82. Kirschenbaum, *Mechanisms*, 10–11.

83. Ibid., 12–13.

84. Bogost, "The Cathedral of Computation."

85. Pariser, *The Filter Bubble*.

86. Stephenson, *Snow Crash*, 434.

87. For more on the relationship between desire, materiality and masculinity see Mackenzie, "A Troubled Materiality: Masculinism and Computation."

88. Ramsay, *Reading Machines*.

89. Madrigal, "How Netflix Reverse Engineered Hollywood."

Chapter 2

1. Manjoo, "Where No Search Engine Has Gone Before."

2. Diderot, "Letter on the Blind for the Use of Those Who See," 109.

3. "Apple Launches iPhone 4S, iOS 5 & iCloud."

4. For the account of Siri's early development I am indebted to Bosker, "SIRI RISING."

5. Mark and Perrault, "Cognitive Assistant That Learns and Organizes."

6. Ibid.

7. Bosker, "SIRI RISING."

8. Quoted in Stiegler, *Technics and Time, 1*, 69.

9. Bosker, "SIRI RISING."

10. Ibid.

11. Newitz, "Why Is My Digital Assistant So Creepy?"

12. Vaidhyanathan, *The Googlization of Everything*, 113–114.

13. Kay, "Behind Apple's Siri Lies Nuance's Speech Recognition."

14. Ibid.

15. Rogowsky, "Without Much Fanfare, Apple Has Sold Its 500 Millionth iPhone."

16. "Note to Self."

17. Zax, "Siri, Why Can't You Understand Me?"

18. "How Siri Works—Interview with Tom Gruber, CTO of SIRI"; See also Domingos, *The Master Algorithm*, 162. Of course, word order can still shape Siri's interpretation, but only through probabilities, not a formal grammatical structure.

19. Bosker, "SIRI RISING."

20. Poeter, "Siri, Are You Anti-Abortion?"

21. "Shit That Siri Says—Baby Stores."

22. Journalist Mat Honan made this argument with passion in the early months after Siri's release: Honan, "Siri Is Apple's Broken Promise."

23. Labovitz, "Google Sets New Internet Record."

24. Vaidhyanathan, *The Googlization of Everything*, 16.

25. Gertner, "The Truth About Google X."

26. Tsukayama, "FAQ."

27. Jenkins, "Google and the Search for the Future."

28. Manjoo, "Where No Search Engine Has Gone Before."

29. Kolbe, "Evolution."

30. Bleecker, "Design Fiction: A Short Essay on Design, Science, Fact and Fiction."

31. Thanks to Sam Arbesman for this insight: Arbesman, "Email Correspondence."

32. Darnton, *The Business of the Enlightenment*, 520.

33. Schwab, "Translator's Introduction."

34. D'Alembert, "Preliminary Discourse."

35. Ibid.

36. Diderot and Stewart, "Encyclopedia."

37. "Knowledge Graph 2.0," 0.

38. *Google I/O 2013*.

39. *The Evolution of Search*.

40. *Google I/O 2013*.

41. Manjoo, "Where No Search Engine Has Gone Before"; Mitchell, "How Google Search Really Works."

42. Discourse on the Method, Part V, quoted in Oppy and Dowe, "The Turing Test."

43. Hafner, "Researchers Yearn to Use AOL Logs, but They Hesitate"; "AOL User 927 Illuminated."

44. Anderson, "U Are What U Seek"; Engelberts and Plug, *I Love Alaska*.

45. *Parisian Love*.

46. Hayles, *My Mother Was a Computer*, 173.

47. Jonze, *Her*.

48. Ibid.

49. Ellwood et al., "'Her' Q&A."

50. The Loebner Prize promises a solid gold medal and $100,000 "for the first computer whose responses [are] indistinguishable from a human's." "Home Page of the Loebner Prize."

51. Turing, "Computing Machinery and Intelligence," 443.

52. Adams, *The Education of Henry Adams*, XXV.

53. Plato, *Symposium*, 9:211d.

Chapter 3

1. Willimon, *House of Cards*.

2. "Global Internet Phenomenon Report."

3. Evers, "The Post: New ISP Performance Data For December."

4. "The Netflix Prize Rules."

5. Töscher, Jahrer, and Bell, "The BigChaos Solution to the Netflix Grand Prize."

6. Hallinan and Striphas, "Recommended for You."

7. Buley, "Netflix Settles Privacy Lawsuit, Cancels Prize Sequel."

8. Strogatz, "The End of Insight."; Arbesman, "Explain It to Me Again, Computer."

9. Amatriain, "Netflix Recommendations."

10. "Introducing Netflix Social."

11. Amatriain, "Netflix Recommendations."

12. Madrigal, "How Netflix Reverse Engineered Hollywood."

13. Ibid.

14. Fritz, "Cadre of Film Buffs Helps Netflix Viewers Sort through the Clutter."

15. "Netflix Tagger Shares What It's like to Have the Internet's Dream Job."

16. And, presumably, Bollywood and related industries, though Netflix's mainstream American focus may not offer good data for this.

17. "Save the Cat!."

18. Carr, "For 'House of Cards,' Using Big Data to Guarantee Its Popularity."

19. Madrigal, "How Netflix Reverse Engineered Hollywood."

20. For a deeper consideration of these layers see Stephenson, *In the Beginning ... was the Command Line.*

21. "Video Streaming Services Could Make More Money than the US Box Office by 2017."

22. "Netflix Is Now Available Around the World."

23. Ibid.

24. Leonard, "How Netflix Is Turning Viewers into Puppets."

25. Baldwin, "Netflix Gambles on Big Data to Become the HBO of Streaming | Gadget Lab."

26. Spangler, "Comcast Cuts Sony Deal to Sell 'House of Cards,' Early-Release Movies."

27. Wu, "Netflix's Secret Special Algorithm Is a Human."

28. Carr, "For 'House of Cards,' Using Big Data to Guarantee Its Popularity"; Roettgers, "For House of Cards and Arrested Development, Netflix Favors Big Data over Big Ratings."

29. For the seminal work on the auteur theory, see Sarris, *The American Cinema*

30. Abele, "Playing With a New Deck—Directing House of Cards with David Fincher and Colleagues."

31. Kim, Queena. "What Happens at Netflix When House of Cards Goes Live."

32. Wallenstein, "'House of Cards' Binge-Watching."

33. Spangler and Spangler, "Netflix Data Reveals Exactly When TV Shows Hook Viewers—And It's Not the Pilot."

34. "Netflix Spoiler Foiler."

35. Rodriguez, "Are You Part of the 2% That Watched 'House of Cards' Season 2 In One Weekend?"

36. It's worth pointing out that entertainment and cultural experiences ask us to do this all the time: theaters ask us to silence our mobile phones, museums forbid photographs, etc. This Netflix example simply illustrates a central tension between abstraction and reality.

37. "Netflix's View: Internet TV is Replacing Linear TV."

38. Rohit, "Personalization, Not House Of Cards, Is Netflix Brand."

39. The streaming video platform dictates that such skipping around typically requires the stream to be rebuffered before playback resumes, creating an annoying pause. Netflix has also implemented an auto-play feature that cues up the next installment in a series to start a few seconds after the previous one has ended, passively encouraging serial viewing of multiple episodes.

40. Maragos, "Andrew Geraci Interview."

41. Habermas, and McCarthy, *The Theory of Communicative Action.*

42. Van Camp, "Stiegler, Habermas and the Techno-Logical Condition of Man."

43. Willimon, *House of Cards*, "Chapter 13."

44. One might speculate about how long it will be before such moments are truly personalized, with streaming video edited to include the viewer's name or other personal details, as is already happening with on-the-fly generations of advertising videos.

45. Sandvig, "Corrupt Personalization"; Baker, *Media, Markets, and Democracy*; on the subject of disingenuous Facebook "likes," see Kosner, "Facebook Is Recycling Your Likes to Promote Stories You've Never Seen to All Your Friends."

46. Ciancutti, "Does Netflix Add Content Based on Your Searches?" Emphasis in original.

47. Habermas, and McCarthy, *The Theory of Communicative Action*, 395.

48. Quoted in Pasquale, *The Black Box Society: The Secret Algorithms That Control Money and Information.*

49. On the manipulations of traditional advertising, see for example Packard, *The Hidden Persuaders.*

50. Habermas, and McCarthy, *The Theory of Communicative Action*, 392.

51. Bowker, *Memory Practices in the Sciences.*

52. Gillespie, "The Relevance of Algorithms."

53. "Egypt."

54. Langlois, "Participatory Culture and the New Governance of Communication."

55. Manovich, *The Language of New Media.*

Chapter 4

1. Čapek and Kussi, *Toward the Radical Center*, 58.

2. Helft, "The 'Facebook Class' Built Apps, and Fortunes."

3. Ibid.

4. Stanford Persuasive Tech Lab, Stanford University, http://captology.stanford
.edu; Fogg, Persuasive Computers.

5. Zichermann, "The Purpose of Gamification."

6. Kosner, "Stanford's School Of Persuasion."

7. Frum, "Five Years On, Millions Still Dig 'FarmVille.'"

8. Jackson, "The Zynga Abyss."

9. Lowensohn, "Virtual Farm Games Absorb Real Money, Real Lives."

10. Bogost, "Persuasive Games."

11. Tanz, "The Curse of *Cow Clicker*."

12. Ibid.

13. Ibid.

14. Bogost, "Cow Clicker."

15. Bogost, *Unit Operations*, 157.

16. Bogost, "Cow Clicker."

17. Wark, *Telesthesia*, 166.

18. "Company Info | Facebook Newsroom"; "Internet Used by 3.2 Billion People in 2015."

19. Galloway, *The Interface Effect*, 135.

20. On social rituals in virtual worlds, see Hillis, *Online a Lot of the Time*; on gamification in the workplace see, for example, Kumar and Raghavendran, "Gamification, the Finer Art"; Rauch, "Best Practices for Using Enterprise Gamification to Engage Employees and Customers."

21. "Essential Facts about the Computer and Videogame Industry: 2014 Sale, Demographic and Usage Data."

22. Castronova, *Synthetic Worlds*, 147.

23. Galloway, *Gaming*, 17.

24. Nardi, *My Life as a Night Elf Priest*, 26, 17.

25. Castronova, *Synthetic Worlds*, 148.

26. See, for example, Lehdonvirta and Castronova, *Virtual Economies*.

27. Manovich, *The Language of New Media*, 223.

28. Galloway, *Gaming*, 85.

29. Ibid., 89–90.

30. Markoff, *Machines of Loving Grace*, 68–75.

31. "Radio 4 Revives Hitchhiker's Game," 4.

32. Belsky, "The Interface Layer."

33. Kleinman, "You're Allowed to Tip Your Uber Driver (and Maybe You Should)"; "Do I Need to Tip My Driver?"

34. Knack, "Pay As You Park."

35. Stein, "Baby, You Can Drive My Car."

36. Lawler, "Lyft-Off."

37. See an extensive list of such incidents at: "The Comprehensive List of Uber Incidents, Assaults and Accusations."

38. Wortham, "Ubering While Black"; Rivoli, Marcius, and Greene, "Taxi Driver Fined $25K for Refusing Ride to Black Family."

39. Wortham, "Ubering While Black."

40. Sandvig, "Seeing the Sort: The Aesthetic and Industrial Defense of 'The Algorithm.'"

41. Carruth, "The Digital Cloud and the Micropolitics of Energy," 342.

42. Much of the following section is based on McClelland's remarkable exposé of cloud warehouse labor practices: McClelland, "I Was a Warehouse Wage Slave."

43. Soper, "Inside Amazon's Warehouse."

44. Duhigg and Barboza, "Apple's iPad and the Human Costs for Workers in China."

45. "Foxconn Says Underage Workers Used in China Plant."

46. Blodget, "CEO of Apple Partner Foxconn."

47. Markoff, *Machines of Loving Grace*, 97–98.

48. Cf. Bogost, *Unit Operations*; this sampling of tasks was offered on the site on August 15, 2014.

49. Ipeirotis, "Analyzing the Amazon Mechanical Turk Marketplace," 21.

50. "Mechanical Turk Concepts."

51. Riskin, "Machines in the Garden."

52. Ibid., 27.

53. Zuniga, "Kasparov Tries New Strategy to Thwart Computer Opponent."

54. Finley, "Did a Computer Bug Help Deep Blue Beat Kasparov? | WIRED."

55. Silver, *The Signal and the Noise*, 288.

56. Isaacson, "'Smarter Than You Think,' by Clive Thompson."

57. Ipeirotis, "Analyzing the Amazon Mechanical Turk Marketplace," 21.

58. Glanz, "Data Centers Waste Vast Amounts of Energy, Belying Industry Image."

59. Cooper, Ipeirotis, and Suri, "The Computer Is the New Sewing Machine: Benefits and Perils of Crowdsourcing"; "Amazon Mechanical Turk."

60. Limer, "My Brief and Curious Life As a Mechanical Turk."

61. Thurston, Wershler, and Wark, *Of the Subcontract*, 47.

62. Ibid., 26.

63. Ibid., 135.

64. Galloway, *The Interface Effect*, 136.

65. Rice, *Minding the Machine*.

66. Quoted in ibid., 32.

67. Ibid., 36.

68. Hardt and Negri, *Multitude*, 108.

69. Purdy, "Why Your Waiter Hates You."

70. Bort, "A GoFundMe Campaign Raised So Much Money for an Uber Driver, He Stopped Taking Donations."

Chapter 5

1. My account of the financial markets here is indebted to Lewis's book. Lewis, *Flash Boys*.

2. Ibid., 35.

3. Ibid., 263; Schneiderman, "Remarks on High-Frequency Trading & Insider Trading 2.0."

4. Lewis, *Flash Boys*, 169.

5. Leal et al., "Rock Around the Clock."

6. Lewis, *Flash Boys*, 100.

7. Ibid., 217–218.

8. McCloud, *Understanding Comics*.

9. Liu, *The Laws of Cool*.

10. Sullivan, "The Recirculation Gap."

11. Page, Method for node ranking in a linked database. It is interesting to note that Page, Brin, and Google do not own the patent at the heart of Google's empire; Stanford University does, and licenses it to Google.

12. Beyer and Gorris, "SPIEGEL Interview with Umberto Eco."

13. Brutlag, "Speed Matters for Google Web Search."

14. Lanham, *The Economics of Attention*.

15. "2014 Financial Tables—Investor Relations—Google."

16. Owens, "Biz Break."

17. Kim, "How Many Ads Does Google Serve in a Day?"

18. Salmon, "Ad Tech Is Killing the Online Experience"

19. Liu, *The Laws of Cool*, 181.

20. Ibid., 451 n. 54. You might argue that we gradually left behind what Coleridge called the "translucence" of symbols that contained complex, conflicting, transcendent meanings precisely because they were hand-crafted by human beings. The fecund weirdness of Geocities, LiveJournal, or other lost kingdoms from the early web was worth waiting for on the 1990s' tenuous baud modem connections because it came replete with such translucent symbols. Liu offers an extensive list of these early "cool" sites in multiple categories: Ibid., 187–89.

21. Hill, "How Google Can 'Forget' People without the Rest of Us Forgetting It Happened."

22. Esguerra, "Google CEO Eric Schmidt Dismisses the Importance of Privacy."

23. Schwartz and Leyden, "The Long Boom."

24. Nakamoto, "Bitcoin."

25. Greenberg, "Follow the Bitcoins."

26. "Controlled Supply."

27. Castranova, *Wildcat Currency.*

28. Scott, "So You Want to Invent Your Own Currency."

29. "Understanding Deposit Insurance."

30. Nakamoto, "Bitcoin."

31. Castronova, *Wildcat Currency,* 139.

32. Parker, "Stanford Scholars Say Bitcoin Offers Promise, Peril."

33. Denton, "Back to Blogging."

34. LaFrance, "Facebook Is Eating the Internet."

35. In a rare moment of newsroom justice, the story was broken by the Gawker Media technology blog Gizmodo: Nunez, "Want to Know What Facebook Really Thinks of Journalists?"; for the instruction memo itself, see Thielman, "Facebook News Selection Is in Hands of Editors Not Algorithms, Documents Show."

36. I borrow these lines from an editorial I wrote on the scandal: Finn, "Facebook Trending Story."

37. Brian Stelter, "Peter Thiel."

38. Habermas, *The Structural Transformation of the Public Sphere.*

39. Thiel, "The Education of a Libertarian.

40. Miller, "I'm Maria Popova, and This Is How I Work."

41. Bourdieu, *The Field of Cultural Production.*

42. Greenfeld, "Faking Cultural Literacy."

43. This disparity has created its own arbitrage opportunities, like the Congress-Edits Twitterbot that announces each anonymous edit to Wikipedia made from IP addresses at the U.S. Congress. Summers, *Congress-Edits.* Wikipedia also struggles with its nominal objectivity and the significant demographic disparities of its largely male, white editorial community. Glott, Schmidt, and Ghosh, "Wikipedia Survey— Overview of Results"; Hill and Shaw, "The Wikipedia Gender Gap Revisited."

44. Agre, "Surveillance and Capture"; Galloway, *Gaming.*

45. Agre, "Surveillance and Capture," 755.

Coda

1. Mnih et al., "Human-Level Control through Deep Reinforcement Learning."

2. Reese, "Google DeepMind."

3. Metz, "Google's AI Takes Historic Match against Go Champ with Third Straight Win."

4. Turing, "Computing Machinery and Intelligence," 457.

5. Domingos, *The Master Algorithm*, 4.

6. Madrigal, "How Netflix Reverse Engineered Hollywood"; Strogatz, "The End of Insight."

7. Lem, *Solaris*.

8. Ptolemy, *Transcendent Man*. Thanks to Corey Pressman for bringing this reference to my attention.

9. Bush, "As We May Think."

10. Arbesman, *The Half-Life of Facts*.

11. Sparrow, Liu, and Wegner, "Google Effects on Memory."

12. Owston, Murphy, and Wideman, "The Effects of Word Processing on Students' Writing Quality and Revision Strategies"; Greenhow and Robelia, "Informal Learning and Identity Formation in Online Social Networks."

13. Sample, "Criminal Code."

14. Rajko, Standley, and Wernimont, "Vibrant Lives."

15. Sample, "A Protest Bot Is a Bot So Specific You Can't Mistake It for Bullshit."

Works Cited

Abele, Robert. "Playing with a New Deck—Directing *House of Cards* with David Fincher and Colleagues." *Directors Guild of America Quarterly*, Winter 2013. http://www.dga.org/Craft/DGAQ/All-Articles/1301-Winter-2013/House-of-Cards.aspx.

Adams, Henry. *The Education of Henry Adams*. University of Virginia Hypertext Edition. Charlottesville: University of Virginia, 1996. http://xroads.virginia.edu/~hyper/HADAMS/ha_home.html.

Agre, Philip E. "Surveillance and Capture: Two Models of Privacy." In *The New Media Reader*, 740–760. Cambridge, Mass.: MIT Press, 2003.

"Algorithms—Inside Search—Google." Accessed March 16, 2015. http://www.google.com/insidesearch/howsearchworks/algorithms.html.

Amatriain, Xavier. "Netflix Recommendations: Beyond the 5 Stars (Part 1)." *The Netflix Tech Blog*, April 6, 2012. http://techblog.netflix.com/2012/04/netflix-recommendations-beyond-5-stars.html.

Anderson, Nate. "U Are What U Seek: New Play Sparked by AOL Search Query Leak." *Ars Technica*, May 22, 2008. http://arstechnica.com/uncategorized/2008/05/uare-what-u-seek-new-play-sparked-by-search-queries.

"AOL User 927 Illuminated." *Consumerist*. Accessed June 2, 2014. http://consumerist.com/2006/08/07/aol-user-927-illuminated.

"Apple Launches iPhone 4S, iOS 5 & iCloud," *Apple Press Info*, October 4, 2011. https://www.apple.com/pr/library/2011/10/04Apple-Launches-iPhone-4S-iOS-5-iCloud.html.

Arbesman, Samuel. "Email Correspondence," October 8, 2015.

Arbesman, Samuel. "Explain It to Me Again, Computer." *Slate*, February 25, 2013. http://www.slate.com/articles/technology/future_tense/2013/02/will_computers_eventually_make_scientific_discoveries_we_can_t_comprehend.single.html.

Arbesman, Samuel. *The Half-Life of Facts: Why Everything We Know Has an Expiration Date*. 1st ed. Current, 2012.

Arbesman, Samuel, and Nicholas A. Christakis. "Eurekometrics: Analyzing the Nature of Discovery." *PLoS Computational Biology* 7 (6) (June 2011). doi:10.1371/journal.pcbi.1002072.

Baker, C. Edwin. *Media, Markets, and Democracy.* New York: Cambridge University Press, 2001.

Baldwin, Roberto. "Netflix Gambles on Big Data to Become the HBO of Streaming." *WIRED*, November 29, 2012. http://www.wired.com/2012/11/netflix-data-gamble.

"Behind Apple's Siri Lies Nuance's Speech Recognition." *Forbes.* Accessed May 28, 2014. http://www.forbes.com/sites/rogerkay/2014/03/24/behind-apples-siri-lies-nuances-speech-recognition.

Belsky, Scott. "The Interface Layer: Where Design Commoditizes Tech." *Medium*, May 30, 2014. https://medium.com/bridge-collection/the-interface-layer-when-design-commoditizes-tech-e7017872173a.

Bendeich, Mark. "Foxconn Says Underage Workers Used in China Plant." *Reuters*, October 17, 2012. http://www.reuters.com/article/2012/10/17/us-foxconn-teenagers-idUSBRE89F1U620121017.

Berlin, Brent, and Paul Kay. *Basic Color Terms: Their Universality and Evolution.* Stanford, Calif.: Center for the Study of Language and Information, 1999.

Berlinski, David. *The Advent of the Algorithm: The Idea That Rules the World.* 1st ed. New York: Houghton Mifflin Harcourt, 2000.

Beyer, Susanne, and Lothar Gorris. "Interview with Umberto Eco: 'We Like Lists Because We Don't Want to Die.'" *SPIEGEL ONLINE*, November 11, 2009. http://www.spiegel.de/international/zeitgeist/spiegel-interview-with-umberto-eco-we-like-lists-because-we-don-t-want-to-die-a-659577.html.

Bleeker, Julian. "Design Fiction: A Short Essay on Design, Science, Fact and Fiction." Near Future Laboratory, March 2009. http://blog.nearfuturelaboratory.com/2009/03/17/design-fiction-a-short-essay-on-design-science-fact-and-fiction.

Blodget, Henry. "CEO of Apple Partner Foxconn: 'Managing One Million Animals Gives Me A Headache.'" *Business Insider*, January 19, 2012. http://www.businessinsider.com/foxconn-animals-2012-1.

Bogost, Ian, and Nick Montfort. "Platform Studies." *Platform Studies.* Accessed January 27, 2016. http://platformstudies.com/index.html.

Bogost, Ian. "Persuasive Games: Exploitationware." *Gamasutra*, May 3, 2011. http://www.gamasutra.com/view/feature/6366/persuasive_games_exploitationware.php.

Bogost, Ian. "The Cathedral of Computation." *The Atlantic*, January 15, 2015. http://www.theatlantic.com/technology/archive/2015/01/the-cathedral-of-computation/384300.

Bogost, Ian. "Cow Clicker." Bogost.com. July 21, 2010. http://bogost.com/writing/blog/cow_clicker_1

Bogost, Ian. *Unit Operations: An Approach to Videogame Criticism.* Cambridge, Mass.: MIT Press, 2008.

Bort, Julie. "A GoFundMe Campaign Raised So Much Money for an Uber Driver, He Stopped Taking Donations." *Business Insider,* April 19, 2015. http://www.businessinsider.com/gofundme-for-an-uber-drive-goes-crazy-2015-4.

Bosker, Bianca. "SIRI RISING: The Inside Story of Siri's Origins—And Why She Could Overshadow the iPhone." *Huffington Post,* January 22, 2013. http://www.huffingtonpost.com/2013/01/22/siri-do-engine-apple-iphone_n_2499165.html.

Bostrom, Nick. *Superintelligence: Paths, Dangers, Strategies.* New York: Oxford University Press, 2014.

Bourdieu, Pierre. *The Field of Cultural Production.* Ed. Randal Johnson. New York: Columbia University Press, 1993.

Bowker, Geof. "How to Be Universal: Some Cybernetic Strategies, 1943–70." *Social Studies of Science* 23 (1) (1993): 107–127.

Bowker, Geoffrey C. *Memory Practices in the Sciences.* Cambridge, Mass.: MIT Press, 2005.

Brutlag, Jake. "Speed Matters for Google Web Search." Google, Inc., June 22, 2009. http://services.google.com/fh/files/blogs/google_delayexp.pdf.

Buley, Taylor. "Netflix Settles Privacy Lawsuit, Cancels Prize Sequel." *Forbes,* March 12, 2010. http://www.forbes.com/sites/firewall/2010/03/12/netflix-settles-privacy-suit-cancels-netflix-prize-two-sequel.

Bush, Vannevar. "As We May Think." *The Atlantic,* July 1945. http://www.theatlantic.com/magazine/archive/1945/07/as-we-may-think/303881.

Čapek, Karel, and Peter Kussi. *Toward the Radical Center: A Karel Capek Reader.* Highland Park, N.J.: Catbird Press, 1990.

Carr, David. "For 'House of Cards,' Using Big Data to Guarantee Its Popularity." *New York Times,* February 24, 2013, sec. Business Day / Media & Advertising. http://www.nytimes.com/2013/02/25/business/media/for-house-of-cards-using-big-data-to-guarantee-its-popularity.html.

Carr, Nicholas. *The Glass Cage: Automation and Us.* 1st ed. New York: W. W. Norton & Company, 2014.

Carruth, Allison. "The Digital Cloud and the Micropolitics of Energy." *Public Culture* 26 (2) (April 1, 2014): 339–364. doi:10.1215/08992363-2392093.

Castronova, Edward. *Synthetic Worlds: The Business and Culture of Online Games*. Chicago: University of Chicago Press, 2005.

Castranova, Edward. *Wildcat Currency: How the Virtual Money Revolution Is Transforming the Economy*. New Haven: Yale University Press, 2014. http://www.myilibrary .com/?ID=614046.

Chun, Wendy Hui Kyong. *Programmed Visions: Software and Memory*. Software Studies. Cambridge, Mass.: MIT Press, 2011. http://site.ebrary.com/lib/alltitles/docDetail .action?docID=10496266.

Ciancutti, John. "Does Netflix Add Content Based on Your Searches?" *Quora*, March 13, 2012. https://www.quora.com/Does-Netflix-add-content-based-on-your -searches/answer/John-Ciancutti.

Clark, Andy, and David J. Chalmers. "The Extended Mind." *Analysis* 58 (1) (1998): 7–19.

Clark, Andy. *Natural-Born Cyborgs: Minds, Technologies, and the Future of Human Intelligence*. Oxford: Oxford University Press, 2003.

"Company Info | Facebook Newsroom." Facebook. Accessed February 19, 2016. http://newsroom.fb.com/company-info.

"The Comprehensive List of Uber Incidents, Assaults and Accusations." *Who's Driving You?* Accessed June 10, 2015. http://www.whosdrivingyou.org/rideshare -incidents.html.

"Controlled Supply." *Bitcoin Wiki*, July 20, 2015. https://en.bitcoin.it/wiki/ Controlled_supply.

Cooper, Matt, Panagiotis G. Ipeirotis, and Siddharth Suri. "The Computer Is the New Sewing Machine: Benefits and Perils of Crowdsourcing." Presented at the WWW 2011, Hyderabad, India, March 28, 2011. http://www.ipeirotis.com/wp-content/ uploads/2012/01/p325.pdf.

Cushing, Ellen. "Amazon Mechanical Turk: The Digital Sweatshop." *Utne*, January/ February 2013. http://www.utne.com/science-and-technology/amazon-mechanical -turk-zm0z13jfzlin.aspx.

D'Alembert, Jean Le Rond. Preliminary Discourse. In *Encyclopedia of Diderot & d'Alembert—Collaborative Translation Project*. Translated by Richard N. Schwab and Walter E. Rex. Ann Arbor: Michigan Publishing, University of Michigan Library, 2009. http://hdl.handle.net/2027/spo.did2222.0001.083.

Darnton, Robert. *The Business of the Enlightenment*. Cambridge, Mass.: Harvard University Press, 1979.

Denton, Nick. "Back to Blogging." *Kinja*, December 10, 2014. http://nick.kinja.com/ back-to-blogging-1669401481.

Diderot, Denis. Encyclopedia. *The Encyclopedia of Diderot & d'Alembert Collaborative Translation Project*. Translated by Philip Stewart. Ann Arbor: Michigan Publishing, University of Michigan Library, 2002. http://hdl.handle.net/2027/spo.did2222 .0000.004.

Diderot, Denis. Letter on the Blind for the Use of Those Who See. In *Diderot's Early Philosophical Works*, edited by Margaret Jourdain. Chicago: The Open Court Publishing Company, 1916. http://tems.umn.edu/pdf/Diderot-Letters-on-the-Blind-and-the -Deaf.pdf.

"Do I Need to Tip My Driver?" Uber. Accessed February 16, 2016. https://help.uber .com/h/1be144ab-609a-43c5-82b5-b9c7de5ec073.

Domingos, Pedro. *The Master Algorithm*. New York: Basic Books, 2015.

Duhigg, Charles, and David Barboza. "Apple's iPad and the Human Costs for Workers in China." *New York Times*, January 25, 2012. http://www.nytimes.com/ 2012/01/26/business/ieconomy-apples-ipad-and-the-human-costs-for-workers-in -china.html.

Edwards, Paul. *The Closed World: Computers and the Politics of Discourse in Cold War America*. Cambridge, Mass.: MIT Press, 1996.

"Egypt: Military Junta Launches Facebook Page." *The Telegraph*, February 17, 2011, sec. World. http://www.telegraph.co.uk/news/worldnews/africaandindianocean/ egypt/8332008/Egypt-military-junta-launches-Facebook-page.html.

Eliade, Mircea. *Shamanism: Archaic Techniques of Ecstasy*. Bollingen Series 76. Princeton, N.J.: Princeton University Press, 1974.

Ellwood, Gregory, Guy Lodge, and Kristopher Tapley. "'Her' Q&A." *HitFix*, Wednesday, Oct. 23, 2013, 12:28 am. Accessed June 3, 2014. http://www.hitfix.com/ galleries/overlay/2014-best-supporting-actress-oscar-contenders.

Engelberts, Lernert, and Sander Plug, directors. *I Love Alaska*. Minimovies, 2009. http://www.minimovies.org/documentaires/view/ilovealaska.

Ensmenger, Nathan. *History of Computing: Computer Boys Take Over: Computers, Programmers, and the Politics of Technical Expertise*. Cambridge, Mass.: MIT Press, 2010. http://site.ebrary.com/lib/alltitles/docDetail.action?docID=10521951.

Esguerra, Richard. "Google CEO Eric Schmidt Dismisses the Importance of Privacy." *Electronic Frontier Foundation*, December 10, 2009. https://www.eff.org/deeplinks/ 2009/12/google-ceo-eric-schmidt-dismisses-privacy.

"Essential Facts about the Computer and Videogame Industry: 2014 Sale, Demographic and Usage Data." Entertainment Software Association, 2014. http://www .theesa.com/wp-content/uploads/2014/10/ESA_EF_2014.pdf.

Evans, James A., and Jacob G. Foster. "Metaknowledge." *Science* 331 (6018) (February 11, 2011): 721–725. doi:10.1126/science.1201765.

Evers, Joris. "The Post: New ISP Performance Data for December." *Netflix US & Canada Blog*. Accessed June 10, 2014. http://blog.netflix.com/2014/01/new-isp-performance-data-for-december.html.

The Evolution of Search, 2011. https://youtu.be/mTBShTwCnD4.

Finley, Klint. "Did a Computer Bug Help Deep Blue Beat Kasparov?" *WIRED*, September 28, 2012. http://www.wired.com/2012/09/deep-blue-computer-bug.

Finn, Ed. "Facebook Trending Story: The Wizard of Oz Algorithm." *CNN*, May 14, 2016, sec. Opinion. http://www.cnn.com/2016/05/13/opinions/facebook-trending-humans-behind-the-algorithm-opinion-finn/index.html.

Fogg, B. J. Persuasive Computers: Perspectives and Research Directions. In *Proceedings of the ACM CHI 98 Human Factors in Computing Systems Conference*, edited by Clare-Marie Karat, Arnold Lund, Joëlle Coutaz, and John Karat, 225–232. Los Angeles, California, April 18–23, 1998. http://www.acm.org/pubs/articles/proceedings/chi/274644/p225-fogg/p225-fogg.pdf.

Fritz, Ben. "Cadre of Film Buffs Helps Netflix Viewers Sort through the Clutter." *Los Angeles Times*, September 3, 2012. http://articles.latimes.com/2012/sep/03/business/la-fi-0903-ct-netflix-taggers-20120903.

Frum, Larry. "Five Years On, Millions Still Dig 'FarmVille.'" *CNN*, July 31, 2014, sec. Tech. http://www.cnn.com/2014/07/31/tech/gaming-gadgets/farmville-fifth-anniversary/index.html.

Galloway, Alexander R. *Gaming: Essays on Algorithmic Culture*. Minneapolis: University of Minnesota Press, 2006. http://site.ebrary.com/lib/alltitles/docDetail.action?docID=10151343.

Galloway, Alexander R. *Protocol: How Control Exists after Decentralization*. Leonardo. Cambridge, Mass.: MIT Press, 2004. http://hdl.handle.net/2027/heb.31968.

Galloway, Alexander R. *The Interface Effect*. 1st ed. Cambridge, UK: Polity, 2012.

Gertner, Jon. "The Truth About Google X: An Exclusive Look Behind the Secretive Lab's Closed Doors." *Fast Company*, April 15, 2014. http://www.fastcompany.com/3028156/united-states-of-innovation/the-google-x-factor.

Gibson, William. *Neuromancer*. 1st ed. New York: Ace, 1984.

Gillespie, Tarleton. The Relevance of Algorithms. In *Media Technologies: Essays on Communication, Materiality, and Society*, edited by Tarleton Gillespie, Pablo J. Boczkowski and Kirsten A. Foot, 167–193. Cambridge, Mass.: MIT Press, 2014. http://www.myilibrary.com?ID=572413.

Glanz, James. "Data Centers Waste Vast Amounts of Energy, Belying Industry Image." *New York Times*, September 22, 2012, sec. Technology. http://www.nytimes .com/2012/09/23/technology/data-centers-waste-vast-amounts-of-energy-belying -industry-image.html.

"Global Internet Phenomenon Report." Sandvine, 1H 2014. https://www.sandvine .com/downloads/general/global-internet-phenomena/2014/1h-2014-global-internet -phenomena-report.pdf.

Glott, Ruediger, Philipp Schmidt, and Rishab Ghosh. "Wikipedia Survey—Overview of Results." United Nations University, March 2010. http://www.ris.org/uploadi/ editor/1305050082Wikipedia_Overview_15March2010-FINAL.pdf.

Golumbia, David. *The Cultural Logic of Computation*. Cambridge, Mass.: Harvard University Press, 2009.

Google I/O 2013: Keynote, 2013. http://www.youtube.com/watch?v=9pmPa _KxsAM&feature=youtube_gdata_player.

Goonan, Kathleen Ann. Girl in Wave: Wave in Girl. In *Hieroglyph: Stories and Visions for a Better Future*, edited by Ed Finn and Kathryn Cramer. 38–73. New York: William Morrow, 2014.

Greenberg, Andy. "Follow The Bitcoins: How We Got Busted Buying Drugs on Silk Road's Black Market." *Forbes*, September 5, 2013. http://www.forbes.com/sites/ andygreenberg/2013/09/05/follow-the-bitcoins-how-we-got-busted-buying-drugs -on-silk-roads-black-market.

Greenfeld, Karl Taro. "Faking Cultural Literacy." *New York Times*, May 24, 2014. http://www.nytimes.com/2014/05/25/opinion/sunday/faking-cultural-literacy .html.

Greenhow, Christine, and Beth Robelia. "Informal Learning and Identity Formation in Online Social Networks." *Learning, Media and Technology* 34 (2) (June 1, 2009): 119–140. doi:10.1080/17439880902923580.

Habermas, Jurgen, and Thomas McCarthy. *The Theory of Communicative Action: Lifeworld and System: A Critique of Functionalist Reason*. New York: Beacon Press, 1985.

Habermas, Jürgen. *The Structural Transformation of the Public Sphere: An Inquiry into a Category of Bourgeois Society*. Cambridge, Mass.: MIT Press, 1989.

Hafner, Katie. "Researchers Yearn to Use AOL Logs, but They Hesitate." *New York Times*, August 23, 2006, sec. Technology. http://www.nytimes.com/2006/08/23/ technology/23search.html.

Hallinan, Blake, and Ted Striphas. "Recommended for You: The Netflix Prize and the Production of Algorithmic Culture." *New Media & Society* 18 (1) (January 1, 2016): 117–137. doi:10.1177/1461444814538646.

Hansen, Mark B. N. *Bodies in Code: Interfaces with Digital Media.* 1st ed. New York: Routledge, 2006.

Hardt, Michael, and Antonio Negri. *Multitude: War and Democracy in the Age of Empire.* New York: Penguin, 2004.

Hardy, Quentin. "Using Algorithms to Determine Character." *New York Times,* July 26, 2015, sec. Bits. bits.blogs.nytimes.com/2015/07/26/using-algorithms-to -determine-character.

Hayles, Katherine N. Foreword. In *Embodying Technesis: Technology Beyond Writing,* by Mark Hansen. iv–x. Ann Arbor: University of Michigan Press, 2000.

Hayles, N. Katherine. *How We Became Posthuman: Virtual Bodies in Cybernetics, Litera-ture, and Informatics.* 1st ed. Chicago: University of Chicago Press, 1999.

Hayles, Katherine N. *How We Think: Digital Media and Contemporary Technogenesis.* Chicago: University of Chicago Press, 2012. http://www.myilibrary.com?id=355452.

Hayles, N. Katherine. *My Mother Was a Computer: Digital Subjects and Literary Texts.* Chicago: University of Chicago Press, 2005.

Helft, Miguel. "The 'Facebook Class' Built Apps, and Fortunes." *New York Times,* May 7, 2011, sec. Technology. http://www.nytimes.com/2011/05/08/technology/08class .html.

Hill, Benjamin Mako, and Aaron Shaw. "The Wikipedia Gender Gap Revisited: Characterizing Survey Response with Propensity Score Estimation." *PLoS One* 8 (6) (2013).

Hill, Kashmir. "How Google Can 'Forget' People without the Rest of Us Forgetting It Happened." *Forbes,* May 15, 2014. http://www.forbes.com/sites/kashmirhill/2014/ 05/15/how-google-can-rebelliously-comply-with-europes-right-to-be-forgotten -ruling.

Hillis, Ken. *Online a Lot of the Time: Ritual, Fetish, Sign.* Durham, N.C.: Duke Univer-sity Press, 2009.

"Home Page of the Loebner Prize." Accessed May 28, 2014. http://www.loebner.net/ Prizef/loebner-prize.html.

Honan, Mat. "Siri Is Apple's Broken Promise." *Gizmodo.* Accessed May 28, 2014. http://gizmodo.com/5864293/siri-is-apples-broken-promise.

"Internet Used by 3.2 Billion People in 2015." *BBC News,* May 26, 2015. http://www .bbc.com/news/technology-32884867.

"Introducing Netflix Social." *Netflix Media Center.* Accessed February 6, 2016. https:// media.netflix.com/en/company-blog/introducing-netflix-social.

Ipeirotis, Panagiotis G. "Analyzing the Amazon Mechanical Turk Marketplace." *XRDS* 17 (2) (December 2010): 16–21. doi:10.1145/1869086.1869094.

Isaacson, Walter. "'Smarter Than You Think,' by Clive Thompson." *New York Times*, November 1, 2013. http://www.nytimes.com/2013/11/03/books/review/smarter -than-you-think-by-clive-thompson.html.

Jackson, Benjamin. "The Zynga Abyss." *The Atlantic*, January 24, 2012. http://www .theatlantic.com/technology/archive/2012/01/the-zynga-abyss/251920/.

Jenkins, Holman W. "Google and the Search for the Future." *Wall Street Journal*, August 14, 2010, sec. Opinion. http://www.wsj.com/articles/SB10001424052748704 901104575423294099527212.

Jonze, Spike, director. *Her.* Warner Bros., 2013.

Kabas, Marisa. "Netflix Tagger Shares What It's like to Have the Internet's Dream Job." *TODAY.com*, July 8, 2014. http://www.today.com/money/netflix-tagger-shares -what-its-have-internets-dream-job-1D79900963.

Kay, Paul, Brent Berlin, Luisa Maffi, William R. Merrifield, and Richard Cook. *The World Color Survey.* 1st ed. Stanford, Calif.: Center for the Study of Language and Information, 2011.

Kay, Roger. "Behind Apple's Siri Lies Nuance's Speech Recognition." *Forbes*, March 24, 2014. http://www.forbes.com/sites/rogerkay/2014/03/24/behind-apples-siri-lies -nuances-speech-recognition/#3b1b09f8421c.

Kim, Larry. "How Many Ads Does Google Serve in a Day?" *Business 2 Community.* Published November 2, 2012. Accessed May 30, 2014. http://www .business2community.com/online-marketing/how-many-ads-does-google-serve-in -a-day-0322253.

Kim, Queena. "What Happens at Netflix When House of Cards Goes Live." *Marketplace.* NPR, February 27, 2015. http://www.marketplace.org/topics/business/ what-happens-netflix-when-house-cards-goes-live.

Kirschenbaum, Matthew G. *Mechanisms: New Media and the Forensic Imagination.* Cambridge, Mass.: MIT Press, 2008.

Kleinman, Alexis. "You're Allowed to Tip Your Uber Driver (And Maybe You Should)." *The Huffington Post*, March 5, 2015. http://www.huffingtonpost.com/ 2015/03/05/tip-uber-driver_n_6810296.html.

Kline, Ronald R. *The Cybernetics Moment: Or Why We Call Our Age the Information Age.* Johns Hopkins University Press, 2015.

Knack, Ruth Eckdish. "Pay As You Park." *Planning Magazine*, May 2005. http:// shoup.bol.ucla.edu/PayAsYouPark.htm.

Knuth, Donald E. "Ancient Babylonian Algorithms." *Communications of the ACM* 15 (7) (July 1972): 671–677. doi:10.1145/361454.361514.

Kolbe, Winrich, director. "Evolution." *Star Trek: The Next Generation*, September 23, 1989. http://www.imdb.com/title/tt0708710.

Kosner, Anthony Wing. "Facebook Is Recycling Your Likes to Promote Stories You've Never Seen to All Your Friends." *Forbes*, January 21, 2013. http://www.forbes.com/sites/anthonykosner/2013/01/21/facebook-is-recycling-your-likes-to-promote-stories-youve-never-seen-to-all-your-friends/#410fca25777c.

Kosner, Anthony Wing. "Stanford's School of Persuasion: BJ Fogg on How to Win Users and Influence Behavior." *Forbes*, December 4, 2012. http://www.forbes.com/sites/anthonykosner/2012/12/04/stanfords-school-of-persuasion-bj-fogg-on-how-to-win-users-and-influence-behavior.

Kumar, Hari, and Satish Raghavendran. "Gamification, the Finer Art: Fostering Creativity and Employee Engagement." *Journal of Business Strategy* 36 (6) (November 16, 2015): 3–12. doi:10.1108/JBS-10-2014-0119.

Labovitz, Craig. "Google Sets New Internet Record." *DeepField Blog*, July 22, 2013. http://www.bespacific.com/deepfield-blog-google-sets-new-internet-record.

LaFrance, Adrienne. "Facebook Is Eating the Internet." *The Atlantic*, April 29, 2015. http://www.theatlantic.com/technology/archive/2015/04/facebook-is-eating-the-internet/391766/.

Langlois, Ganaele. "Participatory Culture and the New Governance of Communication: The Paradox of Participatory Media." *Television & New Media* 14 (2) (March 1, 2013): 91–105. doi:10.1177/1527476411433519.

Lanham, Richard. *The Economics of Attention: Style and Substance in the Age of Information.* Chicago: University of Chicago Press, 2006.

Lanier, Jaron. *You Are Not a Gadget: A Manifesto.* 1st ed. New York: Alfred A. Knopf, 2010.

Lawler, Ryan. "Lyft-Off: Zimride's Long Road to Overnight Success." *TechCrunch*, August 29, 2014. https://techcrunch.com/2014/08/29/6000-words-about-a-pink-mustache.

Leal, Jacob, Mauro Napoletano Sandrine, Andrea Roventini, and Giorgio Fagiolo. "Rock Around the Clock: An Agent-Based Model of Low- and High-Frequency Trading." SSRN Scholarly Paper. Rochester, N.Y.: Social Science Research Network, January 31, 2014. http://papers.ssrn.com/abstract=2390682.

Lehdonvirta, Vili, and Edward Castronova. *Virtual Economies: Design and Analysis.* Cambridge, Mass.: MIT Press, 2014.

Lem, Stanislaw. *Solaris*. Translated by Bill Johnston. Kindle. Pro Auctore Wojciech Zemek, 2014. http://www.amazon.com/gp/product/B00Q21MVAI/ref=dp-kindle -redirect?ie=UTF8&btkr=1.

Leonard, Andrew. "How Netflix Is Turning Viewers into Puppets." *Salon*, February 1, 2013. http://www.salon.com/2013/02/01/how_netflix_is_turning_viewers_into _puppets.

Levy, Steven. "The Definitive Story of 'Information Wants to Be Free.'" *Backchannel*, November 21, 2014. https://backchannel.com/the-definitive-story-of-information -wants-to-be-free-a8d95427641c.

Levy, Steven. *Hackers: Heroes of the Computer Revolution—25th Anniversary Edition*. 1st ed. Sebastopol, Calif.: O'Reilly Media, 2010.

Lewis, Michael. *Flash Boys: A Wall Street Revolt*. 1st ed. New York: W. W. Norton & Company, 2014.

Limer, Eric. "My Brief and Curious Life As a Mechanical Turk." *Gizmodo*, November 28, 2014. http://gizmodo.com/my-brief-and-curious-life-as-a-mechanical -turk-1587864671.

Liu, Alan. *The Laws of Cool: Knowledge Work and the Culture of Information*. 1st ed. University of Chicago Press, 2004.

Loreto, Vittorio, Animesh Mukherjee, and Francesca Tria. "On the Origin of the Hierarchy of Color Names." *Proceedings of the National Academy of Sciences of the United States of America* 109 (18) (May 1, 2012): 6819–6824. doi:10.1073/ pnas.1113347109.

Lowensohn, Josh. "Virtual Farm Games Absorb Real Money, Real Lives." *CNET*, August 27, 2010. http://www.cnet.com/news/virtual-farm-games-absorb-real-money -real-lives.

Mackenzie, Adrian. "A Troubled Materiality: Masculinism and Computation." *Discourse* 18 (3) (1996): 89–111.

Madrigal, Alexis C. "How Netflix Reverse Engineered Hollywood." *The Atlantic*, January 2, 2014. http://www.theatlantic.com/technology/archive/2014/01/how -netflix-reverse-engineered-hollywood/282679.

Malinowski, Bronislaw. *Magic, Science and Religion and Other Essays*, edited by Robert Redfield. Boston: Beacon Press, 1948.

Manjoo, Farhad. "Where No Search Engine Has Gone Before." *Slate*, April 11, 2013. http://www.slate.com/articles/technology/technology/2013/04/google_has_a _single_towering_obsession_it_wants_to_build_the_star_trek_computer.2 .html.

Manovich, Lev. *The Language of New Media*. Cambridge, Mass.: MIT Press, 2002.

Maragos, Alexandros. "Andrew Geraci Interview. Netflix—House of Cards: The Making of the Opening Sequence." *Momentum*. Accessed June 18, 2014. http://www .alexandrosmaragos.com/2013/02/andrew-geraci-interview.html.

Mark, William, and Raymond C. Perrault. "Cognitive Assistant That Learns and Organizes." *SRI International's Artificial Intelligence Center*. Accessed May 27, 2014. http://www.ai.sri.com/project/CALO.

Markoff, John. *Machines of Loving Grace: The Quest for Common Ground Between Humans and Robots*. 1st ed. Ecco, 2015.

McClell. Mac. "I Was a Warehouse Wage Slave." *Mother Jones*, March/April 2012. http://www.motherjones.com/politics/2012/02/mac-mcclelland-free-online -shipping-warehouses-labor.

McCloud, Scott. *Understanding Comics: The Invisible Art*. Reprint ed. New York: William Morrow Paperbacks, 1994.

McCulloch, Warren S., and Walter Pitts. "A Logical Calculus of the Ideas Immanent in Nervous Activity." *Bulletin of Mathematical Biophysics* 5 (4) (December 1943): 115–133. doi:10.1007/BF02478259.

"Mechanical Turk Concepts." In *Amazon Mechanical Turk Requester UI Guide*, API Version 2014-08-15. Amazon. Accessed May 21, 2015. http://docs.aws.amazon.com/ AWSMechTurk/latest/RequesterUI/mechanical-turk-concepts.html.

Metz, Cade. "Google's AI Takes Historic Match against Go Champ with Third Straight Win." *WIRED*, March 12, 2016. http://www.wired.com/2016/03/third -straight-win-googles-ai-claims-victory-historic-match-go-champ.

Meyers, Peter J. "Knowledge Graph 2.0: Now Featuring Your Knowledge." *Moz*, March 25, 2014. http://moz.com/blog/knowledge-graph-2-now-featuring-your -knowledge.

Miller, Tessa. "I'm Maria Popova, and This Is How I Work." *Lifehacker*, September 12, 2012. http://lifehacker.com/5942623/im-maria-popova-and-this-is-how-i-work.

Mitchell, Jon. "How Google Search Really Works." *ReadWrite*, February 29, 2012. http://readwrite.com/2012/02/29/interview_changing_engines_mid-flight_qa_with _goog.

Mnih, Volodymyr, Koray Kavukcuoglu, David Silver, Andrei A. Rusu, Joel Veness, Marc G. Bellemare, Alex Graves, et al. "Human-Level Control through Deep Reinforcement Learning." *Nature* 518 (7540) (February 26, 2015): 529–533. doi:10.1038/ nature14236.

Morozov, Evgeny. *To Save Everything, Click Here: The Folly of Technological Solutionism*. New York: PublicAffairs, 2013.

Moschovakis, Yiannis N. What Is an Algorithm? In *Mathematics Unlimited: 2001 and Beyond*, edited by Björn Engquist and Wilfried Schmid, 919–936. Berlin: Springer-Verlag, 2001.

Nakamoto, Satoshi. "Bitcoin: A Peer-to-Peer Electronic Cash System." Accessed July 28, 2014. https://bitcoin.org/bitcoin.pdf.

Nardi, Bonnie. *My Life as a Night Elf Priest: An Anthropological Account of World of Warcraft*. Ann Arbor: University of Michigan Press, 2010. http://site.ebrary.com/lib/alltitles/docDetail.action?docID=10395616.

"Netflix Is Now Available Around the World." *Netflix Media Center*. Accessed February 8, 2016. https://media.netflix.com/en/press-releases/netflix-is-now-available-around-the-world.

"The Netflix Prize Rules." *Netflix Prize*. Accessed June 9, 2014. http://www.netflixprize.com//rules.

"Netflix's View: Internet TV is Replacing Linear TV." Accessed June 11, 2014. http://ir.netflix.com/long-term-view.cfm.

"Netflix Spoiler Foiler." *Netflix*. Accessed June 11, 2014. http://www.spoilerfoiler.com/.

Newitz, Annalee. "Why Is My Digital Assistant So Creepy?" *Gizmodo*, January 28, 2015. http://gizmodo.com/why-is-my-digital-assistant-so-creepy-1682216423.

Nunez, Michael. "Want to Know What Facebook Really Thinks of Journalists? Here's What Happened When It Hired Some." *Gizmodo*, May 3, 2016. http://gizmodo.com/want-to-know-what-facebook-really-thinks-of-journalists-1773916117.

Nunokawa, Jeff. *Note Book*. Princeton, N.J.: Princeton University Press, 2015.

Ogburn, William F., and Dorothy Thomas. "Are Inventions Inevitable? A Note on Social Evolution." *Political Science Quarterly* 37 (1) (March 1, 1922): 83–98. doi:10.2307/2142320.

Oppy, Graham, and David Dowe. "The Turing Test." In *The Stanford Encyclopedia of Philosophy*, edited by Edward N. Zalta, Spring 2011. http://plato.stanford.edu/archives/spr2011/entriesuring-test.

Owens, Jeremy C. "Biz Break: Apple and Google Now World's Two Most Valuable Companies—San Jose Mercury News." *San Jose Mercury News*, February 7, 2014. http://www.mercurynews.com/60-second-business-break/ci_25087437/biz-break-apple-and-google-now-worlds-two.

Owston, Ronald D., Sharon Murphy, and Herbert H. Wideman. "The Effects of Word Processing on Students' Writing Quality and Revision Strategies." *Research in the Teaching of English* 26 (3) (October 1, 1992): 249–276.

Ozer, Nicole A. "Note to Self: Siri Not Just Working for Me, Working Full-Time for Apple, Too." *ACLU of Northern California*, March 12, 2012. https://www.aclunc.org/blog/note-self-siri-not-just-working-me-working-full-time-apple-too.

Packard, Vance Oakley. *The Hidden Persuaders*. New York: Random House, 1957.

Page, Lawrence. Method for node ranking in a linked database. US6285999 B1, filed January 9, 1998, and issued September 4, 2001.

Pariser, Eli. *The Filter Bubble: What the Internet Is Hiding from You*. New York: Penguin, 2011.

Parisian Love. Google Stories, 2009. https://youtu.be/nnsSUqgkDwU.

Parker, Clifton B. "Stanford Scholars Say Bitcoin Offers Promise, Peril." *Stanford University*, February 18, 2014. http://news.stanford.edu/news/2014/february/bitcoin-athey-srinivasan-021814.html.

Pasquale, Frank. *The Black Box Society: The Secret Algorithms That Control Money and Information*. Cambridge, Mass.: Harvard University Press, 2015.

Plato. *Symposium*. Translated by Harold N. Fowler. Vol. 9. Cambridge, Mass.: Harvard University Press, 1925. http://data.perseus.org/citations/urn:cts:greekLit:tlg0059.tlg011.perseus-eng1:211d.

Poeter, Damon. "Siri, Are You Anti-Abortion?" *PCMAG*, November 30, 2011. http://www.pcmag.com/article2/0,2817,2397090,00.asp.

Ptolemy, Robert Barry. *Transcendent Man*. Documentary, 2011.

Purdy, Jedediah. "Why Your Waiter Hates You." *Daily Beast*, October 26, 2014. http://www.thedailybeast.com/articles/2014/10/26/there-s-a-reason-your-waiter-hates-you.html.

"Radio 4 Revives Hitchhiker's Game." *BBC*, August 31, 2004, sec. Entertainment. http://news.bbc.co.uk/2/hi/entertainment/3615046.stm.

Rajko, Jessica, Eileen Standley, and Jacqueline Wernimont. "Vibrant Lives." *Vibrant Lives*, Fall 2015. https://vibrantdata.wordpress.com.

Ramsay, Stephen. *Reading Machines: Toward an Algorithmic Criticism*. 1st ed. Urbana: University of Illinois Press, 2011.

Rauch, Marta. "Best Practices for Using Enterprise Gamification to Engage Employees and Customers." In *Human-Computer Interaction. Applications and Services*, edited by Masaaki Kurosu, 276–283. Lecture Notes in Computer Science 8005. Berlin: Springer, 2013. http://link.springer.com.ezproxy1.lib.asu.edu/chapter/10.1007/978-3-642-39262-7_31.

Reese, Hope. "Google DeepMind: The Smart Person's Guide." *TechRepublic*, August 3, 2016, http://www.techrepublic.com/article/google-deepmind-the-smart-persons -guide.

Rendell, Paul. *Turing Machine Universality of the Game of Life*. Cham, Switzerland: Springer, 2016. Emergence, Complexity, and Computation 18.

Rice, Stephen P. *Minding the Machine: Languages of Class in Early Industrial America*. Berkeley: University of California Press, 2004.

Rid, Thomas. *Rise of the Machines*. New York: Norton, 2016.

Riskin, Jessica. "Machines in the Garden." *Republics of Letters* 1 (2) (April 30, 2010): 16–43.

Rivoli, Dan, Chelsia Rose Marcius, and Leonard Greene. "Taxi Driver Fined $25K for Refusing Ride to Black Family." *New York Daily News*, August 6, 2015. http://www .nydailynews.com/new-york/taxi-driver-fined-25k-refusing-ride-black-family -article-1.2317004.

Rodriguez, Cain. "Are You Part of the 2% That Watched 'House of Cards' Season 2 in One Weekend? Netflix Watches You Watch." *The Playlist*, February 21, 2014. http://blogs.indiewire.com/theplaylist/are-you-part-of-the-2-that-watched-house-of -cards-season-2-in-one-weekend-netflix-watches-you-watch-20140221.

Roettgers, Janko. "For House of Cards and Arrested Development, Netflix Favors Big Data over Big Ratings." *Gigaom*, February 12, 2013. http://gigaom.com/2013/02/ 12/netflix-ratings-big-data-original-content.

Rogowsky, Mark. "Without Much Fanfare, Apple Has Sold Its 500 Millionth iPhone." *Forbes*, March 25, 2014. http://www.forbes.com/sites/markrogowsky/2014/03/25/ without-much-fanfare-apple-has-sold-its-500-millionth-iphone.

Rohit, Parimal. "Personalization, Not House of Cards, Is Netflix Brand." *Westsidetoday* .com, June 17, 2014. http://westsidetoday.com/2014/06/17/personalization-house-cards -netflix-brand/.

Rosenbush, Steven, and Laura Stevens. "At UPS, the Algorithm Is the Driver." *Wall Street Journal*, February 17, 2015, sec. Tech. http://www.wsj.com/articles/at -ups-the-algorithm-is-the-driver-1424136536.

Salmon, Felix. "Ad Tech Is Killing the Online Experience." *The Guardian*, July 19, 2015, sec. Media. http://www.theguardian.com/media/2015/jul/19/ad-tech-online -experience-facebook-apple-news.

Sample, Mark L. "Criminal Code: Procedural Logic and Rhetorical Excess in Video-games." *Digital Humanities Quarterly* 7, no. 1 (2013). http://www.digitalhumanities .org/dhq/vol/7/1/000153/000153.html.

Sample, Mark. "A Protest Bot Is a Bot So Specific You Can't Mistake It for Bullshit: A Call for Bots of Conviction, Bots of Conviction, a Bot Canon of Anger, Protest Bots as Tactical Media." *Medium*, May 30, 2014. https://medium.com/@samplereality/a -protest-bot-is-a-bot-so-specific-you-cant-mistake-it-for-bullshit-90fe10b7fbaa.

Sandvig, Christian. "Corrupt Personalization." *Social Media Collective*, June 26, 2014. http://socialmediacollective.org/2014/06/26/corrupt-personalization.

Sandvig, Christian. "Seeing the Sort: The Aesthetic and Industrial Defense of 'The Algorithm.'" *Media-N, Journal of the New Media Caucus* 10 (3) (Fall 2014). http:// median.newmediacaucus.org/art-infrastructures-information/seeing-the-sort-the -aesthetic-and-industrial-defense-of-the-algorithm.

Sarris, Andrew. *The American Cinema: Directors and Directions 1929–1968*. New York: Da Capo Press, 1996.

Schneiderman, Eric T. "Remarks on High-Frequency Trading & Insider Trading 2.0." presented at the Insider Trading 2.0, New York Law School, March 18, 2014. http:// www.ag.ny.gov/pdfs/HFT_and_market_structure.pdf.

Schwab, Richard N. Translator's Introduction. In *Encyclopedia of Diderot & d'Alembert—Collaborative Translation Project*, translated by Richard N. Schwab and Walter E. Rex. Ann Arbor: Michigan Publishing, University of Michigan Library, 2009. http://quod.lib.umich.edu/d/did/schwabintro.html.

Schwartz, Peter, and Peter Leyden. "The Long Boom: A History of the Future, 1980– 2020." *WIRED*, July 1, 1997. http://www.wired.com/1997/07/longboom.

Scott, Brett. "So You Want to Invent Your Own Currency." *Aeon*, August 28, 2013. http://aeon.co/magazine/living-together/so-you-want-to-invent-your-own -currency.

Sedgewick, Robert. "Computer Science 226: Algorithms and Data Structures," Fall 2007. http://www.cs.princeton.edu/~rs/AlgsDS07/00overview.pdf.

"Shit That Siri Says—Baby Stores." Accessed May 27, 2014. http://knowyourmeme .com/photos/187708-shit-that-siri-says.

Silver, Nate. *The Signal and the Noise: Why So Many Predictions Fail—but Some Don't*. New York: Penguin, 2012.

Snyder, Blake. "Save the Cat!" Accessed June 10, 2014. http://www.savethecat.com.

Sopor, Spencer. "Inside Amazon's Warehouse." *The Morning Call*, September 18, 2011. http://articles.mcall.com/2011-09-18/news/mc-allentown-amazon-complaints -20110917_1_warehouse-workers-heat-stress-brutal-heat.

Spangler, Todd. "Comcast Cuts Sony Deal to Sell 'House of Cards,' Early-Release Movies." *Variety*, March 10, 2014. http://variety.com/2014/digital/news/comcast -cuts-sony-deal-to-sell-house-of-cards-early-release-movies-1201128558.

Spangler, Todd, and Todd Spangler. "Netflix Data Reveals Exactly When TV Shows Hook Viewers—And It's Not the Pilot." *Variety*, September 23, 2015. http://variety .com/2015/digital/news/netflix-tv-show-data-viewer-episode-study-1201600746.

Sparrow, Betsy, Jenny Liu, and Daniel M. Wegner. "Google Effects on Memory: Cognitive Consequences of Having Information at Our Fingertips." *Science* 333 (6043) (August 5, 2011): 776–778. doi:10.1126/science.1207745.

Spivack, Nova. "How Siri Works—Interview with Tom Gruber, CTO of SIRI." *Nova Spivack*, January 6, 2010. http://www.novaspivack.com/technology/how-hisiri -works-interview-with-tom-gruber-cto-of-siri.

Stelter, Brian. "Peter Thiel: Financing Lawsuits against Gawker Is About 'Deterrence.'" *CNN Money*, May 26, 2016, http://money.cnn.com/2016/05/26/media/ peter-thiel-hulk-hogan-gawker.

Stein, Joel. "Baby, You Can Drive My Car, and Do My Errands, and Rent My Stuff…" *Time* 185 (4) (February 9, 2015): 32–40.

Stephenson, Neal. *In the Beginning … Was the Command Line*. 1st ed. New York: William Morrow, 1999.

Stephenson, Neal. *Snow Crash*. New York: Bantam Dell, 1992.

Sterling, Bruce. *Schismatrix*. New York: Ace, 1986.

Stiegler, Bernard. *Technics and Time, 1: The Fault of Epimetheus*. Translated by Richard Beardsworth and George Collins. Stanford, Calif.: Stanford University Press, 1998.

Strogatz, Steven. "The End of Insight." *Edge: The World Question Center*, 2006. http:// edge.org/q2006/q06_8.html#strogatz.

Sullivan, Danny. "The Recirculation Gap: Why Google Sends More Traffic Than Its Search Market Share Suggests." *Search Engine Land*, May 28, 2014. http:// searchengineland.com/recirculation-gap-192597.

Summers, Ed. *Congress-Edits*. Twitter, 2014. https://twitter.com/congressedits.

Tanz, Jason. "The Curse of Cow Clicker: How a Cheeky Satire Became a Videogame Hit." *WIRED*, January 2012. http://archive.wired.com/magazine/2011/12/ff _cowclicker.

Thiel, Peter. "The Education of a Libertarian." April 13, 2009, *Cato Unbound*, Cato Institute. http://www.cato-unbound.org/2009/04/13/peter-thiel/education -libertarian.

Thielman, Sam. "Facebook News Selection Is in Hands of Editors Not Algorithms, Documents Show." *The Guardian*, May 12, 2016. http://www.theguardian.com/ technology/2016/may/12/facebook-trending-news-leaked-documents-editor -guidelines.

Thrift, Nigel. "Remembering the Technological Unconscious by Foregrounding Knowledges of Position." *Environment and Planning D* 22 (1) (February 2004): 175–190. doi: 10.1068/d321t.

Thurston, Nick, Darren Wershler, and McKenzie Wark. *Of the Subcontract: Or Principles of Poetic Right.* information as material, 2013.

Töscher, Andreas, Michael Jahrer, and Robert M. Bell. "The BigChaos Solution to the Netflix Grand Prize," September 24, 2009. http://www.commendo.at/UserFiles/commendo/File/GrandPrize2009_BigChaos.pdf.

Tsukayama, Hayley. "FAQ: Google's New Privacy Policy." *Washington Post*, January 25, 2012, sec. Tech. http://www.washingtonpost.com/business/technology/faq-googles-new-privacy-policy/2012/01/24/gIQArw8GOQ_story.html.

Tully, C., ed. *ISPW '88: Proceedings of the 4th International Software Process Workshop on Representing and Enacting the Software Process.* New York: ACM, 1988.

Turing, Alan M. "Computing Machinery and Intelligence." *Mind.* New Series 59 (236) (October 1, 1950): 433–460.

Turner, Fred. *From Counterculture to Cyberculture: Stewart Brand, the Whole Earth Network, and the Rise of Digital Utopianism.* Chicago: University of Chicago Press, 2006.

"2014 Financial Tables—Investor Relations—Google," Q1 2014. http://investor.google.com/financial/tables.html.

"Understanding Deposit Insurance." *Federal Deposit Insurance Corporation*, June 3, 2014. http://www.fdic.gov/deposit/deposits/.

Vaccari, Andrés, and Belinda Barnet. "Prolegomena to a Future Robot History: Stiegler, Epiphylogenesis and Technical Evolution." *Transformations: Journal of Media & Culture* 17 (2009). http://www.transformationsjournal.org/issues/17/article_09.shtml.

Vaidhyanathan, Siva. *The Googlization of Everything: (And Why We Should Worry).* Berkeley: University of California Press, 2011.

Van Camp, Nathan. "Stiegler, Habermas and the Techno-Logical Condition of Man." *Journal for Cultural Research* 13 (2) (April 2009): 125–141. doi: 10.1080/14797580902786473.

"Video Streaming Services Could Make More Money than the US Box Office by 2017." *The Verge*, June 4, 2014. http://www.theverge.com/2014/6/4/5781104/netflix-and-peers-will-make-more-money-than-box-office-by-2017.

Vinge, Vernor. "The Coming Technological Singularity: How to Survive in the Post-Human Era." Proceedings of Vision-21 Symposium. NASA Lewis Research Center: NASA, March 30, 1993. http://ntrs.nasa.gov/archive/nasa/casi.ntrs.nasa.gov/19940022855.pdf.

Wallenstein, Andrew. "'House of Cards' Binge-Watching: 2% of U.S. Subs Finished Entire Series Over First Weekend" *Variety*. February 20, 2014. http://variety.com/2014/digital/news/house-of-cards-binge-watching-2-of-u-s-subs-finished-entire-series-over-first-weekend-1201114030.

Waltz, David, and Bruce G. Buchanan. "Computer Science. Automating Science." *Science* 324 (5923) (April 3, 2009): 43–44. doi: 10.1126/science.1172781.

Wark, McKenzie. *Telesthesia: Communication, Culture & Class*. Cambridge, UK: Polity Press, 2012.

Weizenbaum, Joseph. *Computer Power and Human Reason: From Judgment to Calculation*. San Francisco: W.H. Freeman, 1976.

Wiener, Norbert. "Men, Machines and the World About." In *The New Media Reader*, 67–72. Cambridge, Mass.: MIT Press, 2003.

Wiener, Norbert. *Cybernetics; Or, Control and Communication in the Animal and the Machine*. New York: Wiley, 1949.

Wiener, Norbert. *The Human Use of Human Beings: Cybernetics and Society*. 2nd ed. Garden City, N.Y.: Doubleday, 1954.

Williams, Raymond. *Keywords: A Vocabulary of Culture and Society*. Re. ed. New York: Oxford University Press, 1985.

Willimon, Beau, creator. *House of Cards*. Netflix, 2013.

Wolfram, Stephen. *A New Kind of Science*. 1st ed. Champaign, Ill.: Wolfram Media, 2002.

Wortham, Jenna. "Ubering While Black." *Matter*, October 23, 2014. https://medium.com/matter/ubering-while-black-146db581b9db#.zfzrxm8xm.

Wu, Tim. "Netflix's Secret Special Algorithm Is a Human." *New Yorker*, January 27, 2015. http://www.newyorker.com/business/currency/hollywoods-big-data-big-deal.

Zax, David. "Siri, Why Can't You Understand Me?" *Fast Company*, December 7, 2011. http://www.fastcompany.com/1799374/siri-why-cant-you-understand-me.

Zichermann, Gabe. "The Purpose of Gamification." *O'Reilly Radar*, April 26, 2011. http://radar.oreilly.com/2011/04/gamification-purpose-marketing.html.

Zuniga, Janine. "Kasparov Tries New Strategy to Thwart Computer Opponent." *Lubbock Avalanche-Journal (Associated Press Article)*, May 9, 1997. http://lubbockonline.com/news/051097/kasparov.htm.

Figure Credits

Figure 1.1: "This is a Turing Machine implemented in Conway's Game of Life." Designed by Paul Rendell. Source: http://rendell-attic.org/gol/tm.htm.

Figure 1.2: Norbert Wiener and his "moth" circa 1950. Source: Alfred Eisenstaedt / The LIFE Picture Collection / Getty Images.

Figure 2.1: Siri playing up its human affect. Source: http://www.sirihacks.net/best-siri-conversations/.

Figure 2.2: Insert to the *Encyclopédie*, a disruptive knowledge ontology. Image courtesy the ARTFL Encyclopédie Project, University of Chicago https://encyclopedie.uchicago.edu/content/syst%C3%A8me-figur%C3%A9-des-connaissances-humaines

Figure 2.3: "Search Story," an ad for Google Search. Source: https://www.youtube.com/watch?v=nnsSUqgkDwU.

Figure 3.1: "Do You Know When You Were Hooked? Netflix Does." Source: http://www.prnewswire.com/news-releases/do-you-know-when-you-were-hooked-netflix-does-300147700.html.

Figure 3.2: Netflix European Spoiler Foiler campaign for *Breaking Bad*, 2013. Source: "Spoiler Foiler Wins at Eurobest," We Are Social, accessed April 20, 2015, http://wearesocial.net/blog/2014/12/spoiler-foiler-wins-eurobest/.

Figure 3.3: The atomized ideal of Netflix's abstraction aesthetic. Source: "1440+ Netflix Ads - Moat Ad Search," accessed April 20, 2015, http://www.moat.com/search/results?q=Netflix&ad=303381.

Figure 3.4: Screenshot of *House of Cards* opening credits: a city devoid of people. Source: Netflix.

Figure 4.1: *Cow Clicker* Screenshot. Courtesy of Ian Bogost, http://bogost.com/games/cow_clicker/.

Figure 4.2: The cartoon maps Uber provides for its drivers and passengers via the Google Play Store.

Figure 4.3: Uber's homepage offers a message of simultaneous elitism and equality (image from July 2014). Source: Uber, http://mascola.com/insights/ubers-lost-positoning-luxury-car-service/.

Figure 4.4: Lyft advertising takes a very different tack from Uber. Source: http://www.adweek.com/news/technology/lyft-hopes-accelerate-first-integrated-ad-campaign-159619.

Figure 4.5: Amazon Mechanical Turk Interface for Managing Workers. © 2016, Amazon Web Services, Inc. or its affiliates. All rights reserved. http://docs.aws.amazon.com/AWSMechTurk/latest/RequesterUI/ViewingWorkerDetails.html.

Figure 4.6: An engraving of the Turk from Karl Gottlieb von Windisch's 1784 book *Inanimate Reason*.

Figure 5.1: The Blockchain, a system for transparent, public accounting of Bitcoin transactions. Creative Commons: Matthaus Wander; https://commons.wikimedia.org/wiki/File:Bitcoin_Block_Data.png.

Figure 6.1: Vannevar Bush's Memex. Creative Commons: http://2014.hackinghistory.ca/wp-content/uploads/2014/09/wpid14-wpid-Bush-Memex-lg1.jpg.

Index